2238943

D1551555

Strangers on
Their Native Soil

Strangers on Their Native Soil

Opposition to United States' Governance in Louisiana's Orleans Territory, 1803–1809

JULIEN VERNET

University Press of Mississippi   Jackson

www.upress.state.ms.us

The University Press of Mississippi is a member of the Association
of American University Presses.

First printing 2013
∞
Library of Congress Cataloging-in-Publication Data

Vernet, Julien (Julien Paul)
Strangers on their native soil : opposition to United States' governance in
Louisiana's Orleans territory, 1803–1809 / Julien Vernet.
pages cm
Includes bibliographical references and index.
ISBN 978-1-61703-753-5 (cloth : alk. paper) — ISBN 978-1-61703-754-2 (eb-
ook) 1. Louisiana—History—1803–1865. 2. Louisiana—Politics and government—1803–1865. 3. Government, Resistance to—Louisiana—History—19th
century. 4. United States—Territorial expansion—Political aspects. 5. Slavery—United States—Extension to the territories. I. Title.
F374.V47 2013
976.3'04—dc23   2012038293

British Library Cataloging-in-Publication Data available

Contents

Acknowledgments

The research for and writing of this book were only possible because of the support of many people over the years. I would like to thank my colleagues in the History Department at the University of British Columbia Okanagan for their consideration as I worked to complete this project. The archivists and librarians at the Historic New Orleans Collection, New Orleans Public Library, and Special Collections at Tulane University were generous with their time and assistance. The staff of the Interlibrary Loan Department at Syracuse University's Bird Library patiently accepted my unceasing requests for sources. My mentor at Syracuse University, William Stinchcombe, encouraged me as I first began to consider writing about protest in Orleans Territory and provided me with excellent scholarly guidance.

I am also grateful for the understanding of my mother and father, Linda and Max Vernet, who always communicated their belief in the value of my work. The incredible energy and joyful interruptions provided by my daughter, Islene, born in July 2010, raised my spirits as the book neared completion. There is no way to adequately express my appreciation for the time and love that my wife, Suki, has devoted to this project. Without her willingness to listen to my ideas, her candid advice, and her acceptance of my research and writing schedule, this book would not exist.

Strangers on
Their Native Soil

Introduction

With the purchase of Louisiana in 1803, Thomas Jefferson and the government of the United States faced a new problem: how to transform a territory dominated by a foreign population into a state. "Previous American territories had been inhabited by people who spoke the English language, who were Protestant, and who had experience in representative government. The people of Louisiana were predominantly French in culture; they were Catholic; and nothing in their history had given them experience in representative government."[1]

In 1804 Congress divided the Louisiana Purchase into two parts, at the thirty-third parallel. The sparsely populated northern section became the Louisiana District, and the southern portion that included New Orleans, an established Atlantic port connected to European markets, became the territory of Orleans.

Through an analysis of territorial newspapers and government records, and of the correspondence of American government officials within the territory of Orleans as well as that of those who led the protest against territorial government, it is possible to gain an understanding of the issues that concerned Louisianans about their new government. Such an analysis is also useful in tracing the evolution of the protest movement and the efforts of Governor William Charles Cole Claiborne to deal with it.

Possibly the greatest concern to Louisianans was whether Congress would allow slavery and the slave trade in the new territory. Many of the wealthiest French, Spanish, and American Louisianans owned plantations. By the 1790s approximately 19,000 slaves inhabited Louisiana and outnumbered the white population of the province by 3,000. Sugar, first successfully cultivated in Louisiana in 1795, fueled a rapid expansion of the plantation economy. Fifty sugar mills were constructed by 1797, and 550,000 pounds of sugar were exported from New Orleans. In 1802, the year before France sold Louisiana, seventy-five sugar plantations operated in the colony and produced 5 million pounds of sugar.[2]

In addition to fears of restrictions on the slave trade, many Louisianans were anxious that the government of the United States might invalidate titles to land obtained under the Spanish and French governments. Titles obtained from Spanish government officials in Louisiana between 1801 and 1803 were dubious because Spain had ceded the colony to France in 1800. Invalidation of such titles would mean the ruin of many of Louisiana's planters.

Louisianans recognized that that they might be forced to defend what they considered to be their rights to property, in government or in the courts. Those who did not speak English considered that they would be at a disadvantage to do this under an American administration that would most likely establish a territorial government and a court system that conducted all business in the English language.

Anxieties over the future of slavery, land, and government prompted some Louisianans to present petitions to the French representative assigned to oversee the transfer of Louisiana to the United States, Pierre Clément de Laussat, and to the American commissioners assigned to receive the colony on behalf of the United States, William Claiborne and James Wilkinson. These petitions requested that Louisianans' property rights in slaves and land be protected, that the French language be used in government business, and that Louisiana be granted immediate statehood in order that these rights would be guaranteed.[3]

It must be recognized, however, that 1803 did not mark the first occasion that Louisianans had faced anxieties about possible threats to their commerce and property under a new regime. A brief examination of Louisianans' concerns after France ceded their home to Spain in 1762 provides some important context for Louisianans' actions to protect their economic interests in 1803. Furthermore, a brief comparison of French Louisianans' experiences to those of French origin who lived under British rule in neighboring West Florida after 1763 reveals a pattern of petition and imperial adjustment that is remarkably similar to that which occurred in American Louisiana after 1803.

Louisiana began its existence as a French colony but was ceded to the Spanish in 1762. Then, in 1800, France assumed control of the colony once again until Napoleon Bonaparte sold it to the United States. Each of these regime changes took place without consultation of Louisiana's inhabitants, who naturally had concerns about the future of their commercial and property interests. After his arrival in Louisiana in March 1766, Spanish governor Antonio de Ulloa worked to implement colonial policy for the assimilation of Louisiana into Spain's imperial mercantilist system. As John Preston Moore humorously concludes, however, it "was hardly less difficult for a camel to go through the eye of a needle than for Louisiana to become an integrated part of the Spanish mercantile system."[4] On May 6, 1766, the Spanish Crown issued the first of a series of decrees affecting foreign commerce. For Louisiana, the ordinance authorized a limited amount of direct trade with certain Spanish colonies and with the French West Indian dependencies. In addition, Ulloa, in September 1766, introduced a decree designed to eliminate smuggling—the nightmare of

Spain everywhere in the Gulf and Caribbean—by requiring the presentation of duly authenticated licenses or passports.[5] In addition, the Spanish Crown later ordered the application of the royal ordinance of March 23, 1768, to Louisiana. This ordinance was of concern to Louisiana's merchants because "colonial trade would be closely tied to Spain, which might eventually shut off commerce with France and especially the West Indies and thus cripple or destroy the lucrative trade in contraband."[6]

Spain's commercial policies and a shortage of currency in the colony caused difficulties for Louisianans, especially for its planters and merchants. "An economic crisis, brought on by the threatened enforcement of the regulations of September 1766, and March 23, 1768 was in the offing. Trade, legal and contraband, had declined; prices had risen; and the confidence in the mercantile community, which dreaded assimilation into the Spanish commercial system was waning."[7] Under these circumstances French colonists made the decision, in October 1768, to rise in revolt against Ulloa's Spanish administration. The leaders of this uprising were "a powerful, discontented group of traders and landowners. Eventually they reached the conclusion that their economic interests were imperiled by the assimilation of Louisiana into the Spanish mercantile system."[8] Lacking sufficient military support to crush the rebels, Ulloa fled New Orleans and sailed to Cuba in November 1768. Very briefly, Louisiana's French revolutionaries controlled Louisiana and petitioned and sent a delegation to Louis XV to request reestablishment of his rule over the colony. As they awaited news from France over the spring and part of the summer of 1769, colonists learned that "General Alexander O'Reilly with a force of more than two thousand men, had arrived at the mouth of the Mississippi. Clearly, Spain intended to reoccupy the province ceded by the treaty of Fontainebleau."[9]

O'Reilly restored Spanish rule of the colony and executed five revolutionary leaders. While the stronger Spanish military presence in the colony might partially explain why French inhabitants of Louisiana remained at peace for the remainder of the Spanish period in Louisiana, it must also be considered that Spanish administrators adjusted trade policies that had upset colonists before the 1768 revolt. "Spanish governors made frequent exceptions to and allowances to the law confining Louisiana commerce to Spanish ships," and Spain allowed Louisianans to trade with France and the French West Indies in 1776.[10] "By the 1780s Louisiana was annually exporting an average of 3,000,000 livres worth of indigo, 1,000,000 livres of tobacco, another 1,000,000 livres of timber products, and some 600,000 livres of furs, most of the last going to France, and additional European countries other than Spain."[11]

Spain further expanded trade prospects for Louisiana's inhabitants through the Cédula of 1782, which permitted Spanish subjects to "trade between

France and Louisiana—West Florida."[12] For Louisianans, "even this concession to foreign trade was not enough. In the course of the late 1780's many others were made and still others demanded. Frequent 'special permissions' enabled American ships to do a profitable if irregular business at St. Augustine and New Orleans," and "in 1788, the sacred Mississippi itself was thrown open to the Kentuckians as far south as New Orleans, and a thriving commerce soon developed."[13] It was also in 1788 that Spain "gave further encouragement to the development of Louisiana by liberalising the immigration laws." In addition, the Spanish government introduced generous land grants and permitted the importation of slaves.[14]

By the time the United States took control of Louisiana in 1803, its residents had established efficient and very profitable legal and illegal trade networks and had a history of protest against legislation that they deemed contrary to their interests. Given this colonial past, it is no surprise that Louisianans had concerns when the United States established an appointed territorial government over them in 1803. Once again, Louisiana's planters and merchants focused on their economic interests—specifically their investments in commerce, land, and slavery—and organized protest against measures they considered contrary to their interests. Unlike their predecessors who had risen in revolt in 1768, however, Louisianans after 1803 worked to assure the new owners of the territory they inhabited of their loyalty and demanded full assimilation into an expanding empire. Louisianans who protested against the territorial government the U.S. Congress established for them without their consent believed that their best option for future protection of their economic interests was as citizens of an American state who possessed the right to elect their own local government.

Louisiana was not unique in terms of rapid regime change and its consequences for local inhabitants in the late eighteenth century in North America. Like Louisiana, Florida (East and West) was a frontier region that changed hands a number of times in the late eighteenth and early nineteenth centuries. By the Treaty of Paris of 1763, East and West Florida became British possessions. Mobile and Pensacola were the two major settlements within West Florida. "All of the Spaniards left Pensacola, which was the only place in the new province where they had settled, but a number of the French remained about Mobile."[15]

On October 20, 1763, Major Robert Farmar arrived at Mobile with British troops and took possession of the settlement.[16] French troops departed two days later. In 1763 Mobile was a small settlement of approximately 350 inhabitants.[17] The first British administration of Mobile was a military government. On the day of his arrival in Mobile, Farmar issued a manifesto to its inhabitants. Under the terms of the Treaty of Paris, all French inhabitants were to take an "oath of allegiance within three months on pain of dispossession and expulsion from the province."[18] In addition, Farmar also decreed that all cases under French civil law should be suspended and that "all complaints in land cases be recorded not more than one year from the publication of the manifesto."[19]

At first it appeared that almost all of French Mobilians might reject the terms dictated to them in Farmar's manifesto. In January 1764 Farmar "feared that of ninety-eight families in the district, only ten would remain and on April 7, he reported that only eight French inhabitants had taken the oath."[20] It is clear that Farmar and his superiors wanted the French Mobilians to remain in the province. Some were valuable as interpreters, and competent French artisans were in demand because the only men of the Thirty-Fourth Regiment trained as gunsmiths had died in Cuba.[21] Farmar's wish that Frenchmen remain in Mobile is demonstrated by the fact that he hoped that news of the cession of Louisiana from France to Spain might induce French inhabitants to return to Mobile and by his plan to "send an officer to New Orleans 'to implant a favorable idea of the English Constitution, and the great means of fixing them under our protection.'"[22] While French inhabitants did not pour into West Florida after France ceded Louisiana to Spain, many French Mobilians decided to remain. Within one year of British occupation of Mobile, 112 Mobilians took the oath of allegiance to Britain.

The reasons why many French Mobilians decided to remain in the British province of West Florida would of course be different for each individual, but the British government's efforts to satisfy their concerns about their lands and religion may have had an important influence on French Mobilians' decisions about whether to leave or to remain in West Florida. Governor George Johnstone was ordered to recognize French Mobilians' "property rights on the basis of occupation and cultivation and to allow them a reasonable period in which to complete their real estate transactions if they decided to leave the province."[23]

The British government of West Florida also made an effort to soothe French inhabitants' anxieties about the future of the Catholic Church in the colony, an issue that Spanish Louisiana's French inhabitants did not have to worry about. In December 1764 the West Florida Council "considered a petition from the French inhabitants for the free practice of their religion, including the maintenance of a church and bells."[24] Recognizing that "it would be highly conducive to the good of the province to grant such indulgence, more specifically at that critical juncture when the Spaniards were taking possession of New Orleans," the council decided to grant the request of the French petitioners.[25] The council resolved "that the French inhabitants of Mobile should be permitted to enjoy the essential parts of the exercise of religion until the

King's further pleasure should be known; that they might have leave to build from their own collections a chapel for the decent exercising of their worship; that bells should be allowed for the chapel, but that public processions in the streets, except for burials should be prohibited."[26]

Protection of their property and religion was a strong incentive for French Mobilians to remain in West Florida. They remained loyal to the British administration of West Florida, as did those of British origin during the American Revolution. During this conflict, Anglo-American colonists settled in West Florida in significant numbers. In November 1775 Governor Peter Chester "declared the area a refuge for loyalists. Between 1775 and 1781 some 1,312 to 1,643 immigrants entered the West Florida area, with the largest proportion hailing from South Carolina (between 262 and 357) and Georgia (278 to 339) although between 115 and 232 came from the British Caribbean islands."[27] Americans entered the region in 1778 in an effort to instigate a revolt against the British, but they failed. Like the Louisianans of European origin who pressed for statehood as a means to protect their interests after the United States obtained Louisiana in 1803, "issues of land, trade and regional stability trumped issues of national loyalty."[28]

Spain used Louisiana as a base to launch an invasion of West Florida after the Spanish had declared war on Britain in 1779. Bernardo de Galvez, governor of Louisiana, launched a campaign against the British in West Florida. In September 1779 Fort Bute at Manchac and Fort New Richmond at Baton Rouge fell to the Spanish.[29] Following the success of this Mississippi campaign, Galvez prepared to attack Mobile.[30] The Spanish secured Mobile in January 1780 and seized Pensacola in May 1781, which ended Britain's effective control of the colony. As a result of the armed conflict that occurred in West Florida in the late 1770s and early 1780s, "West Florida loyalists suffered tremendous losses in land and personal fortune."[31] After Britain ceded West Florida to Spain by the Treaty of Paris of 1783, West Floridians unsuccessfully sought compensation for their losses from the British and American governments. "Loyalty then shifted by default to the Spanish, simply because Spain provided what Britain and the United States could not: a centralized government willing to act in residents' interests as long as those residents displayed a reciprocal loyalty."[32] A major contributing factor to West Floridians' loyalty to Spain was the fact that the Spanish government allowed Anglo-Americans "to obtain and cultivate land through a liberal system of grants."[33] As in the case of the Louisianans who found themselves residents of a new American territory in 1803, national loyalty was clearly tied to economic interest.

Who were the Louisianans who led or played a prominent role in the movement to have Congress meet their demands for protection of their commercial and property interests? An analysis of government documents, correspondence, and newspaper accounts reveals that they were primarily wealthy planters and planters/merchants of French and American origins such as Etienne de Boré, Daniel Clark, Jean Nöel Destréhan, and Pierre Sauvé. Two lawyers, Edward Livingston and Pierre Derbigny, could also be considered to be part of this group and were outspoken about their concerns about the territorial government designed for Orleans in Washington.

The records of congressional debate on American territorial administration of Louisiana demonstrate that Louisianans were not the only people concerned about the future of Louisiana. While the Jeffersonians who controlled the U.S. House of Representatives and Senate had the votes to pass legislation on territorial government, debate over certain issues, such as representation and importation of slaves, was often heated.

In order to understand this debate and its implications for Orleans Territory, it is necessary to identify party and intraparty divisions within Congress. Many Federalists believed that a Republican Louisiana would eliminate any possibility that their party would ever regain national political power. This obviously influenced their positions in congressional debates on matters relevant to the government of Louisiana.

While it is clear that Louisianans and members of Congress played an important part in shaping the territorial government in Louisiana, President Thomas Jefferson's active role in this process must also be considered. Jefferson was instrumental in directing his party to establish a government that more closely resembled a British royal colony than an American territory.

The Northwest Ordinance outlined the process for the establishment of territorial government and the criteria for statehood. This law stipulated that when the population of a territory reached 5,000 free white males, a representative assembly would be established there. Jefferson, however, rejected the Northwest Ordinance as a model for the government of Orleans Territory for the expressed reason that it turned the laws of Louisiana "topsy-turvy."[34]

An additional or perhaps underlying reason for Jefferson's refusal to use the Northwest Ordinance as a blueprint for territorial government in Louisiana is that he did not believe that Louisianans were prepared for representative government. A few weeks earlier Jefferson submitted a plan for Louisiana territorial government to Senator John Breckinridge of Kentucky. Breckinridge, an influential and loyal Republican, had ensured the passage of Jefferson's Kentucky Resolutions in 1798 while serving in Kentucky's legislature and was therefore a suitable champion of Jefferson's vision for Louisiana in Congress. In a letter to New York senator De Witt Clinton Jefferson declared that Louisianans were "as yet incapable of self-government as children."[35]

Most Republican congressmen demonstrated their support for Jefferson's position on the government of Louisiana by voting for An Act Enabling the

President to Take Possession of Louisiana, passed on October 31, 1803. This act empowered Jefferson to vest "all the military, civil and judicial powers exercised by the officers existing government (under France) in such person and persons as the President of the United States shall direct." In effect, this allowed Jefferson to rule Louisiana in the same manner as his predecessor, Napoleon. The president appointed one man, William Claiborne, to "exercise all the powers and authorities heretofore exercised by the Governor and Intendant."[36]

On March 26, 1804, Congress passed An Act for the Organization of Orleans Territory and the Louisiana District. Jefferson, who supported and helped to design this act, retained the powers that he was granted in the act of October 31, 1803. The president still appointed all government officials, and executive power would be vested in a governor whom the president could remove at any time. The only real change was that the governor was to rule in concert with "thirteen of the most discreet individuals in the territory." These men would be appointed by the president and constitute the Legislative Council of the territory of Orleans.

Despite the passage of the Breckinridge Bill, Jefferson faced challenges from within his own party over his plans for the government of Louisiana. Some western Republicans whose states or territories bordered on the Mississippi valley and were commercially connected with New Orleans believed that their bargaining power in Congress on issues of western trade and slavery would be strengthened with the immediate addition of Louisiana as a state. Opposition by these western Republicans and Federalists, however, did not prevent Jefferson from going forward with his government plan for Louisiana.

While Jefferson had little to fear concerning his design to have Louisiana enter the Union as an American state under his terms, he did recognize that he should make some effort to ensure that he did not alienate Louisianans through the introduction of measures that were entirely unpopular to them. On the issues of slavery, land, and language of government and law, Jefferson was willing to compromise as long as it did not interfere with his goal for an American Republican Louisiana.

Jefferson's almost unchallenged control over Orleans territorial government during his two terms as president had implications for future territorial expansion in the American West. Through his rejection of the Northwest Ordinance, which included a clear guideline based on population for introduction of a representative body within territorial government and statehood, Jefferson ensured that territorial inhabitants were more subjects than they were citizens of the United States. Territorial subjects held privileges and not rights. In dealing with the problem of territorial government in Orleans, Jefferson set a precedent by rejecting the Northwest Ordinance as a model for territorial government. The interests of the Union, for Jefferson, far outweighed the privileges of a suspect population in a U.S. territory. The president and Congress, not the population of inhabitants, determined when a territory should have an elected assembly or be admitted as a state. Western expansion after the Louisiana Purchase would be based on this principle.

Louisiana's close neighbor to the north, Missouri, discovered this when petitions for statehood were presented to Congress in 1818. Over many objections, Congress set the timetable for statehood and the rules for establishment of a constitutional convention. When the Missouri convention completed work on a constitution, it was submitted to Congress. The Northern majority in the House opposed to slavery in Missouri prevented final admission from November 1820 until February 1821. Missourians did not accept this. "During the last phase of the contest over admission, in the winter of 1820–1821, Missourians maintained that they were already a state and would never consent to return to a territorial status." Congress, however, and not Missourians determined how and when Missouri was to be admitted to the Union.[37]

CHAPTER ONE

"An Object So Dear to the Heart of Every American"

American Interests and the Purchase of Louisiana

In comparison to other French colonies of the mid-eighteenth century, Louisiana was an economic failure. Efforts to establish a profitable trade in cash crops such as tobacco and indigo were hindered by climate, shortages of slave labor, skeptical merchants in France, and the duties of the Farmers General and the Crown. The capital of the colony, New Orleans, was founded in 1718. Located 100 miles up the Mississippi River, it was an Atlantic gateway to the interior of North America.

French officials and merchants at New Orleans found it difficult to profit from the valuable North American interior fur trade because Indian traders recognized the superiority of English goods: "Anglo-American traders consequently received the best furs and pelts, fastened more tightly their economic hold upon the Indians, and increased Indian dissatisfaction with the French."[1] Because of Louisiana's relatively limited economic growth, the population of Louisiana grew slowly until France was forced to abandon the colony as a result of defeat in the Seven Years' War. In 1763, after half a century of settlement, the population of the lower Mississippi valley was approximately "four thousand whites, five thousand Negro slaves, two hundred mulatto slaves, one hundred Indian slaves and one hundred free people of color."[2]

By the seventh article of the peace treaty of 1763, France ceded its possessions east of the Mississippi to Great Britain, except for the province of Orleans, which was surrendered to Spain. Anglo-American traders poured into the lands abandoned by the French after the Seven Years' War, and they took control of much of the trade along the Mississippi River. "By 1767 Anglo-Americans were diverting trade from Illinois down the Mississippi River to the towns they controlled along the Gulf. On the Mississippi they turned

Natchez and Baton Rouge into fortified settlements; on the Gulf they made Pensacola the hub of their interests."[3]

The extent of Spanish weakness in Louisiana was demonstrated in October 1768 when a rebellion in response to a Spanish decree prohibiting trade between France and Louisiana resulted in the expulsion of the Spanish governor, Antonio de Ulloa. In response, Spain sent a new governor, Alexander O'Reilly, who had recently served Spain at Havana, and 2,000 men to Louisiana in 1769. O'Reilly successfully put down the rebellion in New Orleans, but his attempts to crack down on Anglo-American trade in Louisiana failed.

"Anglo-Americans penetrated as far west as Texas and captured much of Louisiana's commerce. They even supplied New Orleans with the greater part of its food."[4] Oliver Pollock, an Irish American merchant who had engaged in trade at Havana while O'Reilly was there, was one of the first Anglo-Americans to make a fortune in Louisiana. In 1769 he capitalized on a food shortage in New Orleans and brought a cargo of flour from Pittsburgh down the Mississippi.[5] With O'Reilly's permission, Pollock developed a regular trade between Philadelphia and New Orleans.

Anglo-American interest in Louisiana increased during the American Revolution when the Spanish government decided to aid the thirteen colonies in their struggle with Britain. With the support of Spain, Pollock was able to obtain supplies and loans for American military expeditions. For these services, the Continental Congress recognized Pollock as its regular agent in New Orleans in 1778, and he profited handsomely from this position until the Revolution ended in 1783.[6]

As a result of the American Revolution, England lost its colonies in North America, and Spain regained control of East and West Florida. "For Louisiana new disadvantages offset these successes. The Americans of the newly created United States were the same aggressive people who under the British flag had pushed westward and threatened to take over the colony."[7]

The potential for profit from Louisiana trade increased greatly in the period between the end of the American Revolution and the Louisiana Purchase. The introduction of the cotton gin and the first successful mass production of sugar created an economic boom in Louisiana during the 1790s.[8] This prosperity attracted more Americans to Louisiana, and it became apparent that Spain was incapable of preventing them from settling there. "By 1795 it was too late for Spain to take effective steps against the Americans."[9]

As the American presence in Louisiana increased, more colonists were attracted by the potential for commercial profit; Daniel Clark and Evan Jones were two such men. Daniel Clark was born in 1766 at Sligo, Ireland. After completion of his education at Eton, he embarked for Louisiana at the invitation of his uncle of the same name, who was a merchant in New Orleans.[10] Immediately upon arrival at New Orleans, in December 1786, Daniel Clark began working in his uncle's store as a minor clerk. Eager to improve his language skills, Clark, who was fluent in both English and French, was able to learn Spanish while he worked as a translator in the office of Governor Esteban Miro, where he made important contacts among the key families of the city and also met influential American officials such as General James Wilkinson. Wilkinson had managed to make a personal arrangement with the Spanish government for trading concessions and had entered into a tobacco trading partnership with Daniel Clark's uncle.[11]

By 1788 the younger Daniel Clark had assumed most of the responsibilities of the Clark merchant house. He expanded business through a partnership with Daniel Coxe, a merchant and landowner of Philadelphia, for the trade of sugar, cotton, and tobacco.[12] Clark's commercial activities encouraged his first interest in a political appointment after the signing of the Pinckney Treaty in 1795.

The Pinckney Treaty marked the culmination of a decade of negotiations between Spain and the United States over boundaries in North America, Atlantic trade, and navigation of the Mississippi River. In the wake of the American Revolution, many Americans considered free navigation of the Mississippi River essential to American territorial and commercial expansion. Spain, however, had accepted Louisiana from France in 1762 and received West Florida from Britain in 1783. In control of territory on both banks of the Mississippi River, Spain temporarily planned to bar American vessels from the region. "The year after the peace settlement of 1783, the Governor of Louisiana was instructed to proclaim that, until the boundaries of Louisiana and the Floridas were settled, Americans would not be allowed to navigate the Mississippi within Spanish territory."[13]

The Spanish government dispatched Diego de Gardoqui to negotiate a boundary treaty with the United States in 1784. Congress commissioned Secretary for Foreign Affairs John Jay to deal with Gardoqui. As part of his instructions, Jay was to insist on "the free navigation of the Mississippi, from the source of the ocean as established in the treaties with Great Britain."[14] This American claim of a right to free navigation of the Mississippi proved to be a major point of contention throughout Jay's negotiations with Gardoqui. At one point Jay proposed that the United States give up its claim to navigation of the Mississippi for twenty-five to thirty years, but opposition in Congress, especially from Southern states, ensured the death of this idea.

Gardoqui left the United States in 1789, but negotiations between Spain and the United States continued through the first half of the 1790s. Thomas Pinckney, a South Carolinian who had served as minister to Britain, arrived in Madrid on June 28, 1795, as envoy extraordinary to Spain.[15] Following his instructions, Pinckney adamantly demanded that the Spanish government recognize his nation's right of free navigation of the Mississippi, and he attempted "to procure the cession of a port or at least a landing place in Spanish territory near the mouth of the river for transshipment of goods from river boats to ocean-going vessels."[16]

Fortunately for Pinckney, Spain had secretly signed the Peace of Basle on August 3, 1795, ending a costly war with France. Fearful that England would soon attack Spanish possessions, including those in North America, in retaliation for Spain's desertion of the Anglo-Spanish alliance, Spain strove to maintain a good relationship with the United States. A week after it was announced in Madrid that the war with France had ended, Spain decided to concede the right of navigation to the United States.[17] The Spanish government was not prepared, however, to satisfy Pinckney's demand for a right of deposit at the mouth of the Mississippi River. Unwilling to sign a treaty without a guarantee of a right of deposit, Pinckney decided to end his involvement in negotiations on October 24 and asked for his passports.[18]

Pinckney's request for his passports was not intended as a bluff, but it forced the hand of the Spanish, who were warned in September of England's negative reaction to Spain's signing of a peace treaty with France.[19] Called to a conference the day after he had asked for his passports, Pinckney learned that Spain "consented to the principle of *permitting* the *privilege* of deposit for three years at New Orleans with the liberty of continuing it at the expiration of the period."[20] Two days later the document known as Pinckney's Treaty was signed at San Lorenzo.

In order to ensure that the Spanish observed Americans' privilege to deposit goods at New Orleans, President George Washington appointed Oliver Pollock's son, Jacinto, U.S. consul to that city on March 2, 1797.[21] The younger Pollock did not go to New Orleans, however, and eventually resigned from this post. Like other New Orleans merchants with interests in American commerce, Daniel Clark worried as months passed and New Orleans remained without a U.S. consul. In a letter to Daniel Coxe, Clark explained why he believed that this official was vital to Louisiana's Americans. "We are here without a Consul and his presence is highly necessary to prevent and put a stop to the numerous abuses which the Spanish Governm't force the Americans to submit to." The "abuses" that American merchants complained of included a 21 percent export tax for American vessels engaged in the shipment of goods produced in Louisiana. Spanish merchants by comparison paid a duty of 12 percent for Spanish vessels exporting Louisiana produce.[22] Of course most merchants took steps to avoid payment of these duties. "It was only good sense for ships['] captains to carry as many sets of papers as they could obtain and to be prepared at all times to show a different set of colors."[23]

American Interests and the Purchase of Louisiana

By March 1798 Americans in Louisiana decided to appoint their own U.S. representative in New Orleans. Andrew Ellicott, U.S. boundary commissioner for Louisiana, and Captain Isaac Guion, commander of U.S. forces at Natchez, asked Daniel Clark to serve as U.S. vice-consul to New Orleans until a consul appointed by the president arrived in Louisiana.[24] Clark agreed to serve in this capacity, and Governor Manuel Luis de Gayoso officially approved his appointment.

In the same month that Clark accepted his position as vice-consul to New Orleans, however, Adams nominated Dr. William Empson Hulings of Philadelphia for the same position, and the Senate approved this nomination on March 14, 1798.[25] Hulings arrived in Louisiana in June 1798. Meanwhile, Clark served in his place.

In his unauthorized capacity as vice-consul to New Orleans, Clark gained two important concessions for Americans from the Spanish government of Louisiana in 1798. Clark convinced the intendant, Juan Ventura Morales, to permit American vessels to export the produce of the colony by paying a 6 percent duty and to allow exporters to ship goods to any American territory along the Mississippi from New Orleans without payment of duty.[26] With this success, Clark's friends presented his name to the State Department for a full consular appointment. In the meantime, however, Hulings arrived in Louisiana and presented his commission to Governor Gayoso. Gayoso approved Hulings's commission, but the government of Spain rejected it eleven months later.[27]

Because of the Spanish rejection of Hulings, Clark had reason to hope that a consular appointment would go to him. To his disappointment, however, on April 12, 1799, Secretary of State Pickering recommended Evan Jones, formerly a prominent merchant of West Florida, for the consular appointment. President Adams agreed and issued Jones a commission while the Senate was in recess.[28]

Evan Jones was born and raised in the province of New York. He and his brother, James, became involved in commerce and established themselves in West Florida after it became a British province in 1763. Hoping to advance his career, Jones attached himself to the party of Lieutenant Governor Elias Durnford. In 1767 Jones was involved in a factional struggle between Durnford and his predecessor, Montfort Browne.[29] Durnford had examined Browne's accounts and accused him of providing his family with supplies from presents designated for Native American nations. Durnford's accusations resulted in a duel between Jones, "one of the Durnford adherents," and Browne. Jones almost paid the ultimate price for his loyalty to Durnford. A witness to the duel reported that Jones fired first and missed; Brown returned fire and shot Jones "through the body so that his life" was "despaired of." Jones's wound healed, however, and Browne left West Florida.[30]

The fortunes of the Jones brothers improved after the duel. James Jones served as a member of the Governor's Council, and on April 24, 1769, the council granted them a tract of 2,000 acres on the Mobile River. After this the brothers asked the council to sell them more land so that they in turn could sell it to settlers from New York. On July 10, 1773, the governor of West Florida agreed to this plan and granted James and Evan Jones 25,000 acres.[31]

Following their success in West Florida, the Jones brothers began to do business in Louisiana. At New Orleans, Evan Jones served as the agent of merchants Thomas and Clifford of Philadelphia.[32] James and Evan Jones were also agents of Nicholas Low of New York. They purchased the planters' crops and sold them to Low.[33] As a result of his business acumen and his ability to speak Spanish, Evan Jones obtained commissions in the Spanish militia that gave him a degree of status in the colony. In 1787 he became a sublieutenant and in 1792 a militia captain. Five years later Governor Gayoso appointed Jones commandant of the Lafourche District in Louisiana, where he served from September 13, 1797, until he resigned on September 27, 1798. Jones's superiors described him as a tactful and useful official.[34]

After Jones resigned his commission as commandant, he traveled to Philadelphia on business. Pickering believed that Jones would be of valuable service as consul to New Orleans and explained to Hulings as he replaced him that Jones's "character as well in the U.S. of which he is a native, as in Louisiana, where he lived many a year, and his knowledge and experience presented him as a fit person" to serve as consul. Hulings was not, however, completely dismissed from service. Pickering ordered him to "continue the usual functions of Vice-Consul, but in subordination to Mr. Jones as Consul of the United States and its dependencies."[35]

Upon receipt of his commission, Evan Jones departed for New Orleans, where he arrived in August 1799. He met with Colonel Francisco Bouligny, who was acting as temporary governor of Louisiana as a result of the death of Governor Gayoso. Bouligny claimed that only the Marquis de Someruelos, captain-general of Cuba and Louisiana at Havana, could approve of Jones's commission as U.S. consul, and so Jones's credentials were sent to Cuba. In September the newly selected permanent governor of Louisiana, the Marquis de Casa Calvo, informed Jones that the captain-general had refused to recognize Jones as a consul because Jones was still a subject of Spain.[36] Even worse, Someruelos had ordered that Jones be arrested and sent to Cuba for his treasonous acceptance of a commission from the president of the United States. Governor Casa Calvo, however, wrote the captain-general and stated that Jones was "a person of independent fortune, married, with grown up children and a large family connection, and enjoying the esteem of the principal men" and that his arrest would cause problems with the American government.[37]

American Interests and the Purchase of Louisiana

Someruelos then rescinded the order of arrest but refused to recognize Jones as American consul to New Orleans. Despite this, Jones continued to act as consul.[38]

Because he had no influence with the Spanish government and was provided with little guidance from Pickering, Jones became frustrated with his consular duties. On May 15, 1801, he expressed his dissatisfaction with his position to the new secretary of state, James Madison. He complained that he had written a number of letters to Pickering "respecting the situation of the Citizens of the U.S." but that he had not "had the honor to receive an answer to most of them" and that this had "almost discouraged [him] from writing any more." An additional problem for Jones was that he had been "ordered in the most positive terms to refrain from *every consular function*" and that he had "no power to resist this order."[39]

In this same letter Jones complained of what he believed were violations of the Pinckney Treaty. He claimed that American ships in the Mississippi River bound for New Orleans were often delayed or lost as a result of the negligence of Spanish pilots.[40] The free navigation of the Mississippi, Jones argued, surely implied that American pilots should be able to take Americans in and out of the river, but an American captain had been arrested for attempting to sound the channel in order to take his ship out of New Orleans. An American warship on the Mississippi, Jones suggested, would solve this problem.

In addition to Spanish harassment of American pilots, Jones stated that U.S. vessels on the Mississippi suffered embargoes "contrary to the letter as well as the spirit of the treaty between France and Spain." There were also, according to Jones, "gross abuses" in the depositing and reshipping of American cotton. For example, cotton grown in Louisiana was reported as having been grown in Mississippi Territory: this allowed shippers to avoid payment of duty on foreign cotton at American ports. Furthermore, there were "people" who acted in concert with clerks at the Spanish customhouse to ship Spanish cotton as American cotton. "Thus," concluded Jones, "almost all the Cotton of Louisiana, and the quantity is very considerable, goes into the Atlantick states free of duty."[41]

In closing his letter Jones declared that the increase of commerce between Spanish subjects and American citizens demanded the creation of a law that defined the powers of the consul and stipulated which American citizens were required to apply to him on arrival and departure. Without this law, Jones predicted, "the Consul will always be a Cypher, and the rights and interests of Americans will be trampled on."[42] The law that Jones demanded was never created, but he was relieved from the burdens of his office. Because Spanish rejection of Jones appeared final, President Thomas Jefferson appointed Daniel Clark U.S. consul to New Orleans on July 16, 1801.[43]

American Interests and the Purchase of Louisiana

Clark was in Philadelphia on business in January 1802 when he received his commission. He was disappointed to find that it described him as a subject of Spain. To correct this, Clark traveled to Washington and told Jefferson that he "had never been a Spanish subject, but had been naturalized as an American citizen, in the latter part of the year in 1798, at Natchez." Whether this was true or not, Clark did receive a new commission signed by Jefferson on January 26, 1802, that declared Clark a "citizen of the United States."[44] Clark had little time to savor this victory, however: when he returned to New Orleans in April 1802, he found that the Spanish government, which had accepted him as an unofficial representative of U.S. interests, was not willing to accept him as consul to New Orleans.

Despite his rejection by the Spanish, Clark was still recognized by Jefferson and Madison as the U.S. consul to New Orleans. Clark continued to work and reported new problems Americans faced as Spain attempted to restrict increasing U.S. economic expansion in Louisiana. For example, he noted that the intendant had placed a duty of 3 percent on all money deposited at New Orleans to be shipped to the United States on American vessels. Clark concluded that the extension of this principle, "if not avoided by the Merchants," would "put a stop to all Commerce" and that the "immediate interference of the Government" was required to prevent this from happening.[45]

Clark's information was of value to Jefferson, who had become increasingly interested in the possibility of an American territorial acquisition in the lower Mississippi valley during his first months as president. In June 1801 Jefferson and Madison had learned through "well-substantiated rumor" that Spain had ceded Louisiana to France by treaty in 1800.[46] This was cause for concern. If Napoleon Bonaparte used his military might to control Louisiana, the Floridas, and St. Domingue (present-day Haiti), he could unite these colonies in an exclusive trade network. "He would be master of four hundred miles of Atlantic coast, master of the Caribbean, the Gulf of Mexico, the commerce of the Mississippi, the Eldorado of its valley, in short an American empire richer and more dangerous than anything ever ruled by the Bourbon monarchs."[47]

Bonaparte's scheme for an American empire was hindered by the fact that Spain had not yet given in to the first consul's demands for the Floridas. This presented a possible but slim chance for the United States to gain valuable territory in the lower Mississippi valley and to prevent total French control of the region. On September 28, 1801, Madison had instructed the newly appointed minister to France, Chancellor Robert Livingston, to discover whether the rumor of cession was true and, if it was, to attempt to obtain "at least West Florida" in return for the U.S. government assuming claims of American citizens against France.[48]

Livingston arrived in Paris in December 1801 and began to make inquiries about the cession of Louisiana to France, which at first the French government flatly denied. Minister of Foreign Affairs Charles-Maurice de Talleyrand informed Livingston that he could not discuss the terms of a treaty that had not been communicated to the U.S. government.[49] The reason for this denial was that Bonaparte was still engaged in negotiation for the Floridas.

In April 1802 Jefferson wrote to Livingston to make it clear that the possession of New Orleans was essential to the prosperity of the United States because the produce of the expanding West had to pass through New Orleans to get to market. Jefferson feared that if France gained control of New Orleans, the French government would use its military power to close the port to American trade. This situation, Jefferson concluded, would force the United States to "marry" the "British fleet and nation," which would also hinder American commerce.[50]

Madison supported Jefferson's position on New Orleans in a letter of May 1, 1802, and he further asked Livingston to find out if New Orleans and the Floridas had been ceded to France and, if so, to discover if there might be a price for those possessions. Livingston's prospects for success appeared grim through the autumn of 1802, as everything appeared to proceed according to plan for the first consul. Control of St. Domingue was his first priority, and it was the key to Louisiana. In June he learned that Toussaint L' Ouverture, leader of the resistance to French rule, had surrendered to General Charles Leclerc. In October 1802 Carlos IV officially announced the retrocession of Louisiana to France. Bonaparte commissioned his brother-in-law, Claude Emmanuel Victor, as captain-general of Louisiana to prepare a military expedition that would set sail for New Orleans as soon as the Spanish government delivered the royal order of cession.[51]

Like Jefferson, Madison, Livingston, and other Louisiana businessmen, Clark became anxious about the implications of French control of Louisiana for American interests. He traveled to France, after he had completed a business trip to England in October 1802, to investigate what the French government planned to do with its recovered colony and to seek some commercial advantage from its future rulers. With the help of Livingston, Clark secured an interview with General Victor.[52] Victor told Clark that treaties between Spain and the United States were "waste paper."[53] Clark understood this to mean that France might close the port of New Orleans to American shipping. He also met with Pierre Clément de Laussat, the appointed prefect for Louisiana. Of this meeting, Laussat wrote that he found Clark to be witty and ambitious and that the American consul to New Orleans had established connections with the Spanish officials in Louisiana and wanted to do the same with the new French regime. Laussat recorded that he responded to Clark in a friendly but noncommittal manner.[54]

American Interests and the Purchase of Louisiana

After his meetings in France, Clark returned to England and sailed for the United States on December 24, 1802. Clark arrived in New Orleans on February 25, 1803, and on March 8 he wrote to Madison and stated that his excursion had convinced him that the French were coming to Louisiana with "a determined resolution to injure us essentially on all occasions."[55] As proof of this, Clark cited unlikely conversations that he had with Antoine Roustan, "the confidential agent of the French Capt. General Victor," who had traveled with Clark to New Orleans. According to Clark, Roustan told him that the French would "under various pretences and by means of Jobs and Favors plunder the country in conjunction and divide the Spoil among them." Roustan also described a plan to "detach the Western States from the Union" by opening the French islands to American produce and by excluding U.S. shipping from the Mississippi.[56]

Clark went on to declare that this information had convinced him that the United States should assume control of the colony and told Madison that this could be accomplished through the use of force. He was convinced that Creoles, Spaniards, and Americans could unite to overthrow the government of Louisiana in a bloodless coup. Clark urged the U.S. government to support such an action since it was in the best interests of the United States to do so, and he warned that there would be negative consequences if it hesitated.

> The Inhabitants . . . cry out against our temporising when our dearest interests imperiously call upon us to embrace the favorable moment for acting and they tremble when they see it pass and themselves on the point of falling under the lash of a government they detest and in whose cause they may be afterwards by a military force obliged to sacrifice their lives, by bearing arms against whom they now invite as deliverers.[57]

While Clark was sailing home to New Orleans, negotiations for the possible acquisition of Louisiana by the United States had taken a new turn. In November 1802 Jefferson and Madison learned that the Spanish had closed the port of New Orleans to U.S. shipping in retaliation for American smuggling.[58] To placate American inhabitants in the West and to silence Federalists calling for war, Jefferson wrote to James Monroe on January 10 to inform him that he was to go to France to assist Livingston in his negotiations for the purchase of New Orleans and the Floridas. Monroe and Livingston were authorized to offer as much as $9,375,000 for those possessions. There was some reason to believe in the success of this mission because Bonaparte learned of the defeat of the French force sent to St. Domingue in December 1802. American negotiations would now be conducted "against a great dissolving background—nothing less than the disintegration of Bonaparte's dreams of an American empire."[59]

American Interests and the Purchase of Louisiana

Despite a lack of official support from Madison, Clark did not give up on his plan for the overthrow of the government in Louisiana, however. After he "returned from Europe in the beginning of 1803" and "found the deposit at New Orleans suspended and the French making immediate preparations to take possession of Louisiana," Clark approached William Claiborne, governor of Mississippi Territory, and General James Wilkinson in March 1803 with a plan for armed resistance against French occupation of Louisiana. Clark proposed that New Orleans be taken and "assured them of a certainty of success in consequence of the proffered assistance of the people of the country." To entice Claiborne to support his plan, Clark offered "him, in provisions and money, a sum of $150,000." Claiborne, however, refused to accept this gift. Clark claimed that the Mississippi governor's reason for doing so was that he feared that if the expedition failed, "he being a public officer dependent on the public, would be ruined." Next, Clark offered to put his "whole estate in trust, to be divided between him and me in case the expedition failed." Claiborne responded that he "was afraid of the consequences" and refused to support Clark's plot.[60]

While Clark was unhappy with Claiborne over his failure to support an armed conquest of Louisiana, his attention was diverted to the arrival of Pierre Clément de Laussat, French prefect for Louisiana, on March 26, 1803. Almost immediately after he had established himself in New Orleans, Laussat, following his orders, began to make preparations for the arrival of an expected 3,000 French troops. Clark was delighted to report that the Spanish government of Louisiana was reluctant to help Laussat complete this work. Clark believed that the interests of the United States demanded that he make a bad situation worse for Laussat. This would not be difficult, Clark assured Madison, because Laussat, who was his own worst enemy, could not "always sufficiently command himself" and used a "tone of authority" that angered the rich and frightened the poor. Clark promised that he would take every advantage to "heighten these unfavorable impressions" of the prefect.[61]

In addition to capitalizing on the defects of Laussat's character and the suspicions of Louisianans, Clark hoped to exploit divisions within Laussat's circle of administrators to disrupt his rule. In order to ensure animosity between Laussat and Victor, Clark informed Roustan that Laussat had a negative opinion of him and the captain-general. "In hopes of deriving advantage from their mutual hatred I shall endeavor to foster it; it will prevent all concert in public Measures, the people will be worse governed by their eternally thwarting each other, and will be less inclined to oppose us."[62] Clark also declared that, if desired, he would allow Laussat to believe that he had become the "dupe" of Laussat and possibly a "Convert to his Views and useful to his Government."[63]

Throughout the spring and early summer, Clark continued to criticize Laussat and blamed him for many of the problems that Americans faced in Louisiana. On July 21, 1803, Clark wrote Madison to report that Laussat had "violently opposed" the restoration of the deposit that the Spanish government had suspended for seven months, "even after the Royal Order had been received." Furthermore, Clark declared, Laussat "proposed a variety of vexatious regulations respecting Searches and Visits of our Shipping" and defined Americans "not as a Corps de Nation but as a number of Hordes spread over the Country." Clark was quick to add that he was not certain whether these were the views of Laussat or those of the French government but that Americans "should not have the less to suffer from them." In the end, however, Clark's machinations to discredit Laussat and disrupt his rule proved unnecessary.[64]

In August Clark learned from Madison that Louisiana had become an American possession on April 30, 1803. Monroe had reached France on April 10, and on the same day Bonaparte had confided to his minister of finance, Francois Barbe-Marbois, that he believed that if war between England and France occurred, Louisiana would be England's first target.[65] Bonaparte went on to tell Marbois that he had considered the cession of Louisiana to the United States. Although the Americans had asked for "only one town in Louisiana," Napoleon admitted that he believed "the colony entirely lost."[66]

While he was certain that France would be unable to keep Louisiana, Bonaparte also believed that a formal cession of Louisiana would secure the friendship of the United States. Napoleon was warned repeatedly by his consul general in the United States, Louis Andre Pichon, that the Jefferson administration was hostile to French possession of Louisiana.[67] Madison told Pichon, in their first discussion about Louisiana on July 22, 1801, that French possession of the colony would cause a "collision" between France and the United States.[68] Such a collision could cause problems for Napoleon. Pichon recognized this and in November 1801 reported that the United States maintained "60,000 sailors and 90,000 tons of shipping" and that obstacles to American trade would "then make this people warlike."[69]

Bonaparte also clearly considered that a concrete benefit of cession might be improved trade with a nation that was on course to become a maritime power. Napoleon's decision to cede his North American colony then, was based on his conclusion that Louisiana would "be more useful to the policy and even to the commerce of France than if I should attempt to keep it."[70] Upon reaching this conclusion, Napoleon ordered immediate commencement of real negotiations for the sale of Louisiana. These progressed rapidly, and on April 30, 1803, Louisiana became an American possession.

Napoleon did face some opposition for his sale of Louisiana. Once they learned of their brother's decision, Lucien and Joseph Bonaparte rushed to the Tuileries and expressed their disappointment to Napoleon as he bathed. Outraged at their behavior, Napoleon drenched both of them.[71]

After Clark received the news that Napoleon had ceded Louisiana to the United States, his antagonism toward Laussat abated somewhat as he recognized that the prefect would be forced to end French rule in Louisiana.[72] Clark wrote back to Madison to express his "sincerest joy on the accomplishment of an object so dear to the Heart of every American."[73] According to Clark, the news of the sale gave "general Satisfaction to the Planters and Spaniards (even in Office)" and was disliked by "a few of the merchants and lower Classes of the Towns People only" who were influenced by Laussat.[74]

During the months of August and September 1803, Clark busied himself with preparation of a report on Louisiana for Congress. On July 17, 1803, President Thomas Jefferson had written to the governor of Mississippi Territory, William Claiborne, to request information on Louisiana for Congress "to enable them to take understandingly the best measures for incorporating that country with the Union & for its happy government." The president went on to state that "for this purpose I have sent a set of queries, of which the enclosed is a copy to mr. Daniel Clarke of New Orleans to obtain and forward answers before the meeting of Congress."[75]

Jefferson was thorough in his queries. He asked forty-three questions on subjects ranging from maps, population, militia, land titles, public buildings, and the legal system, to education, government officials, taxation, and the economy.[76] Clark was equally thorough in his responses to the president. He was able to list every officer appointed for the general government and their function, and he estimated that the annual expenditure to govern the colony was six times its annual revenue. Clark was also able to compile very useful estimates on the annual amount of American exports from Louisiana. Clark noted that the United States annually exported 20,000 bales of cotton valued at $1.2 million. Annual sugar exports consisted of about 5,000 casks of sugar valued at $260. Clark was also very familiar with the taxation system and was able to list all of the taxes paid in the colony and the total amount of import and export duties paid to Spain between 1801 and 1803.[77]

Clark provided information not only to Madison and Jefferson but also to Claiborne. On September 20 Clark responded to questions Claiborne asked him regarding Spanish land grants. He reported that the government operated a land office in New Orleans but that it only sold land in West Florida. He also noted that "some years past" the Spanish government had ordered that grants of land would only be given to those who resided in Louisiana, and "that no grants of land shall be made to Americans who may be desirous of settling upon it."[78]

American Interests and the Purchase of Louisiana

In addition to his reports on commerce, government, and land, Clark wrote a description of the Native Americans of Louisiana. *An Account of the Indian Tribes in Louisiana* listed the location and populations of villages. He provided some brief commentary on relations between some of these nations and the white inhabitants of Louisiana.[79]

Daniel Clark was not the only American in Louisiana who provided useful information to the U.S. government. Evan Jones, for his part, wrote Madison a memo on the importance of the establishment of a judicial system that would be best suited to the needs of Louisiana. Jones gave this document, entitled *Hints of Evan Jones: Administration of Justice*, to Clark, who forwarded it to Madison with his own brief comments. Clark stated that he had been induced to send this brief treatise to demonstrate that he was "not singular" in his idea "of a military force being indispensably necessary to maintain Order here."[80] Clark declared that Jones's talents were known to Madison since he had acted as consul. As a personal endorsement, Clark honored Jones with his claim that he had "a great reliance on his Judgement & Experience."[81]

The major point of Jones's report was that the American government and judicial system of Louisiana should be acceptable to its inhabitants. This would ensure Louisianans' support of the U.S. government.

> The most important consequences that may finally flow, from the first impression given to the inhabitants of a newly acquired Country—Of this the natives especially of Louisiana, afford an ample proof—It will therefore be well worthy the wisdom of the U.S. to adopt such a form of Government, and to make such a choice of Magistrates, as may induce the inhabitants at large, to regard the people of America, rather as their fathers & brothers, than as their masters or tyrants![82]

Jones further suggested that magistrate appointment should be given to Americans because even the most powerful Louisianans were ignorant of the laws of the United States. Perhaps with the hope that he would be selected for a judicial post, Jones also declared that "pretty considerable salaries must be annext to the offices, to induce fit persons to accept them."[83]

As they assembled the information sent to them by Americans in Louisiana such as Clark and Jones, Madison and Jefferson became concerned about the possibility of armed resistance to U.S. possession of Louisiana. Madison wrote Clark that there was no need to worry about opposition on the part of Laussat or the French government because France was in the middle of a war with Great Britain. The real danger, Madison warned, was "that Spain, either alarmed by the cession of so much Territory to the United States, or hoping to make her consent the price of concessions on their part, may be so unwise as to oppose the execution of the measure."[84] Because of this possibility, Madison instructed Clark that the president wanted him "to watch every symtom [sic] that may show itself."[85] Clark was further ordered to provide details on Spanish military strength and to find out whether Louisianans would support a U.S. force if it were marched to New Orleans.

Clark wrote back to Madison and asked him to "assure the President" that he would advise him on "every symptom indicative of a hostile or hostile intention toward us from any Quarter whatever" and that he would "spare no pains or exertions to increase the attachment of the People of this Country to the Government of the U.S."[86] Clark confirmed Madison's hypothesis that Laussat would see the necessity of cooperation with, rather than resistance to, the government of the United States. He reported that the prefect's "decided enmity to the Individuals and Government of the U.S." had "given place to more Pacific and friendly Views."[87]

In addition, Clark reassured Madison that he foresaw no real possibility of opposition to the transfer to the United States from Spain. Specifically, Clark suggested that because of the "animosities between the two authorities, French and Spanish," each authority would attempt to serve the United States at the "expence of the other." The result of this, Clark predicted, would be that French and Spanish officials would "mutually betray and lay open each others Plans."[88] Real opposition, Clark declared, would appear after Louisiana became a territory of the United States.

> On the whole I am fearful of very little trouble with respect to taking possession—the trouble I apprehend will be more likely to occur afterwards when all the Evils attendant on a Change of Government viz a new Language, new Officers, new Laws, new Courts, and new forms of Justice, etc. etc. etc. are felt and before the blessings expected can be realized. . . . Add to this the anarchy now existing, the necessity of immediate organization, the diversity of nations of which we are composed, our jarring political Sentiments, our entire ignorance of political Liberty, the different Opinions of what would best suit us, the violence and impatience of the Creole Character, and you will conceive a part of the difficulties the Man will have to labor under, who will have the task of governing us imposed on him and the necessity that he should be a person of talents, experience and even Consequence at home, in order to inspire Confidence in his measures.[89]

If that were not enough to suggest that he should be selected as governor, Clark went on to suggest that the "Government of this country may at first be made so lucrative as to make it desireable [sic] to persons of the first talents and character in the U.S."[90]

American Interests and the Purchase of Louisiana

In his ambition to serve as U.S. governor of Louisiana, Clark would be disappointed. On October 31, eleven days after Clark wrote his letter to Madison that hinted at his qualifications and experience, Congress passed An Act Enabling the President to Take Possession of Louisiana. This act gave Jefferson the power to use the army and navy to secure possession if necessary. In addition, the president was granted the power to direct and appoint all government officials in Louisiana unless Congress provided for a temporary government before the session of Congress ended.[91] Jefferson used his new powers to appoint the governor of Mississippi, William Claiborne, governor of Louisiana. Madison immediately sent Claiborne his governor's commission and two additional commissions for Claiborne and General Wilkinson to receive Louisiana from France on behalf of the United States.[92]

On the same date that Jefferson appointed Claiborne governor of Louisiana, Madison wrote letters to Clark and Claiborne in which he again mentioned his fears of Spanish resistance to the future cession of Louisiana to the United States. Madison ordered Claiborne to determine whether a U.S. force with the support of "well disposed inhabitants" could "dispossess the Spanish authorities."[93] On this subject, Madison instructed Claiborne to communicate with Laussat and Clark, "[w]hose sanction to the use of force, and co-operation therein, is particularly to be wished." In his letter to Clark, Madison suggested that the U.S. consul possessed "knowledge of local circumstances" and an "acquaintance with the disposition of the people" that would enable him to direct a "cooperating movement of the well disposed part of the Inhabitants" against the Spanish if it proved necessary.[94]

In addition to military preparations, the U.S. government took additional steps to ensure the peaceful transfer of Louisiana to the United States. On November 15 Congress issued an *Address to the People of New Orleans* to warn Louisianans that it would not be in their best interests to participate in any Spanish resistance to the transfer. The address declared that it would be the "peculiar happiness" of Louisianans to come under the rule "of a philosopher who prefers justice to conquest."[95] In another move to win support of Louisianans, the U.S. government, possibly on the basis of a suggestion from Clark, set a transition period for the transfer of Louisiana. France would be granted a symbolic period of rule of the colony for a few weeks. As a result, Laussat ruled Louisiana from November 30 to December 20, 1803.[96]

At noon on November 30, 1803, Laussat assumed control of the government of Louisiana. He issued a proclamation to announce this and the sale of Louisiana to the United States. After he expressed sentiments of friendship for the United States, Laussat spoke about Louisianans' future under American rule. He focused his remarks on the third article of the treaty of cession and specifically noted the clause that stated that Louisianans would be "incorporated into the union of the United States, & admitted as soon as possible according to the principles of the Federal Constitution, to the enjoyment of rights advantages & immunities of citizens of the United States." Laussat also pointed out that the third article stated that until Louisianans enjoyed the rights of citizenship, they would be "maintained and protected in the enjoyment [of] their liberties and possessions and in the practice of the religions they possess." Based on the "nature of the government of the United States" and the guarantees made in the third article of the treaty, Laussat concluded that Louisianans would have even

> under a provisional system, popular leaders, subject with impunity to your protests and your censure, & who will have need of your votes & your affections. Public affairs & interests far from being prohibited to you, will be your own affairs and interests, over which wise and impartial opinions will be sure to obtain preponderant influence in the long run, & to which even you could not remain indifferent without experiencing bitter repentance.[97]

In addition to spoken promises, Laussat made real changes in the government of the colony. The most important of these was his elimination of the Spanish city administration of New Orleans and the creation of a French municipal council. Laussat claimed that he wanted "some merchants, some Americans, and some experienced businessmen for his council."[98] All of his choices for the key positions in this council, however, went to prominent French Louisianans.

For mayor of New Orleans he chose Etienne de Boré, whom he described as "a wealthy, industrious settler, who never flinched before Spanish officials and who had a well-earned reputation for patriotism and integrity."[99] Laussat also "looked about for a secretary registrar who might make this political machine function—one who might be its soul and who might have honesty, talent, diplomacy and popularity."[100] He finally settled upon Pierre Derbigny, an accomplished lawyer. His choice for first deputy was Jean Nöel Destréhan. The prefect had come to know Destréhan during a visit to his plantation and described him as "the most active and intelligent sugar planter of the colony."[101] Another planter, Jean Sauvé, was Laussat's choice for second deputy.

Although they received no executive positions, Laussat did appoint three Americans to the nine-member municipal council. One of these was Evan Jones, "a wealthy American and a naturalized Spaniard of long standing." To enforce the rule of the city council, Laussat required a commander of militia. He chose Joseph de Ville de Goutin Bellechasse, a Spanish officer who had retired "under hardly favorable conditions because of the intrigues of the Marquis de Casa Calvo, whom he had defied."[102]

American Interests and the Purchase of Louisiana

Laussat described his establishment of the municipal council as the "dominant act of my short-lived reign and the one to which I attached the greatest importance because of its possible long-term consequences for the future of Louisiana."[103] Clark suggested that Laussat's "Experiment" would "give the lower classes a hankering for French Government and arouse that Spirit which I have long attempted to subdue."[104]

Despite the fact that he did not support Laussat's government, Daniel Clark advised the prefect on municipal and military appointments. On November 29, 1803, Clark wrote Madison and informed him that he had spoken with Laussat, who had outlined the structure of his proposed municipal government and "communicated his Plans with the names of the Persons he designed to fill the different Offices civil and military."[105] According to Clark, Laussat told the governor about his plan to create these positions, and so it was "too late to dissuade him from his purpose, but he made no difficulty in making such Changes among the administrative Officers as I thought necessary." One of the appointments that Clark declared he had involved himself with was that of the commander of militia. Initially, Bellechasse refused to accept this office and informed Clark of his refusal. Clark told Madison that he advised his "friend to accept the command being better pleased to see it in his hands than in those of a Person in whom I could not confide."[106]

In addition to assisting Laussat with the establishment of a municipal government, Clark also aided the prefect and advanced his own career by taking measures to preserve the peace in Louisiana during the three weeks of French rule. At George King's coffeehouse, "the general rendezvous for Americans," Clark and other Americans in New Orleans met and discussed the possibility of raising a militia company to serve Prefect Laussat until Commissioners Claiborne and Wilkinson arrived to take possession of Louisiana. A witness to this meeting, Woodson Wren, recorded that "Daniel Clark was requested to raise the company and take command of it which he did."[107]

On November 30, 1803, the date of a ceremony to mark the transfer of Louisiana from Spain to France, Laussat was happy to note in his journal that Clark had offered the services of an American militia that he had formed.[108] According to Laussat, he and Clark "agreed that we would call on them only when needed and that during the ceremonies they would be prepared for any eventuality."[109] To the relief of the prefect and the U.S. consul, no uprising occurred to threaten French government of Louisiana. Clark's militia, which consisted of 150 Americans and fifty "inhabitants," kept order in the city of New Orleans throughout Laussat's brief reign.[110]

By December Clark was even more convinced and relieved that the transfer of Louisiana to the United States would occur without any serious problems. He wrote to Madison to report that he had received a letter from Claiborne and Wilkinson dated December 7, 1803, stating that they would be prepared to depart from Fort Adams the next day. This was good news for Clark, who hoped that they would "shortly arrive to relieve us of the irksome situation we are in."[111]

Less than a week after Clark wrote Madison to report that he expected Wilkinson and Claiborne to arrive in New Orleans, Laussat met with them on December 19 to discuss the procedure and ceremony for the transfer of Louisiana to the United States. Wilkinson had some last-minute fears that the transfer ceremony would be interrupted after Clark provided him with information of a conspiracy to "fire the town," but New Orleans remained quiet.[112] The next day Laussat ordered the reading of the treaty of transfer, and the American flag was raised in front of the city hall. Daniel Clark's role as U.S. consul to New Orleans had effectively ended.

In Washington, members of the Jefferson administration joyfully received news of the peaceful transfer of Louisiana. "For some it seemed incongruous for a republic aspiring to democracy to glory in an imperial venture but the event was important enough for rejoicing in grand style."[113]

For many Louisianans the reality of the United States' "imperial venture" would prove unworthy of celebration. On the first day of American rule of Louisiana General Wilkinson wrote to the secretary of war and requested him to

> dispose of a Garrison of 500 Regulars for the place as soon as possible, for indeed I apprehend difficulties from various causes—The formidable aspect of the armed Blacks & Malattoes, officered and organized, is painful and perplexing and the people have no Idea but of Iron domination at this moment.[114]

If Wilkinson was truly concerned that the administration in Washington might not consider that Louisianans were accustomed to "Iron domination," he need not have worried. As Jefferson's appointed representative, Governor William Claiborne exercised almost unlimited power. There was little to distinguish the garrison government structure of American government in Louisiana from that of its predecessors. Louisiana, once a colony of Spain and France, had become an imperial territory of the United States.

CHAPTER TWO

A Conquered People

The View from Washington

Jefferson declared that the purchase of Louisiana enlarged America's "empire of liberty," despite the fact that the American government established for Louisiana lacked any representative features. The president considered the acquisition of this new western territory as essential to the future prosperity of the United States. "I look to this duplication of area for the extending a government so free and economical as ours, as a great achievement to the mass of happiness which is to ensue." When he wrote this in January 1804, Louisianans clearly did not yet enjoy any of the benefits of a free government. The territory was administered under an act of October 31, 1803, entitled An Act Enabling the President to Take Possession of Louisiana. This act, written by Jefferson himself, gave the president the power to vest "all the military, civil and judicial powers exercised by the officers of the existing government (under France) in such person and persons . . . as the President of the United States shall direct." Jefferson appointed one man, William Claiborne, to "exercise all the powers and authorities heretofore exercised by the Governor and Intendant."[1] Because he was granted the powers of two colonial administrators Claiborne was a more powerful figure in Louisiana than any of the Spanish officials who had ruled Louisiana in the past. Claiborne was also granted an unprecedented amount of freedom to make his own decisions as he exercised his authority at the beginning of his reign. In a letter that accompanied Claiborne's commission, Madison informed Claiborne that his powers were "very extensive by law" and that "for the manner of exercising those ample powers no particular instructions are now given by the president." Like Jefferson, Madison also provided no specific instructions to Claiborne. "You will be led by your own judgement and your correct principles and dispositions to a prudent moderation."[2]

While Jefferson had helped to create an American viceroy in Louisiana, it is clear that he did not intend Claiborne to rule until his death. The Louisiana government established by the act of October 31, 1803, was defined as temporary. Claiborne's commission stated that he was to hold power until "the end of the present session of Congress unless provision to be sooner made for the temporary government of the territory so ceded by France to the United States." As Claiborne began his rule as governor, Senator John Breckinridge of Kentucky, who had a great interest in the purchase, presented a bill for the government of Louisiana on behalf of a Senate committee appointed for that purpose.[3]

While Congress debated the Breckinridge Bill for the government of Louisiana, Claiborne worried about the power that Jefferson had granted him to rule the new American province. During his second week as governor, he admitted that he did not feel equal to the task assigned him. He was uneasy with "the great latitude of powers" that were "temporarily entrusted" to him and found the "exercise of discretionary power in matters of the moment" an "irksome duty." Claiborne "indulged the anxious hope" that Congress would soon relieve him from "the weight of responsibility" that was placed upon him.[4]

Claiborne was not alone in his belief that he was not equipped to govern Louisiana. Jefferson had wanted a governor who was skilled in diplomacy, who could speak French, and who could win the trust of the people of Louisiana.[5] With these criteria in mind, Jefferson first considered Thomas Sumter Jr. for the position. Sumter spoke French and had served on Robert Livingston's staff as secretary to the legation to Paris. Sumter was eliminated, however, as a possible candidate after he had a serious disagreement with Livingston. The president also considered the Marquis de Lafayette for the position and then turned to James Monroe, who was fluent in French, well versed in the history and politics of the region, and served the United States during the Jay-Gardoqui discussions and in the Paris negotiations for the Louisiana Purchase. Monroe wrote Jefferson from London and rejected the offer with the argument that an "appointment to Louisiana" would be "incompatible" with his efforts to conclude treaties with England and Spain.[6]

In addition to those who were offered the post of governor of Louisiana by Jefferson, there were some who wanted to be considered but were not asked, such as Andrew Jackson; Fulwar Skipwith, who at the time was in Paris as commercial agent of the United States; and Daniel Clark. Clark's acquaintances and government officials in Washington questioned his trustworthiness. On August 11, 1803, Benjamin Morgan, a New Orleans merchant, wrote to a friend, Chandler Price, and advised that Clark wanted to be appointed governor. Morgan noted that he and Clark were "good friends" but that Clark was too "deficient in dignity of Character and sterling veracity to fill the office of governor" and that he was "liked by few of the Americans" in Louisiana except those "dependant upon him."[7] Like Morgan, Secretary of the Treasury

Albert Gallatin also distrusted Clark. On September 3, 1803, Gallatin suggested that Clark could be informed of the government's plans for Louisiana if he could be trusted to that extent.[8]

Clark was not offered the office of governor, and Jefferson's first two choices for this position, Lafayette and Monroe, had refused it. William Claiborne was appointed governor because Jefferson trusted him and because he would accept the post. In a letter to John Dickinson written in 1807, Jefferson reflected on his choice for Louisiana and declared that he had selected Claiborne because he was a "firm republican" and because he was the only available choice for the job. "There were characters superior to him whom I wished to appoint but they refused the office; I know of no better man who would accept of it, and it would not be right to turn him out for one not better." The fact that Claiborne had previously served as the governor of Mississippi Territory was probably an additional reason that Jefferson chose him.[9]

Despite his anxiety about his position, Claiborne recognized his own shortcomings as a "stranger in the Country" and promised Madison that he would govern the colony according "to the intentions of the President, and the expectations of the inhabitants." Claiborne, however, indicated in a letter to Madison of January 2 that he had little regard for the expectations of the inhabitants or for the inhabitants themselves. He found that the people expressed a desire and an admiration for republicanism because there "was something in the plain principle of equal rights which comes within the Scope of the meanest Capacity." Few of those who were friends of republicanism, however, according to Claiborne, "had cultivated an acquaintance with her principles."[10]

While Claiborne was critical of Louisianans' expectations and capacities in general, he was specific in his condemnation of Louisiana's elite.

The Merchants as well as the planters in this Country appear to be wealthy, their habits of living are luxurious and expensive. . . . The attainments of *some of the first people* consist of only a few exterior accomplishments. Frivolous diversions seem to be among their primary pleasures, and the display of Wealth and the parade of power constitute their highest objects of admiration.[11]

As Claiborne secretly expressed his negative impressions of Louisianans, they began to form an unfavorable opinion of their governor. An incident that contributed to this occurred on January 22, 1804. Although he apparently disliked frivolous diversions, Claiborne served as master of ceremonies for a public ball that was interrupted by a disturbance. George W. Morgan, an American who attended the ball, reported that toward the end of an English country-dance headed by Governor Claiborne, "some individuals called (in the French language) for the Waltz in so loud a manner as to stop the Musick of the English dance." Claiborne halted the ball and, with General James Wilkinson, attempted to restore order. As Wilkinson began to remove a Frenchman who continued to cry for the waltz, "disorder" resulted, and the Americans "being desirous to protect their chiefs rallied around them and sang Hail Columbia (a Patriotic Air) which was attempted to be interrupted by some Frenchmen singing the Marseilles Hymn."[12] Morgan noted that Claiborne was unable to quell the disturbance. "His Excellency Governor Claiborne seemed much distressed by this unfortunate difference, finding that his best efforts to maintain good order by the mildest means had been to no avail."[13]

Claiborne wrote to Madison on February 7 and provided his own account of the incident at the ball. He noted that the fracas itself was not serious, but that it had dangerous consequences. "A Difference of rather a serious nature, has sprung up from apparently from a very trivial Source, between the American and French Citizens (in which hitherto, the Creoles or natives of this Province, have taken no Open Part, though we suppose them to favor decidedly the French interest)."[14]

While it is not clear that the Creoles favored the French interest, it is certain that some viewed the incident at the ball as proof that Claiborne was not suitable for the office of governor of Louisiana. The mayor of New Orleans, Etienne de Boré, attended the ball and suggested this in a letter to Jefferson. Boré wrote that he wanted to put Jefferson in a position to "see our situation and our feelings through other eyes than foreign eyes or eyes which are new among us."[15] Boré claimed that it was "not in the midst of pleasures, at balls, in the midst of a great throng of women who constituted their charm and agreeableness, that one would expect to see this spirit of disturbance and discord arise" but that differences and disturbances such as those that occurred at the ball were "favoured or even aggravated by those who had the duty to suppress them."[16]

The source of Claiborne's failure as governor, Boré asserted, was his inability to speak French. It was "indispensable" that the "heads of Louisiana should know the French language as well the English language." If the rulers of Louisiana "had had this advantage, we should not have experienced the occurrences which have produced so bad a Feeling and the course of business would not languish and Would not be exposed to numberless embarrassments." The language barrier between the governor and his subjects, according to Boré, had frustrated municipal councilors who became even more upset when Claiborne "began from the start by suggesting to us that we should draw up our public acts in English."[17]

This was a change of policy that Louisianans considered an attack on custom that the Spanish had respected. Because "despotic" Spain respected their customs, Boré argued, Louisianans should expect the same from a "Republican government, in which the principles of natural rights have so many Safeguards" and which the people of Louisiana were "associated Under the guarantees of a treaty" that included "Sacred Stipulations" in their favor.[18]

Boré claimed that Louisianans also hoped that Congress would grant them a better system of government. He knew that Congress was at work on a bill to establish a new form of government for Louisiana and claimed that Louisianans were "in extreme impatience for the Bills which must fix our internal Organization." Until Louisiana became a state, Boré warned, Louisianans would only be satisfied with one form of government. The "continual object" of the "hopes" and conversations of "all louisianians" was that they be given "your *Second degree* of Government." This second degree of government would include a constitution "in agreement with our needs and wishes."[19]

It is unclear where Boré learned of the "*Second degree*" of government, but this was probably a reference to the Northwest Ordinance of 1787: a three-stage plan for territorial government devised by James Monroe that replaced an earlier plan designed by Jefferson. In recommending his plan, Monroe advised Jefferson that he thought it best to create a "Colonial Govt. similar to that which prevail'd in these states previous to the revolution." In the first stage of government, Congress appointed a governor who would have absolute executive and legislative power. A five-man council and a secretary were to assist the governor. In the second stage of government, elections for an assembly would be held when the population of a territory reached 5,000 free male inhabitants. One representative would be elected to the assembly for every 500 inhabitants. This assembly did not have the power to make or pass legislation; this was reserved for the governor and his council. In the third stage, three to five states were to be formed out of the Northwest, and population for statehood was set at 60,000.[20]

Compared to state governments in existence at the time of the establishment of the Northwest Ordinance, the first and second stages of territorial government appear despotic. "In the first stage it did not afford even the most meager elements of popular government to be found in the colonies in the seventeenth century." The second stage of the ordinance "did not simply revert to the second British stage of representative government; it made all of the changes made in the British system after 1763 that strengthened the governor's office."[21]

While territorial government was clearly less democratic than state government, Louisiana in 1804 did not have the stage one government outlined in the Northwest Ordinance. Boré, speaking for Louisianans, clearly expected more from Congress than a government that consisted of a governor appointed by the president. While he recognized that Louisiana would not be admitted as a state until its population was counted, he had reason to believe that at the very least Congress would grant it the "second degree" of government. Louisiana met the 5,000 free male requirements for this stage of territorial government.

Boré was unaware, however, that Jefferson had rejected the Northwest Ordinance as a format for government of Louisianans in November 1803 because "it would turn all their laws topsy-turvy." Despite this, Jefferson still believed it best to "appoint a governor and three judges, with legislative powers; only providing that the judges shall form the laws, & the Governor have a negative only, subject further to the negative of the National Legislature." By his abandonment of the Northwest Ordinance as the principle for the organization of the government of Louisiana, Jefferson committed himself to the creation of a new form of territorial government. He again turned to Breckinridge to present his plan for the government of Louisiana to the Senate in the form of a bill. Jefferson suggested that strong executive government was necessary and prepared an outline for territorial government for Breckinridge. Jefferson was nervous that his role in the preparation of this bill would be discovered, as he warned Breckinridge "to never let any person know that I have put pen to paper on the subject and that if you think that the enclosed can be of any aid to, you will take the trouble to copy it and return me the original."[22]

Congress passed An Act for the Organization of Orleans Territory and the Louisiana District on March 26, 1804.[23] What is striking about the structure of government created by this act is that it had none of the limited representative features of the Northwest Ordinance. Section 2 of the act declared that the executive power would be vested in a governor who would "hold his office during the term of three years unless sooner removed by the President of the United States." The governor was also granted the position of commander in chief of the militia. Finally, the governor was given the authority to "appoint and commission all officers civil and of the militia" whose appointments were not already provided for by law. In essence, Claiborne's powers, as outlined by the act of March 26, 1804, were no different than those that Jefferson had granted through the act of October 31, 1803.[24]

As in the act of October 31, 1803, the governor was granted legislative powers. By the fourth section of the act of March 26, 1804, however, the governor was to share these powers "with thirteen of the most fit and discreet persons of the territory, to be called the Legislative Council." The president was to appoint the Legislative Council, and the governor had the authority to convene or prorogue it whenever he deemed it "expedient." With the advice and consent of the Legislative Council, the governor had "power to alter, modify or repeal the laws." The only real restriction on the governor and council was that Congress could strike down any territorial laws.[25]

Finally, section six outlined the selection process for officials. "The governor, secretary, judges, district attorney, marshal and all general officers of the militia, shall be appointed by the President of the United States, in the recess of the Senate; but shall be nominated at their next meeting for their advice and consent."[26]

In sum, the act passed on March 26, 1804, empowered the president, through his appointed officials, to govern Louisiana. Why had Jefferson not included any representative features in this plan for territorial government? While he had rejected the Northwest Ordinance, which included a provision for elected assemblies, on the basis that it would turn the laws of Louisiana "topsy-turvy," Jefferson also expressed a belief that Louisianans were not suited for popular government. A few weeks before he sent his plan for the government of Louisiana to Breckinridge, the president had declared that Louisianans were "as yet incapable of self-government as children."[27]

Jefferson was not alone in making this assertion. Daniel Clark had warned Jefferson of Louisianans' "entire ignorance of political liberty." William Claiborne shared Clark's opinion. "The more I become acquainted with the inhabitants of this province," Claiborne declared, "the more I am convinced of their unfitness for representative government." Claiborne stated that Louisianans were "uninformed, indolent, luxurious—in a word, illy fitted to be useful citizens of the Republic." Because Louisianans were incapable of governing themselves, Claiborne suggested that "territorial government of the *first grade*" was "best suited to this province."[28]

There were a few Americans, however, who were outspokenly critical of the Jefferson administration's plan to govern Louisiana as England had governed the thirteen colonies. Before the passage of An Act for the Organization of Orleans Territory and the Louisiana District, some senators and congressmen voiced opposition to various aspects of Jefferson's proposal for Louisiana government, known as the Breckinridge Bill, for the Kentucky senator's role in championing it in Congress. Foremost among these was Senator John Quincy Adams of Massachusetts, who was appalled that the Jefferson administration planned to tax Louisianans, despite the fact that the Breckinridge Bill did not include a provision for an elected assembly. While he did not express sympathy for Louisianans, Adams was not prepared to accept taxation without representation for any people governed by the United States.

In early January Adams worked on "resolutions" that he planned to introduce to the Senate in an attempt to amend the Breckinridge Bill so that Louisianans were not taxed without their consent. Adams admitted that this effort caused him some anxiety and that his resolutions would be as futile as the use of a "feather against a whirlwind," but in his diary on January 8, he noted that their presentation to the Senate was necessary as a matter of principle.

> Varied the resolutions, which I have concluded to offer to the Senate on the subject of the Louisiana revenue. The subject has already given me one sleepless night. Yet for what? For the Constitution I have sworn to support—for the Treaty that binds our national faith—for the principles of Justice—and for opposing to the utmost of my power those who in this measure will violate them all.[29]

When the Senate debate on the Breckinridge Bill for the government of Louisiana began on January 10, 1804, Adams introduced three resolutions. His first of these was that "the people of the United States" had "never, in any manner delegated to this Senate, the power of giving its legislative concurrence to any act for imposing taxes upon the inhabitants of Louisiana, without their consent." In his second resolution, Adams warned the Senate that the taxation of Louisianans without their consent would set a dangerous precedent. "Resolved that by concurring in any act of legislation for imposing taxes upon the inhabitants of Louisiana without their consent, this Senate would assume a power, unwarranted by the Constitution & dangerous to the liberties of the people of the United States." Finally, in his third resolution Adams declared that "the power for originating bills for raising revenue" was "exclusively vested in the House of Representatives." Because of this, Adams claimed that his resolutions should be carried to the House and that the members of the House should "adopt such measures as to their wisdom may appear necessary & expedient, for raising and collecting a revenue from Louisiana."[30]

After he read his resolutions, Adams urged that they be "taken up in the usual course of business, be postponed and till tomorrow, be printed & laid upon the table." This was refused. Adams then went on to defend his resolutions by quoting from the Declaration of Independence and the journals of Congress of 1774 and 1775, "to prove that they were the very principles on which the American Revolution was founded." This failed to persuade the Senate to adopt Adams's resolutions.[31]

On January 16, 1804, the Senate received a message from Jefferson. The president congratulated Congress for the purchase, which secured fertile lands, ensured a prosperous future for western citizens, and contributed to the "peace and security of the nation in general." Finally, Jefferson stated that the citizens of the United States had obtained "new brethren to partake of the blessings of freedom and self-government."[32]

Federalist politicians in the Senate and in the House of Representatives did not rejoice in the president's message of congratulations. In fact, many such as William Plumer, Federalist senator from New Hampshire who, like John Quincy Adams, later joined the Republicans, considered the Republican achievement the death knell of New England's political influence. This fundamental fear underlay all of the Federalist arguments against the Breckinridge Bill in the House and the Senate. Plumer believed that Jefferson's plan for the government of Louisiana, which placed control of the territory in the hands of the president, was a model designed to ensure a Republican "empire of liberty."

> This [bill] gives an encreased weight of patronage to the Executive; and lays a foundation to make new States. These new States, if we may judge from those lately made, will prove so many satellites moving round and subordinate to Virginia. The weight & influence of New England in the councils & legislation of the Union, will soon be reduced to a cypher.[33]

Oliver Wolcott Jr. shared Plumer's concerns about Louisiana. As he had explained earlier to Fisher Ames, Wolcott informed Roger Griswold in January 1804 that an American Louisiana would be "connected with the dismemberment of the existing Union, and the subjugation of the Southern States." Wolcott went on to imply that this was the goal of the Republicans. Division of the Union and control of the Southern states were "two events which in charity, we are bound to suppose, were not foreseen by the present administration, unless they suppose the reelection of Mr. Jefferson for the term of four years, an equivalent for these consequences."[34]

Given that the Federalists believed that their political existence depended on successful resistance to the Breckinridge Bill, it is not surprising that they worked to oppose it and limit the influence of a potential Republican-controlled Louisiana government. For Republicans, the potential elimination of the Federalist Party and expansion of a Republican empire were incentive enough for most Republicans to toe the line on the bill. There were exceptions, however. Republican senators and congressmen in western states commercially connected to the Mississippi, such as Ohio, Kentucky, and Tennessee, recognized that an additional western representative government would share their interests and support them in Washington. Because of this, some western Republicans in Congress pushed for representative government in Orleans Territory. Matthew Lyon was one of these.

Lyon had served as a congressman for Vermont in Congress during the 1790s. During that time he had "played the role of ideologue of Republicanism." In 1801, however, Lyon moved to Kentucky and became engaged in western trade, shipping meats such as pork and venison hams to New Orleans and cotton for the cities of the East. By 1802 Lyon expanded his operations and became a cotton planter. After he had successfully established his business affairs, Lyon ran for Congress and was elected, but "he was no longer a spokes-man for a crusading political movement." It was evident that "during his sec-ond congressional career, his position in Congress reflected his new concerns both as a merchant and as a representative of the southwestern frontier."[35]

Another major factor that influenced the debate over the Breckinridge Bill was the fact that Congress had to devise a government in a territory where the majority of Louisianans, whether they were French, Spanish, Acadian, or Creole, were Catholics who lived alongside a growing minority of American Protestants. The British government had faced a similar situation with regard to Quebec after 1763. A majority of French and French Canadian Catholics lived with a growing minority of British Protestants. Parliament attempted to establish a government structure for that province in 1774 through the Quebec Bill, which included provisions for the establishment of an appointed gover-nor and council. There was some debate in Parliament over the question of representation for the inhabitants of the province, as there was a sense "that representative institutions were the birthright of all British subjects, and to deny them was to support despotism." Opponents of the bill considered that an administration by an appointed governor and council would subvert the constitution and that the king of England would simply replace the king of France and "have a taste of what is deemed so delicious, arbitrary power." An additional opposition argument was that the establishment of arbitrary rule in Quebec would lead to arbitrary rule in England. "If the government was able to get away with it in the colonies, who would stop it in Britain?"[36]

Despite opposition and petitions for representation from both English and French inhabitants of Quebec, "it was a foregone conclusion that the new con-stitution would not provide for an assembly." The reason for this was that "not the most ardent advocate of representative institutions would have suggested that, fifteen years after the Conquest, when there was strong suspicion that France had not forgotten her old colony, the assembly should be turned over to the Roman Catholic majority."[37]

Instead of a representative assembly, the Quebec Act of 1774 established a council that was to have between seventeen and twenty-three members, whom the governor could suspend or dismiss at will. It would meet with the governor for the first four months of every year. With the consent of the gov-ernor, the council could pass laws that would be sent to London for review and disallowed if necessary before the next meeting of the council.[38]

In terms of structure, the system of government established by the Quebec Act is remarkably similar to that proposed in the Breckinridge Bill for Loui-siana. In both cases, absence of representative institutions would ensure that Catholic inhabitants could exert little influence within provincial government. English inhabitants of Quebec, however, did not believe that the Quebec Act went far enough in limiting the possibility of Catholic participation in government. They wanted a guarantee of an "exclusively Protestant council, or at least one including 'only a few of the more moderate sort of Roman Catholics.'" The desire of the English inhabitants of Quebec to limit the influence of Catholics was rooted in their belief that "Roman Catholics were unreliable citizens, rendered incapable by their religion of offering full and single-minded loyalty to the state."[39]

Fear of Roman Catholic influence in North America was not limited to British subjects of Quebec. The Continental Congress vehemently protested the Quebec Act's provision for the existence of the Roman Catholic Church in a British province. In a statement to the people of Great Britain in September 1774, the Continental Congress declared its "astonishment that British Parliament should ever consent to establish in that country a religion that has deluged your island in blood and dispersed impiety, bigotry, persecution, murder and rebellion through every part of the world." Alexander Hamilton repeated this belief in 1775, in a pamphlet entitled *Remarks on the Quebec Bill*. Tom Paine declared that "an aim of Parliament was to subvert the Protestant Religion" by "the Roman Catholic Religion not tolerated but established."[40]

The anti-Catholic attack on the Quebec Act by the Continental Congress and Revolutionary leaders became part of American Revolutionary heritage. "In a sense, the tradition of anti-popery facilitated the creation of a new nation by permitting England to be cast off as morally corrupt and by allowing colonists to proudly assert that they were the real guardians of a Protestant ideal that had been lost elsewhere." Less than twenty-five years after the American Revolution, the belief that the United States was a Protestant republic threatened by the pope and his Catholics in North America existed alongside the widespread belief in popular representation for all. These beliefs collided during the Breckinridge Bill debate on representation for the inhabitants of Louisiana.[41]

Immediately after Jefferson's message of congratulations for the purchase of Louisiana was read, on January 16, 1804, the Senate resumed debate on the Breckinridge Bill. Republican Thomas Worthington of Ohio moved to amend the fourth section of the bill to allow the Legislative Council to elect a representative to Congress who would have the right to debate but not vote. This motion was rejected by Timothy Pickering, an "old school" Massachusetts Federalist who declared that Louisiana was "a purchased province" and that it was "therefore absurd to admit a delegate from that country to debate in our national councils."[42] Republican James Jackson of Georgia supported his party's position on the bill and argued that "the people of that country ought not to be represented in Congress." Federalist John Quincy Adams also "reluctantly" rejected the motion on the basis that it was a violation of the

Constitution and because, as the Federalists most feared, the delegate would be "the representative of the Executive & not of the people."[43]

Republican Joseph Anderson of Tennessee, however, used Adams's argument against taxation without consent to support the motion for the amendment. "If this amendment does not obtain," the senator from Tennessee exclaimed, "I must vote agt. the section. What tax the people without their being represented!" Republican William Cocke, the other Tennessee senator, also strongly supported the proposed amendment. "Gentlemen confound things—this man will not be a representative but a delegate. . . . I know *that* the people are ignorant, but ignorant people will always elect learned and wise men to represent them, they know the necessity of it."[44] These arguments did not sway the majority of senators, however. The proposal was rejected in a vote by a margin of eighteen to twelve.

What is most apparent about this vote is that western Republicans voted in favor of a delegate to Congress. John Breckinridge of Kentucky, William Cocke and Joseph Anderson of Tennessee, John Smith and Thomas Worthington of Ohio, and George Logan of Pennsylvania all voted in favor of a Louisiana delegate to Congress. All of the Federalist senators voted against the proposed amendment. This is not surprising given their fear of expanded Republican representation. Eastern Republicans, with the exception of Israel Smith of Vermont and Samuel Potter and Christopher Ellery of Rhode Island, supported the Breckinridge Bill and voted against the proposed amendment.[45]

As debate continued in the Senate on January 24, 1804, a proposed amendment to the fourth section of the Breckinridge Bill for the popular election of the Legislative Council was discussed. Republican senators James Jackson of Georgia, Samuel Smith of Maryland, and William C. Nicholas of Virginia and Federalist senator Timothy Pickering of Massachusetts all opposed popular election of the Legislative Council for the expressed reason that Louisianans were too ignorant to elect a government. Jackson stated plainly that Louisianans were "too ignorant to elect a legislature" and that they would "consider jurors as a curse to them." Smith echoed this belief and stated that "those people are absolutely incapable of governing themselves, of electing their rulers or appointing jurors." Smith promised, however, that he would support popular government in Louisiana when its people were "capable & fit to enjoy liberty and a free government." Nicholas approved of the bill as it was and opposed giving Louisianans "the rights of election or the rights of having jurors." And Pickering claimed that "that people are incapable of performing the duties or enjoying the blessings of a free government—They are too ignorant to elect suitable men."[46]

Republican senators Samuel Maclay of Pennsylvania and Anderson and Cocke challenged Jackson, Nicholas, Pickering, and Smith. Maclay was the first to attack the assertion that ignorance of a people was a basis for the denial of self-government: "Those people are men and capable of happiness—they ought to elect a legislature & have jurors." Cocke rejected the entire Breckinridge Bill: "The people of that country are free—let them have liberty & a free government—This bill I hope will not pass—it is tyrannical." Anderson went further in his criticism of the bill: "This bill has not a single feature of our government in it—it is a system of tyranny destructive of elective rights—We are bound by treaty, & must give that people a free elective government."[47]

On January 24 senators who supported the idea of some form of popular participation in the government of Louisiana again attempted to modify the fourth section of the Breckinridge Bill. A motion was introduced to have the governor divide the territory into twenty-four districts. The residents of each district would then elect "two of the most fit and discreet" landholders. Out of these representatives, the governor was to select one from each district for the Legislative Council. Opinion on this motion was almost evenly divided; it was defeated by only one vote (fifteen nays to fourteen yeas).[48]

Immediately after this vote was held, Jefferson, determined to ensure that Louisianans did not receive a representative government from Congress, presented a letter from Governor Claiborne to "throw light on the government of Louisiana, under contemplation of the legislature." This letter was Claiborne's of January 2, 1804, in which he noted that Louisianans knew nothing about republicanism. Because senators in support of the Breckinridge Bill also attempted to prove that Louisianans were incapable of self-government, it is not surprising that Jefferson had the letter read to a Senate that was closely divided over the issue of representation for Orleans Territory.[49]

On the same day that the motion to allow Louisianans to vote for representatives for the Legislative Council was voted down, the Senate began the possibility of a ban on the slave trade in Louisiana. This coincided with Congress's reading of a petition by the American Convention for Promoting the Abolition of Slavery to "prohibit the importation of slaves into the Territory of Louisiana, lately ceded to the United States." The petition consisted of four arguments. The first of these was that men should abhor slavery out of a love for their fellow man. Second, the petitioners argued that the Constitution made "all men equally entitled to liberty." Third, they claimed that God had preserved peace in North America and that it was "the duty of a nation so crowned with the blessings of peace and plenty and happiness, to manifest its gratitude to the whole world by acts of justice and virtue." In addition, the petitioners argued that Congress should heed the example of the earlier Congress that passed the Northwest Ordinance, which excluded the expansion of slavery to the Northwest Territory.[50]

In the Senate, James Jackson began discussion of the Louisiana slave trade by asserting that slaves were necessary for agriculture in Louisiana. Jackson's claim opened debate on the possibility of the extension of the act of February 28, 1803, which forbade "importation of slaves into States which prohibited their importation." This resulted in a two-day general debate on slavery in the United States.[51]

The debate over the prohibition of slavery in the Senate was largely a partisan one. Federalists for the most part opposed a ban on importation while Republicans supported it. The fact that many New England Federalists were prepared to vote against a measure that was designed to limit slavery demonstrates that, no matter what their personal feelings were on this issue, they were prepared to do whatever it took to hinder the passage of the Breckinridge Bill. There were, as in the debate over representation, however, exceptions to the rule. Some Southern Federalist senators supported the proposed ban on slave importation to Louisiana. As he made notes on the Senate debate on this issue, Senator William Plumer suggested a reason for this. He claimed that that the senators "from the Slave States" desired prohibition of foreign importation of slaves into Louisiana because it would result in an increase of the value of their own slaves and give them a captive market for the export of their most dangerous slaves.

An expressed argument against importation of slaves, however, was that an increase in isolated Louisiana's slave population might lead to an outbreak of a slave revolution. Republicans Breckinridge and Jesse Franklin of North Carolina supported the idea of a ban on slave importation because they feared that "our slaves in the South will produce another St. Domingo."[52]

Other senators who did not follow their party on the issue of slavery in Louisiana included Federalist senator James Hillhouse of Connecticut, who was adamantly opposed to slavery, and Republican Samuel Smith of Maryland, who believed that government should not make a decision on slavery on behalf of the people of a state or territory.[53]

Federalists Jonathan Dayton of New Jersey and John Quincy Adams and Republicans Israel Smith and Samuel Smith argued against the prohibition of importing slaves to Louisiana. Dayton echoed Jackson's argument, and added that "slaveholders in the United States" would "collect and send into that country their slaves of the very worst description" if foreign imports were prohibited. Israel Smith, although opposed to slavery in general, argued that the Constitution allowed states to import slaves from Africa until 1808. A ban on foreign importation, Smith concluded, would "operate as an encouragement to South Carolina to import slaves."[54]

Republican Samuel Smith flatly stated that he was opposed to the motion. "The people of that country wish for African slaves & we ought to give them a supply—we have a constitutional right to prohibit slavery in that country, but

I doubt as to the policy of it." Adams argued against a ban on importation because although he considered slavery a "moral evil," he believed that "connected with commerse it has important uses."[55]

Republican John Smith of Ohio argued for a prohibition against the importation of slaves because he wished that "our Negroes were scattered more equally not only through the United States, but through our territories—that their power might be lost."[56]

Perhaps the most radical position on slavery in Louisiana was that expressed by Hillhouse, who suggested that slavery be abolished. "If that country cannot be cultivated without slaves, let slaves hold it—or let it remain a wilderness forever. Those are the real friends of liberty who extend it to others, as well as to themselves." On January 26 Hillhouse introduced an amendment to make it unlawful for anyone to import slaves into Orleans, "from any part or place within the limits of the United States, or to cause or procure to be imported or brought, or knowingly to aid in so importing or bringing any slave or slaves."[57]

Arguments for and against this proposed amendment included all of those presented in the first two days of debate on slavery in Louisiana and some important additional ones. Federalist Israel Smith, who was opposed to the ban, argued that it would damage any possibility of a good relationship between the people of Louisiana and those of the United States. "The people of Louisiana ought not to be subject to much change in government, laws, or habits at present—They are not yet bound to us by any ties—This resolution will estrange them from us—It will oppress them." Smith was obviously aware, as other Federalist senators must have been, that the Federalists' position against a proposed ban of the slave trade to Louisiana would help to make their party popular in that territory. Franklin suggested that the proposed amendment did not go far enough. "My wish is to prohibit slaves altogether from that country, except those carried thither by actual settlers from the United States—but I despair of obtaining such a vote in the Senate—I will vote for such a prohibition as I can obtain."[58]

At the close of the day's debate, Franklin voted, as did the majority, for Hillhouse's amendment. The vote was not close. Twenty-one voted for the motion, and six voted against it. This encouraged Hillhouse, who introduced further motions concerning slavery in Louisiana on January 30. Hillhouse first introduced a motion to ensure no male slave of twenty-one years and no female slave of eighteen years "bro't into said territory of Louisiana from any part of the United States, or territories therof, or from any province or colony in America belonging to any foreign prince or state" could be "beholden by law to serve for more than the term of one year." This motion occasioned little discussion, and it was rejected by a vote of seventeen to eleven.[59]

After this motion was rejected, Hillhouse introduced another designed to make it illegal to import slaves to Louisiana from within the United States. The only exception to this law was for people who owned slaves and planned to move to Louisiana to live there. "And no slave or slaves shall directly or indirectly be introduced into said territory, except by a person or persons removing into said territory for actual settlement, & being at the same time of such removal *bona fide* owner of such a slave or slaves."[60]

This amendment was easily passed by twenty-one votes to seven. The next day, however, a motion was made to strike out the provision that allowed settlers to bring slaves to Louisiana. Those senators who supported the motion to strike down this provision expressed different reasons for doing so. Republican senator Stephen Bradley of Vermont was opposed to the provision "because it admits the doctrine of slavery to be just—it is like a law regulating theft or any other crime. . . . I really consider slavery as a violation of the laws of God—of Nature—of Vermont." Jackson opposed the provision but not as an opponent of slavery. He argued that the restriction of slavery in Louisiana would turn its people against the federal government. "If this law with these amendments passes you destroy that country—you render it useless—You will excite alarms in the minds of Frenchmen—you will render a standing army necessary." Despite Jackson's alarming predictions, the majority of senators, including Franklin, supported "restraining foreign importation," but believed it prudent "to proceed no further." The motion to strike out the provision that allowed for the importation of slaves by persons who owned slaves and wanted to settle in Louisiana was defeated by a vote of fifteen to thirteen.[61]

While Franklin stated that he was willing to go no further in the restriction of the slave trade in Louisiana, Hillhouse made a motion to allow only citizens of the United States who owned slaves to import them into Louisiana. Debate over this amendment centered on the issue of foreign immigration. Jackson, Hillhouse, and Pickering presented their positions on this issue. Senator Hillhouse hoped foreigners would "not be permitted to settle in that *distant* country—It is seldom, that any but the *worst* of men leave their own to settle in a foreign country." Jackson rejected this assertion: "I am not afraid of such evils. The *friends of liberty only will come*—let us encourage the settlement of that country as much as possible—It is dangerous to exclude foreigners." Pickering supported Jackson's position on foreign immigration. "I am willing that in Louisiana oppressed humanity should find an asylum, and that the patriots of no country should there find a Country in which no restraints should be imposed upon them."[62]

The arguments made by Jackson and Pickering did not sway a majority of senators to reject the motion for an amendment to limit the import of slaves to slaveholding citizens of the United States who intended to settle in Louisiana.

The View from Washington

Eighteen senators voted in favor of the amendment and eleven against it. The passage of this amendment marked the end of the Senate debate on slavery in Louisiana. Through the passage of three amendments introduced by Hillhouse, Louisianans were, at least on paper, prohibited from engaging in the slave trade.[63]

On February 10 the opponents of the fourth section of the bill, specifically the provisions for government by an appointed governor and appointed Legislative Council, made a last-ditch effort to create a representative body in the Louisiana government. Senator Anderson called for a "General Assembly or Legislature" that was to consist of "the Governor, Legislative Council and a House of Representatives." Members of the House of Representatives were to be elected by the inhabitants of the territory when the population of the territory reached "___ thousand free white male inhabitants." There was to be one representative for "every five hundred free, white male inhabitants," and each representative was to serve for two years.[64]

Anderson's representatives were to have elective and legislative powers, which went far beyond the nonrepresentative system of government outlined in Section 4 of the Breckinridge Bill. After they were elected, the representatives were to prepare a list of nominations for the Legislative Council. This list was to be presented to the president, and from it he would select the Legislative Council. Representatives were to also have a role in the making of laws for the territory. Anderson proposed that "all bills having passed by a majority in the House of Representatives, and by a majority in the Council," would "be referred to the Governor for his assent: but no bill or Legislative act whatever shall be of any force without his consent." Few senators were willing to go as far as Anderson. The motion was easily defeated by a vote of nineteen to five.[65]

A final, less extreme attempt to amend the fourth section of the Breckinridge Bill took place in the Senate on February 13. This motion was similar to that presented on January 24, with the exception that the inhabitants of twenty-four proposed districts would elect "one discreet person" instead of two in each district; these twenty-four representatives would serve as the Legislative Council. The Senate vote on this motion was almost tied, indicating that the Senate had almost come around to the idea of allowing some form of participation of Louisianans in their territorial government. This was of little consolation to those who supported this, as the Senate debate on the fourth section of the Breckinridge Bill ended on February 13, 1804.[66]

As the Senate prepared to vote on the Breckinridge Bill on February 18, 1804, Senator John Quincy Adams "alone" made a speech detailing why he would vote against it. Adams's first reason for rejection of the bill was that it was "forming a government for that people without their consent and against their will." "All power in a republican government," Adams declared, "is derived from the people—We sit here under their authority. The people of that country have given no power or authority to us to legislate for them." Congress "ought to have applied to the inhabitants of Louisiana to recognize our own right to govern them."[67]

Adams's more specific criticism centered on "arbitrary principles—principles repugnant to our Constitution" contained in the Breckinridge Bill. He challenged the provision for the appointment of the Legislative Council by the governor, who was "a creature of the President's." In other territorial governments, Adams declared, "even in the departure from liberty,—there is a reverence for it—for it provides that when its inhabitants are encreased to a certain number they shall elect a representative."[68] The power that Jefferson had to make appointments was also of great concern to Adams. "This bill provides that the officers shall be appointed by the President *alone* in the recess of the Senate," which he found to be a violation of the Constitution.[69]

Finally, Adams further criticized the bill because he believed that it was designed before Congress had adequate data on Louisiana. "We have not the necessary information to pass a law containing the great fundamental principles of government—we know little of that people or Country—In thus passing this bill we commit an act of practical tyranny." The tyranny of the act was demonstrated by its "incongruous articles—establishment of courts—juries—numerous laws—prohibition of slavery etc." Even worse than this, according to Adams, was the fact that the Breckinridge Bill established a tyrannical "colonial government" that would serve as the model for future American territorial expansion. "This is a Colonial system of government—It is the first the United States have established—It is a bad precedent—the U.S. in time will have many colonies—precedents are therefore important."[70]

Despite Adams's objections, the Breckinridge Bill passed in the Senate on February 18 ("yeas twenty nays five"). Privately, Senator Adams noted his regret at the outcome: "and thus terminates the introductory system for the government of Louisiana. I have thought it placed on wrong foundations. It is for time to show the result."[71]

The debate over the Breckinridge Bill was not over, however. On February 20, 1804, the House of Representatives received the message from the Senate that the Breckinridge Bill had passed. The debate in the House of Representatives was different from that which had occurred in the Senate in that the Republicans completely dominated the House. The debate on the bill was not so much between Republicans and Federalists as it was between Republicans who strictly supported Jefferson's plan for the government of Louisiana as outlined in the Breckinridge Bill and Republicans who opposed its denial of representative government to Louisianans. As in the Senate, representatives from western states that were connected commercially to the Mississippi, such as Tennessee, Kentucky, and even Pennsylvania (Pittsburgh), had a vested interest in the creation of a new representative body that would share their economic concerns.

After a bill for the registry for shipping in Louisiana was passed, the House of Representatives began to debate the Breckinridge Bill on February 28. Section 4 of the bill, which vested legislative power in the offices of the appointed governor and the appointed thirteen-member Legislative Council, was the subject of fierce debate. Those who supported the fourth section based their position on the principle that the available information on Louisiana suggested that Louisianans were incapable of self-government and that the appointed government outlined in the fourth section was designed in the best interests of the inhabitants of Louisiana.[72]

On the first day of House debate on the fourth section of the Breckinridge Bill, Republican William Eustis of Massachusetts stated that Louisianans were not prepared to elect a government and that the role of the federal government was to protect their rights as conquered subjects. "The approach of such a people to liberty must be gradual. I believe them at present totally unqualified to exercise it. . . . I consider them as standing in nearly the same relation as if they were a conquered country." Republican John B. C. Lucas of Pennsylvania stated that he was "fully of the opinion with Representative Eustis." Benjamin Huger, Federalist representative from South Carolina, was convinced that "information lately received from Louisiana" (perhaps Claiborne's letter) "convinced him of the propriety of proceeding with the bill immediately." Republican James Elliot of Vermont concurred with Huger but believed that "by the introduction of a small amendment" the fourth section "might be rendered perfectly consistent with the treaty and the Constitution," and the passage of the bill would be "greatly accelerated."[73]

Those representatives who opposed the fourth section of the Breckinridge Bill in the House, like their counterparts in the Senate, did so with arguments that focused on the tyrannical nature of the proposed territorial government. Republican George W. Campbell of Tennessee strongly opposed the fourth section and spoke of it as despotic. "It really establishes a complete despotism, that it does not confer one single right to which they are entitled under the treaty; that it does not extend to them the benefits of the Federal Constitution or declare when hereafter, they shall receive them." Campbell went on to attack the argument that Louisianans were not suited for representative government. "Is their condition such as not to qualify them for the enjoyment of any of the blessings of liberty? Are they blind to the difference between liberty and slavery? Are they insensible to the difference of laws made by themselves and laws made by others?" Campbell answered his own questions and said there was no evidence to prove that Louisianans did not understand or could not appreciate liberty.[74]

Republican Matthew Lyon of Kentucky directly attacked the positions of Huger, Elliot, and Eustis. Lyon proclaimed that the "most ludicrous idea" that he had heard expressed on the subject of the fourth section was that Louisianans should "be kept in slavery until they learned to think and behave like freemen."[75]

Other representatives who opposed the fourth section of the Breckinridge Bill made more specific denouncements of it than had Lyon and Campbell. Republicans Michael Leib and Andrew Gregg of Pennsylvania opposed the power given to the governor. Leib was especially critical of the power granted to the governor to prorogue the Legislative Council, which made that body a "royal appendage." Gregg condemned the provision that empowered the president to appoint the Legislative Council. "It appeared to him a mere burlesque to say they shall be appointed by the President." Republican Speaker Nathaniel Macon of North Carolina made a motion to strike out the fourth section of the Breckinridge Bill on the basis that he recognized only three types of government in the United States: "that of the Union, that of the states, and territorial governments." Macon argued that territorial government as defined by the Northwest Ordinance of 1787 was best suited for the people of Louisiana.[76]

When the debate over the fourth section of the Breckinridge Bill continued on February 29, discussion centered on the extension of elective powers to the inhabitants of Louisiana. Republican John G. Jackson of Georgia spoke first and asked whether it was "proper on the broad principle of political justice" to adopt the fourth section. Jackson then asked the House to consider whether the fourth section was "best calculated to advance the happiness of those who have never tasted the blessings of liberty." He rejected the argument that the people of Louisiana were comparable to slaves. Even if the people of Louisiana were slaves, Jackson argued, this did not prove they were not "fit objects" of free government. "Look at the ensanguined plains of St. Domingo; the oppressed there have broken their chains, and resumed their long lost rights." In addition to Louisianans, Jackson noted that there were also Americans in Louisiana who were perfectly capable of self-government. Finally, Jackson warned that rejection of representative government in Louisiana cast the United States in a negative light. The rest of the world, he argued, would "say we possess the principle of despotism under the garb of Republicanism; and that we are insincere, with whatever solemnity we may declare it, in pronouncing all men equal."[77]

James Holland of North Carolina spoke after Jackson, primarily to challenge the assertion that Louisianans should be permitted some form of self-government. "Does the history of nations show that all men are capable of self-government? No such thing. It shows that none but an enlightened and virtuous people are capable of it; and if the people of Louisiana are not sufficiently enlightened, they are not yet prepared to receive it." Holland concluded that an "elective franchise" should be granted when Louisianans understood the laws of the United States and were attached to its interests.[78]

In response to Holland, Republican James Sloan of New Jersey asked the House whether anything could "be more repugnant to the principles of just government than for a President to appoint a Governor and a Legislative Council, the Governor having a negative on all their acts, and power to prorogue them at pleasure." Sloan stated that he had great respect for the "superior talents, integrity and justice" of the present president but that he could never "consent to delegate that power to a just person, which an unjust person," who might succeed him, might "use for oppressive and tyrannical purposes." There was no basis in fact, Sloan declared, for the argument that granting Louisianans "their just rights" would make them dangerous to the United States. Sloan wanted an elective franchise because it was "not only as their inherent and inalienable right, but as a right we are bound to give them to fulfill the treaty of cession."[79]

Republican representative John Boyle of Kentucky declared that he opposed the structure of government proposed in the fourth section and claimed that the second grade of government was "most fitted to the people of Louisiana." Boyle argued that Louisianans should be granted "all that portion of self-government and independence" that was "compatible with the Constitution." The thirteen colonies, Boyle explained, had "declared to the world our right of being governed by laws of our own making" in response to the passage of the Declaratory Act by the British Parliament. If the right of self-government was an "inalienable right" at that time, he asked, "is it less so now?"

It became clear in the course of the House debate on February 29 that those who opposed the fourth section of the Breckinridge Bill outnumbered those who supported it. A vote was held, and the section was struck down by a margin of sixty-five votes.[80]

On March 14 an amendment to prohibit the importation of slaves to Louisiana from foreign nations and the United States was introduced by Representative Sloan. While the subject of slavery in Louisiana was debated in the Senate over several days, it appears that the House spent little time on this issue. All that is recorded is that "Mr. S. concisely stated his reasons in favor of this provision, when the question was taken, and the amendment agreed to—ayes 40, noes 36."[81] Although there is no explanation for the brevity of the discussion on slavery, it should be noted that Jefferson made an effort to inform the House on this issue.

On March 8 Jefferson had sent a letter to the House from Governor Claiborne "respecting the importation at New Orleans of slaves from Africa, and his impression that he did not possess the power to interpose respecting the same." In this letter, written on January 31, Claiborne reported that he had made inquiries and found that "the bringing of African slaves to Louisiana had been permitted by the Spanish authorities." Because he "doubted whether" he was "vested with the power to forbid their sale," Claiborne allowed the slave trade to continue. The degree to which the reading of this letter influenced the vote in the House on slave importation is not known, but the fact that the Senate had already voted in favor of such a prohibition probably contributed to the brevity of the debate.[82]

Toward the end of the day's discussion on March 14, Republican Peter Early of Georgia proposed a change to the fourth section of the Breckinridge Bill. He suggested that the Legislative Council become an elected body with the power to make laws. After their first year in power, the thirteen appointed councilors were to be replaced annually through elections by all free white males who were residents of the territory. The Legislative Council was to make all regulations for elections, and it had legislative powers, "restricted only by conformity with the Constitution of the United States and the prohibition of interference with the religious freedom of the inhabitants."[83]

On March 15 the House voted on Early's proposed substitution for the fourth section of the Breckinridge Bill, and this passed by a vote of fifty-eight to forty-two.[84] The House then debated a last proposed amendment to the Breckinridge Bill on March 17 to limit the duration of the act to two years. The House agreed to this and then voted on the entire Breckinridge Bill. It passed by a vote of sixty-six to twenty-one. This did not mark the end of debate on the bill, however.

The House heard a message from the Senate on March 17 on the amendments made by the House that the Senate refused to accept. The first of those mentioned was the amendment for the fourth section of the Breckinridge Bill. The House voted on whether to recede from this amendment. Thirty-seven representatives voted for recession, and sixty-three voted against recession.[85]

After the members of the House had voted against recession of their fourth section amendment, another vote was taken on whether the House should insist on it. The House voted to insist on its fourth section amendment by a vote of fifty-three to thirty-six and then resolved to ask for a conference with the Senate on the amendments that the House refused to rescind. Nicholson, Early, and John Rhea of Tennessee were appointed to serve on behalf of the House as "managers" for this conference.

On March 23 the House "managers" made a report on their conference with the Senate representatives. Nicholson suggested that the House recede from its fourth section amendment on the basis that "the election of a Legislative Council by the people of Louisiana would be attended with inconveniences which he, for one, had never perceived before." Nicholson said that he had learned at the conference that some of the parishes of Louisiana were "entirely composed of Spaniards, some of French, and some of Germans, and some of Creoles." If each of these parishes were to send a member, Nicholson concluded, "the Legislative Body would be composed of persons of different languages. . . . This Mr. N. said was the principal reason which induced the House to recommend that the House should recede."[86]

The House voted to accept the report of the House managers and voted in favor of recession from the fourth section amendment by a vote of fifty-one to forty-five. Finally, the House received "a message from the Senate stating their agreement to the report on the committee of conference on the Louisiana bill, which was consequently passed." President Jefferson signed the bill, and it became law on March 26, 1804. The structure of the government for Louisiana established by this act empowered the president to have almost total control over a territorial governor and Legislative Council that he himself appointed. As part of the United States, Orleans Territory was a colony in Jefferson's new "empire of liberty."[87]

Federalist Fisher Ames recognized Jefferson's power over the government of Louisiana and recognized the passage of the Breckinridge Bill as an opportunity to attack the president and the Republicans in the Federalist *Palladium*:

The Romans, in the days of their degeneracy and corruption, set no more bounds to their favor than to their resentments. While Pompey was their idol, they conferred unlimited authority upon him all over the Mediterranean sea, and four hundred stadia (about forty-five miles) within land. We in like manner devolve upon Mr. Jefferson the absolute and uncontrolled dominion of Louisiana. It was thus the Romans were made by their own vote familiar with arbitrary power.[88]

CHAPTER THREE

"A Flame in the District"

The Organization of Protest against
Territorial Government in Orleans

As Congress began to debate the Breckinridge Bill in January 1804, a new wave of American immigrants set out for New Orleans. Many of these sought to increase their fortunes through the establishment of commercial enterprises in that city. Others hoped to obtain a position in the future territorial administration of Louisiana. These Americans, however, faced competition from established native Louisianans. Governor Claiborne recognized that a total distribution of political appointments to Americans would alienate Louisianans and make his rule difficult. Because of this, he made efforts to retain the services of many of those who had served the Spanish and French administrations.

In January 1804 Claiborne dispatched an agent to tour the countryside around New Orleans and instructed him to reappoint the commandants of the parishes if they demonstrated loyalty to the United States. In addition, the agent was to "impress the minds of the Citizens favorably, towards the change of government" and to note the concerns of the inhabitants. The agent, Dr. John Watkins, who had arrived from Philadelphia in 1804, was, according to Claiborne, a "perfect Master of the French and Spanish languages" and an honest man.[1]

Several different groups, primarily of French and Spanish origin, inhabited the parishes. There were the French and Spanish planters along the Mississippi who were the descendants of the first European settlers of Louisiana. While Spain and France controlled Louisiana, they were the colony's wealthiest and most politically influential inhabitants. Claiborne ensured that they would remain so by allowing them to continue in their appointed posts. An additional distinct population in Louisiana at this time was the community of "twenty-five hundred to three thousand Acadian exiles who carved a new homeland in the Mississippi Valley between 1764 and 1803." The majority of these Acadians settled along the Mississippi and South Louisiana bayous and farmed and/or lived on what they were able to trap or catch. By the 1780s, however, some Acadians began to purchase slaves to help them clear land. Between 1790 and 1810 "the fragmentation of the once extremely cohesive Acadian community appears to have taken place," as second- and third-generation Acadians embraced both slavery and the plantation system.[2]

Acadian planters and the planter/merchant elite of Louisiana considered slavery as essential to their economic survival. They and new slave-owning arrivals, such as the French planters who fled St. Domingue during the 1790s, shared a concern about its future under American rule. Dr. Watkins, who returned to New Orleans from his mission to the parishes in February 1804, after reappointing all but three commandants made this absolutely clear to Claiborne in a report of his travels:

> No Subject seems to be so interesting to the minds of the inhabitants of all that part of the Country, which I have visited as that of the importation of brute Negroes from Africa. This permission would go farther with them, and better reconcile them to the Government of the United States, than any other privilege that could be extended to the Country. They appear only to claim it for a few years, and without it, they pretend that they must abandon the culture both of Sugar and Cotton.

From the issue of protection of the Louisiana slave trade Louisianans were "naturally carried to speak of the form of this local and temporary government." They wanted to have a representative in Congress "to represent their true interests and situation." Some Louisianans wanted to go further and "enter immediately into all the benefits and advantages of a State government." Watkins suggested, however, that Louisianans would "generally stop short at the difficulties of popular representation" because of their limited political knowledge.[3]

Claiborne took Watkins's suggestions regarding the Louisiana slave trade and representation in Congress seriously. On March 1, 1804, Claiborne sent Watkins's report to Madison and noted that the people had a "lively interest" in preservation of the slave trade and that the "prevailing opinion" of the people was "that a prohibition would tend generally to the injury of the Province." Claiborne further declared that the desire for a "delegate to Congress" described in Watkins's report was "not greater than that of the Citizens of New Orleans." The governor suggested that Congress make provision for a Louisiana delegate who would have the same rights as other territorial delegates.[4]

Eight days later Claiborne informed Madison that a paper received from

The Organization of Protest against Territorial Government in Orleans

Washington stated that the Senate had passed a law prohibiting the foreign importation of slaves into Louisiana. According to Claiborne, news of this law "occasioned great agitation" in New Orleans and in the parishes as it was viewed as "a serious blow at the Commercial and agricultural interest of the Province." Claiborne was especially concerned because Louisianans knew of South Carolina's importation of slaves. Many Louisianans, Claiborne concluded, would be made to believe that the prohibition of the foreign slave trade was established "with a view to make South Carolina the Sole importer for Louisiana." An additional aggravation for Claiborne was that an "adventurer by the name of Tupper" had taken "advantage of the agitation of the Public mind" and proposed a public meeting to draw up a memorial of grievances.[5]

Benjamin Tupper, according to Claiborne, "was a native of Boston, (and if the report be true, of little respectability)" who had arrived in New Orleans approximately three weeks earlier from France. Aside from Claiborne's notes, there is little recorded history on Benjamin Tupper. In a letter to Madison on March 16, 1804, Claiborne, who had obviously made some inquiries on Tupper's background, reported that "Mr. Tupper" was "known to the Northward as a Swindler, and that a Mr. Moreton a Merchant of Boston has suffered much by his fraudulent conduct. Tupper passes here for a man of fortune, and being very much of a Parisian in his Manners and Politicks has acquired some influence among the uninformed of French Society."[6]

The "themes of discussion" between Tupper and the public included the "Prohibition of the African Trade, the Continuation of the export duties, the want of Registers for Vessels, and the delay in extending to the Louisianans like privileges with those enjoyed by Citizens of the United States." Claiborne believed that Tupper's motive for support of a memorial of grievances at a public meeting was that he wanted to be the agent elected to present the memorial to Congress, and so he worked to discredit Tupper and declared that "few (if any) respectable citizens" would attend the public meeting. At the same time, however, Claiborne clearly feared Tupper's influence and the possibility of popular hostility toward American rule. "The Public mind here may easily be inflamed, and when the inhabitants are put in motion it would be difficult to restrain them from outrage. The success which this man Tupper has met with is a strong proof of the mischief that a single unprincipled Man may do in Louisiana."[7]

At the same time that Claiborne worked to diminish Tupper's influence, the governor attempted to win the favor of the New Orleans planter/merchant elite by granting their request for a "Bank of Discount, Deposit and Exchange" in the city of New Orleans. Claiborne named Evan Jones, Pierre Sauvé, and Beverly Chew, a business partner of Daniel Clark, to a committee that would direct distribution of its shares.[8]

The Organization of Protest against Territorial Government in Orleans

The establishment of Claiborne's "Louisiana Bank" did little or nothing to stop the organization of protest against Congress's plans for the government of Louisiana. Less than a week after Claiborne wrote Madison about the activities of Tupper, the public meeting called by that "adventurer" took place. Claiborne received an account of the proceedings and outlined these for Madison. As it turned out, Tupper was a minor figure in the meeting, which was composed "principally of respectable Merchants of New Orleans, and farmers in its Vicinity, but few Americans."[9] According to Claiborne, Etienne de Boré, not Tupper, presided over the meeting, and he suggested that the assembly send a commissioner or commissioners to Congress "to represent the grievances of Louisiana, but especially the desire of the inhabitants for the continuation of the Slave trade, and their great Solicitude for Speedy relief from their present commercial embarrassments."[10]

After saying this Boré opened the meeting to suggestions on how to proceed with the selection of the commissioners. According to Claiborne, a Mr. Detrion (Destréhan?), a sugar planter, proposed that the commandant of each district assemble the people and that they elect deputies to attend a future meeting in New Orleans. These deputies would elect two of their number to serve as commissioners to Congress. In addition, the deputies would elect a permanent committee that would provide instructions to the commissioners "and more particularly upon the Subjects of the Slave trade, and the present Commercial embarrassments; and that the Governor of Louisiana, be requested to use his influence in Support of these measures." Detrion's proposals were well received, and he was applauded upon completion of his speech.[11]

Tupper spoke after Detrion and stated he believed that only one commissioner to Congress was necessary but that he had no objection to two. Tupper then proceeded to speak of "the oppressive grievances under which the people of Louisiana laboured, the unfortunate consequences which might attend the suppression of the Slave trade, and added that Congress was too neglectful of the important interests of Louisiana." Tupper closed with a promise to support Detrion's propositions.[12]

While Tupper spoke, Claiborne reported, "much discontent was manifested, it was asked by some French Gentlemen, 'Who is this Man? Who has authorized him to speak about our interests? Let us put him down.'" Dr. John Watkins spoke after Tupper and warned of "the impropriety of inviting general meetings of the people, the public agitation which such a measure might produce, and the scenes of tumult which would arise." He also hinted that such meetings were unnecessary because Claiborne had already conveyed the people's sentiments on the slave trade to Washington. Watkins did, however, admit that Louisianans had a right to express their interests. All he wanted "was that the mode of doing so should be prudent and the manner respectful."[13]

The Organization of Protest against Territorial Government in Orleans

Watkins suggested that a committee of three should be appointed to draft a memorial to Congress to be presented at a future meeting. If those assembled at that meeting approved of it, the memorial was to be signed and sent to the governor, who would forward it to the government in Washington. When Watkins had finished, Boré asked him to repeat his speech in French as it was a primarily French assembly.[14] Watkins did so, and the assembly adopted his suggestions unanimously. A Mr. Mericault and Mr. Pitot, "two respectable merchants," and Watkins were then appointed to the committee to draft the memorial. After this was done, "the meeting broke up without fixing any other day for their assembling."[15]

Claiborne was pleased with the outcome of the meeting. He did not believe that the committee to draft the memorial would do so, and even if it did, Claiborne added, it was doubtful that the assembly that elected the committee members would meet again. The governor also hoped that Tupper would "sink into contempt" once the public saw that his interest in the memorial was based on his ambition to serve as a commissioner to Congress.[16]

While Claiborne asserted that the memorial assembly would dissolve, he considered it his "duty to convey to the President, the wishes and Sentiments of the inhabitants on the Subjects of general interest." Not surprising is the fact that the first subject of interest that Claiborne wrote about was the slave trade. Claiborne stated that "the continuation of the slave trade for a few years is viewed by the inhabitants as essential to the Welfare of this Province and no act of Congress would excite more discontent than an immediate Prohibition."[17] Next Claiborne mentioned the "commercial embarrassments" that the merchants in New Orleans faced as a result of the fact that they had not received notice of their status as U.S. merchants. Claiborne was pleased to note, however, that he had read in the proceedings of Congress that the government planned to make a provision to allow citizens of Louisiana to obtain registers for their ships.[18]

Claiborne next suggested "the citizens of Louisiana would be well pleased in having some voice in their local government." This could be achieved, he claimed, if Louisianans were allowed to elect forty-four delegates and the governor selected twenty-four of these to serve as one branch of the legislature. In addition, Claiborne hinted "if the Branch had the power of electing a Delegate to Congress with an authority to speak and not to vote, it would tend still more to conciliate the confidence of the people in the general Government."[19] By the time Madison received these suggestions, Congress had passed the Breckinridge Bill, which prohibited the foreign import of slaves into Louisiana and denied Louisianans a voice in local and federal government.

As Louisianans waited for news of the Breckinridge Bill, Claiborne's political influence among them was damaged when his ideas about the igno-rance of Louisianans became public knowledge. On April 14, 1804, Claiborne informed Madison of the publication of his letter of January 2, 1804, in which he criticized the planters and merchants. This paper was forwarded to New Orleans "in great numbers," and Claiborne noted that his published letter re-sulted "in a day or two much talk, and many of the citizens, expressed some discontent, at my representing the *whole society* (as was erroneously stated by the listen'er in the gallery) as involved in profound ignorance." Claiborne believed that this was true but admitted that he should never have written the letter. "The information I gave was literally correct and such as I thought it my duty to communicate, but I must confess, I did not count on the publication of my letter at the time that I wrote it.—The old adage, that the truth should not be told at all times applies on this present occasion."[20]

Claiborne did not dwell on his unwise criticisms of Louisianans, however. The day after he wrote Madison on the matter, he wrote to Jefferson about his concerns about the Breckinridge Bill. Claiborne noted with satisfaction that Congress had passed a law to allow Louisianans to register their ships but expressed his disappointment with the law that prohibited the foreign im-portation of slaves to Louisiana. The governor insisted that this law would be "viewed by the Citizens as a great Grievance" and that "on this subject much irritation is manifested." Claiborne claimed that he made an effort to convince Louisianans that a prohibition on slave importation was in their best interests. Specifically, Claiborne "instanced the Horrors of St. Domingo, & reminded them of the just cause for apprehension, of similar horrors in this Province at some future day." This argument, however, had no effect, and Claiborne was forced to concede that only an uninterrupted slave trade to Africa for three or four years would satisfy Louisianans.[21]

On May 2 Claiborne finally received a copy of An Act for the Organization of Orleans Territory and the Louisiana District enclosed with an April 2 letter from Madison. At the same time, Claiborne received a packet of letters from Madison dated February 6, 1804, which included a copy of the Breckinridge Bill that was at that time before the Senate.[22] After Claiborne read the Breck-inridge Bill he wrote Madison to inform him that "many of the old inhabitants expected immediate admission into the Union, and the Law does not hold out the means of gratifying the ambition of some of the late adventurers from the United States." Claiborne did not believe, however, that the dissatisfaction of the "old inhabitants" (French and Spanish Louisianans) and adventurers merited an immediate change in the act. He declared that the "constitution temporarily prescribed" was "well adapted to the present situation in Loui-siana." The governor added that he had confidence Congress would modify the government of Louisiana "if previous to the expiration the Law it should be discovered, that a Government managed more immediately by the people would better conduce to their happiness and prosperity."[23]

While Claiborne was not too concerned with the discontent of old inhabitants and adventurers over the territorial status of Louisiana and the system of government established by the Act for the Organization of Orleans Territory and the Louisiana District, he was anxious about a provision of the act that continued to be the focus of increasing widespread protest. Claiborne informed Madison that the citizens of Louisiana were convinced that a "very great supply of Slaves" was essential to the economy. "Hence Sir," Claiborne declared, "you may conclude that the prohibition as to the importation Subsequent to the 1st of October it is at present, a cause of much discontent; Nay Sir, it is at present a cause of much clamour." The governor indulged a hope that Louisianans would see the "justice and policy of the measure" but also noted that importation of slaves continued and was in fact increasing as a result of refugee emigration to Louisiana from the French West Indies. The governor estimated that thousands would be imported to Louisiana before October 1, 1804.[24]

Claiborne was correct in his assessment that protest against the prohibition of the slave trade and against the American territorial system of government had expanded. On May 16, 1804, Mayor Etienne de Boré asked the New Orleans Municipal Council to file a formal protest against the Act for the Organization of Orleans Territory and the Louisiana District. Boré argued that the act was a complete departure from the principles of American government and that it was an "infringement on the natural rights of the people of the territory and of the third article of the treaty of cession." The Municipal Council, however, refused to make this protest because of a belief that the people as a whole should be responsible for it. In response, Boré resigned as mayor.[25]

Etienne de Boré was not the only official to resign during the first months of Claiborne's rule of Louisiana. On March 13 Colonel Joseph de Ville de Goutin Bellechasse, commander of the New Orleans militia, and Pierre Derbigny, secretary registrar of the Municipal Council, resigned from their positions. The fact that these men resigned on the same day is interesting. Derbigny explained that absolute necessity and "powerful motives," which he did not explain, had induced him to resign. In a terse note, Bellechasse explained that his ill health and his inability to explain himself in English compelled him to abandon his post. Claiborne, however, who was anxious about the instability of American control of Louisiana and who recognized Bellechasse's "Talents and Character" as well as "the great share of public esteem and confidence" that he enjoyed, refused to accept his resignation. Taken together, the resignations

The Organization of Protest against Territorial Government in Orleans

offered by Bellechasse, Derbigny, and Boré damaged support for Claiborne's government, as these were three influential men in the French Louisianan community.[26]

A week after Boré resigned, Claiborne received notice from Secretary of the Treasury Albert Gallatin that the Louisiana Bank was an illegal institution because at the time of its establishment, Congress had authorized a branch of the Bank of the United States for New Orleans. The charter of the Bank of the United States prohibited the establishment of any other banks under the authority of the general government.[27] Claiborne immediately wrote Gallatin a letter of apology and explained his reasons for his permission for the establishment of the Louisiana Bank.

> The uncertainty of the people as to their political fate produced much inquietude; the proposed prohibition of the African Trade, had excited dissatisfaction among the farmers; the Merchants were loud in their clamors against the export duties, and the want of Registers for their Vessels many of which had been lying idle for months. And at that critical period there were not wanting persons who from principles of disaffection to the New Government, or motives of personal ambition, were endeavoring to take advantage of the prevailing ferment in the Public mind. Popular meetings were called, Spirited remonstrances were threatened, and the Suppineness of Congress relative to the interests of Louisiana much complained of.

Under these circumstances, Claiborne established the bank to "divert for the moment, the most influential part of the Mercantile interest from the Pale of Political discontent" and to promote the economic interest of the United States.[28]

Claiborne wrote a similar letter of apology to President Jefferson. Although he was initially suspicious of Claiborne's role in the establishment of the Louisiana Bank, Jefferson concluded that the governor was "the dupe" of roguery and ordered the revocation of the bank's charter. Jefferson was aware that this would be unpopular with those men whom Claiborne had attempted to please through appointments to the bank's directorship. The president hinted that many of these men would not be offended, however, as there were on the list of the directors of the Louisiana Bank "several names who will probably be on the list of the branch bank."[29]

Ever loyal to Jefferson, Claiborne canceled the charter of the Louisiana Bank even though he realized this would not be popular. Perhaps conscious of this and of his increasing unpopularity and isolation, Claiborne wrote to Jefferson on May 29 and made suggestions for appointments to the future Legislative Council. Naturally Claiborne recommended men who would support him. Julien Poydras was Claiborne's first choice for a position on the council. Poydras was a wealthy influential sugar planter and commandant of Pointe Coupee. Claiborne expressed confidence in the integrity and abilities of Poydras, who could speak both French and English and had proclaimed his loyalty to Claiborne and the government of the United States.[30]

Claiborne's next recommendation for the Legislative Council was Colonel Bellechasse. The governor was obviously desperate to retain the support of Bellechasse, whom he described to Jefferson as "unquestionably the most popular man in Louisiana." The fact that Bellechasse was a friend of Daniel Clark, who had previously revealed his enmity for the governor, may have contributed to Claiborne's determination to win his loyalty. Benjamin Morgan, a merchant of New Orleans, "a man of business and integrity," was the next candidate for the Legislative Council listed by Claiborne. It seems most likely that Claiborne selected Morgan for his standing in the community and because he was critical of Daniel Clark. Finally, Claiborne recommended that Dr. John Watkins serve on the Legislative Council. Watkins had proved his loyalty on his mission to the parishes and at the public meeting called by Benjamin Tupper.[31]

Claiborne needed the support of friends in Louisiana, such as those he recommended for the Legislative Council, because public criticism of the Act for the Organization of Orleans Territory and the Louisiana District continued in the late spring of 1804. At the end of May 1804 Louisianans were permitted to register their ships, but they were upset with the structure of government that allowed no popular representation and with the prohibition against foreign importation of slaves. Just as the causes of discontent had not changed since March 1804, neither had the popular response. A week after Claiborne received his order to revoke the charter of the Louisiana Bank, approximately twenty-four Louisianans held a public meeting to determine how to persuade Congress to address their grievances regarding the Act for the Organization of Orleans Territory and the Louisiana District.

The "active agents" at the public meeting held on May 31, 1804, according to Claiborne, were Daniel Clark, Evan Jones, ex-mayor Etienne de Boré, and Edward Livingston, who had arrived at New Orleans on February 7, 1804. The circumstances of Livingston's immigration to Louisiana and his rapid ascension in New Orleans society are interesting. Prior to his arrival in New Orleans, Livingston had served as mayor and district attorney of New York. He had received these posts from Jefferson as a reward for his services to the Republican Party after the election of 1800.[32]

Livingston's star was on the rise, but his dual responsibilities as district attorney and mayor of New York left him little time to supervise the work of his assistants who served under him. In June 1803 agents of the Treasury

Department audited the accounts of the district attorney, and it was discovered that one of Livingston's clerks had embezzled a percentage of the federal taxes that he was appointed to collect. On July 2 Secretary of the Treasury Albert Gallatin informed Jefferson "he would not be surprised if the whole deficiency exceeded forty thousand dollars."[33]

Throughout July and early August Gallatin made futile efforts to convince Livingston to resign as district attorney and mayor of New York. Jefferson became impatient by August 18 and advised Gallatin that there "ought to be no further hesitation with E. Livingston."[34]

Livingston finally sent his resignation as mayor and district attorney to Governor George Clinton in the last week of August. Because Livingston had become ill as he supervised city officials' efforts to deal with a yellow fever epidemic, however, the Council of Appointment delayed its acceptance of the mayor's resignation for two months. As he recovered, Livingston came to the obvious conclusion that he had no future in New York as a Republican politician. His case was tried on December 22, 1803, and he did not contest his sentence to pay the federal government $100,000.[35]

At the end of December Livingston departed for Louisiana because the new American territory offered opportunities to a lawyer who could speak French and who was trained in Roman and common law. Upon his arrival, Livingston worked quickly to ingratiate himself with the leading businessmen of New Orleans and with the government of Louisiana. In a letter to Madison written on March 10, 1804, Claiborne reported that Livingston had succeeded in this endeavor.[36]

> My former Congressional acquaintance Edward Livingston, is now in New Orleans, and has acquired considerable influence among the inhabitants, he manifests the best disposition towards the Government, and a desire to render the administration pleasing and the present state of things acceptable to the people.[37]

Livingston also began to make efforts to purchase land along the Ouachita River. Such land would be suitable for the establishment of plantations. Like other Louisiana planters, then, Livingston had a vested interest in protesting the prohibition of the slave trade.[38]

Claiborne demonstrated his confidence in Livingston on March 12, 1804, when he appointed him to the committee to supervise distribution of the shares of the Louisiana Bank. Between March and May 1804, however, Claiborne appeared oblivious to the fact that Livingston began to align himself with those who were involved in protest against Congress's plan for the government of Louisiana.

The Organization of Protest against Territorial Government in Orleans

On June 1, 1804, Livingston and James Pitot, the new mayor of New Orleans, called on Claiborne to present him with an address on behalf of a "number of respectable Planters Merchants and Other inhabitants of Louisiana" who planned to prepare a remonstrance against several of the provisions in the Act for the Organization of Orleans Territory and the Louisiana District. Pitot and Livingston added that the public assembly had directed them to "disavow in their name any other design but that of a respectful address to the Congress stating our rights and praying that they may be speedily restored to us according to the terms of the treaty and the principles of the federal Constitution."[39]

The governor read this address and then told the envoys "the people had a right peaceably to assemble together for the purpose of remonstrating against grievances," but it was the duty of those "who produced such assemblages to prevent tumult and disorders." Claiborne also warned that persons who were not interested in the "permanent welfare" of Louisiana had attempted "to give an improper direction to the public deliberations." Finally, Claiborne told Livingston and Pitot that an examination of the Act for the Organization of Orleans Territory and the Louisiana District would prove that it was "well adapted to the local situation and interests of Louisiana, but that if there were" provisions disagreeable to the people, "a respectful memorial to Congress, was the only means of obtaining redress."[40]

Claiborne considered Livingston's involvement with the protest assembly a personal betrayal. On June 3 Claiborne wrote to Madison and explained that when his "old acquaintance Edward Livingston" had arrived he "expressed an ardent wish to see the present administration prosper, but declared it to be in his interests not to be concerned in public business." Livingston, Claiborne added, had done well for himself. "His talents, address, connexions, and the high stations he had filled, gave him consequence here: his prospects as a Lawyer became flattering, and he has made two to three thousand dollars." Livingston's legal success, according to Claiborne, was not enough to satisfy him, however.

> Mr. Livingston cannot be a stationary character; he has of late become the warm advocate of the *Rights of Louisiana* and is among the most distinguished, and the most active of those who disapprove of the measures of Government, in relation to this territory: *what his real objects are* you can as readily conjecture as myself, but his late conduct here, I consider very imprudent.[41]

Claiborne also blamed Daniel Clark for the organization of protest against the government of Louisiana. "This gentleman, I am inclined to think, is of the opinion that his services at New-Orleans, have not been sufficiently

The Organization of Protest against Territorial Government in Orleans

rewarded, and I view him as very inimical to the present Administration." Claiborne added that Clark, "in conjunction with one or perhaps two other persons," had made efforts to tarnish Claiborne's reputation in Louisiana and in Washington.[42]

While Clark was a ringleader in the protest against Claiborne's administration, he was not directly involved in the drafting of the remonstrance against the Act for the Organization of Orleans Territory and the Louisiana District. The assembly of May 31 selected Evan Jones, Edward Livingston, James Pitot, and Pierre Petit to draft the remonstrance to Congress.[43] While it was technically the work of the committee, Livingston wrote the remonstrance.[44] As Claiborne noticed upon reading the memorial, Livingston adopted "the Language of the Patriots of 76" in his description of the grievances of the inhabitants of Louisiana.[45] More specifically, Livingston's memorial appears loosely modeled on the Declaration of Independence.[46]

The Remonstrance of the People of Louisiana is a straightforward description of the grievances of Louisianans specific to the Act for the Organization of Orleans Territory and the Louisiana District. Livingston explained that the laws created by Congress for the government contravened the rights of Louisianans: the people of Louisiana had not expected this, Livingston argued, because they believed that by the treaty of cession they were promised protection of their rights and American citizenship. Louisianans "calculated with certainty" that Congress would grant them citizenship because a "free people would acquire territory only to extend the blessings of freedom" and because "an enlightened nation would never destroy those principles on which its Government was founded."[47]

The belief that they would become American citizens encouraged Louisianans to submit to the "inconveniences of an intermediate dominion without a murmur." The inconveniences listed by Livingston included a governor vested with almost unlimited civil, military, and judiciary powers; the abrupt introduction of English to government and judicial proceedings; as well as different "forms of French, Spanish and American jurisprudence." Despite all of this, Louisianans submitted to temporary government "with cheerfulness while we supposed your honorable body was employed in reducing this chaos to order, and calling a system of harmony from the depth of a confused, discordant mass."[48]

While Congress worked on the Breckinridge Bill, Livingston noted that the people of Louisiana followed the debates in newspapers. They saw that every amendment introduced on behalf of Louisianans was rejected and that the government of Louisiana outlined in the first five sections of the Act for the Organization of Orleans Territory and the Louisiana District was inconsistent with the principles of the American Revolution.

The Organization of Protest against Territorial Government in Orleans

Taxation without representation, an obligation to obey laws without any voice in their formation, the undue influence of the executive upon legislative proceedings and a dependent judiciary, formed we believe, very prominent articles in the list of grievances complained of by the United States, at the commencement of their glorious contest for freedom; the opposition to them, even by force was deemed meritorious and patriotic. . . . Were the patriots who composed your councils mistaken in their political principles? Did the heroes who died in their defence seal a false creed in blood? No they were not wrong![49]

After he made this argument, Livingston moved on to attack specific aspects of the act. He first challenged the sections that empowered the president to appoint the government of Orleans by rejecting the premise for the denial of representative government: that Louisianans were "sunk in ignorance, effeminated by luxury," and "debased by oppression." He called for Congress to produce evidence that the people of Louisiana had "so far degenerated as to become totally incompetent to the task of legislation." Livingston argued that "local knowledge was necessary to legislate wisely" and insisted that the people "possess exclusively that species of information, with respect to character, conduct, circumstances, and abilities which is necessary to a prudent choice of their representatives."[50]

Following his arguments on the necessity of representative government, Livingston presented a case for Louisiana's immediate incorporation into the Union. He quoted the third article of the treaty of cession: "the inhabitants of the ceded territory shall be incorporated into the Union of the United States as soon as possible, according to the principles of the Federal Constitution." Livingston stated that Congress interpreted this article as reading "the inhabitants of Louisiana shall be incorporated into the Union and admitted to the enjoyment of all the rights, & c., as soon as the principles of the Federal Constitution will permit." Livingston wrote, however, that this interpretation was wrong and that "the article contemplates no other delay to our reception than will be required to pass the necessary laws and ascertain the representation to which we are entitled." The Act for the Organization of Orleans Territory and the Louisiana District, Livingston argued, violated the third article of the treaty of cession because Orleans was not incorporated into the United States. The form of government established for Louisiana, Livingston concluded, "had not one principle of republicanism in its composition" and was therefore "not in compliance with the letter of the treaty" and was "totally inconsistent with its spirit."[51]

The fact that Congress had not guaranteed a date for the incorporation of Louisiana into the United States was another aspect of the act that Livingston criticized. He argued that the power to admit new states was "vested in the Congress without any restriction whatever." But Louisianans feared, Livingston explained, that this would mean that Congress might never consider it necessary to incorporate Louisiana into the United States. "If it may be procrastinated for two years, we saw no reason why it may not be deferred for twenty, or a hundred or totally omitted."[52]

Livingston next criticized Congress for its support of the segment of the act that divided Louisiana into Orleans Territory and the District of Louisiana. Louisianans, Livingston declared, did not know why Congress had "severed" the territory north of the thirty-third degree latitude from Louisiana. The people would have been better served, Livingston suggested, by administering Louisiana as a whole until an increase in population made a division necessary. Livingston hinted, however, that the purpose of the supporters of the act in the division of Louisiana was to postpone statehood for the inhabitants. "If this division should operate so long as to prolong our state of political tutelage, on account of any supposed deficiency of numbers we cannot but consider it as injurious to our rights."[53]

The provision of the Act for the Organization of Orleans Territory and the Louisiana District that had caused popular furor in New Orleans, the prohibition of importation of slaves into Louisiana, was the next issue that Livingston dealt with. He did so with a brief and simple argument: Congress should not have the right to decide on the question of slave importation on behalf of the people of Louisiana. "We ask only the right of deciding this question for ourselves and of being placed in this respect on equal footing with the other states."[54]

Finally, Livingston addressed the problems caused by the "sudden change of language in all the public offices and administration of justice." The Spanish government in Louisiana, he asserted, selected Spanish and French speakers for officials. Judicial proceedings, though conducted in Spanish, were carried out "altogether in writing" so that translations were simple. Under the system of government instituted by Congress, Louisianans required a translator for "the slightest communication." The introduction of viva voce proceedings in the courts subjected a party who could "neither understand his counsel, his judge, nor the advocate of his opponent to embarrassments the most perplexing, and often to injuries the most serious."[55]

Livingston closed the memorial with the "prayer" that Congress would remember the "sacred, self-evident and eternal truths" that the governments of the United States were founded upon, and cancel the Act for the Organization of Orleans Territory and the Louisiana District and incorporate Louisiana as a state in the Union.

Annexed to your country by the course of political events, it depends upon you to determine whether we shall pay you the cold homage of reluctant subjects, or render the free allegiance of citizens attached to your fortunes by choice, bound to you by gratitude for the best of blessings, contributing cheerfully to your advancement and defending, as we solemnly pledge ourselves to do, at the risk of fortune and life, our common constitution, country and laws.[56]

The Remonstrance of the People of Louisiana was presented for approval to a public meeting held in New Orleans on July 1, 1804. Hatch Dent, an American who was present, reported that 250 men attended the meeting and unanimously adopted it. Dent also recorded that a "committee of twelve were appointed to distribute it thro' the different parishes for signatures & three agents chosen to present it to Congress" and that Livingston was "the only American with a few exceptions that had any hand in the business."[57]

Claiborne's account of the meeting of July 1 differs from that of Dent. On the day that the meeting was held Claiborne wrote to Madison to report that the *Remonstrance* was read to the assembly and that "without discussion" 140 men signed it and that a second meeting was scheduled for "Sunday next for the purpose of electing two persons to bear the memorial to congress, and to advocate the same." The governor eventually learned that three men who had served on Laussat's city council were elected: Pierre Derbigny, Jean Nöel Destréhan, and Pierre Sauvé.[58]

Claiborne was disturbed by the plan to send Derbigny, Destréhan, and Sauvé to Congress. In addition to writing Madison on July 1, Claiborne, although suffering from an attack of yellow fever, wrote a lengthy letter to Jefferson. Claiborne admitted that he had not yet seen the memorial but that it had been represented to him as "an ingenious piece of composition, & well calculated to please the people, whose signatures are requested." He also reported that Livingston was "supported by Messrs. Evan Jones and Daniel Clark" and that these men would be joined by French inhabitants.[59]

While he suspected "secret springs" to the "warmpth [sic] of patriotism or Enthusiasm in Messrs. Livingston, Clark and Jones," Claiborne was forced to admit that they had "caused a flame in the District, which," would "not," he feared, "shortly subside."[60] Claiborne was apparently not surprised at the involvement of Clark and Jones in the protest against territorial rule but was clearly disappointed in Livingston. "I once thought that Mr. Livingston would be an acquisition to Louisiana, where men of Science and political Information are so much wanting; but now I fear he will become a troublesome member of our political society, and I do sincerely regret that he ever left New York."[61]

As proof that patriotism had not motivated Clark and Livingston to start a movement for representative government, Claiborne referred to the views expressed to him on that subject by them. Both men, Claiborne stated, had agreed with him that Louisianans were unprepared for representative government. Another individual who had shared this belief was General James Wilkinson. The opinions of these men, however, according to Claiborne, had suddenly reversed, and "these gentlemen" became "the advocates of an entire Representative Government in Louisiana." Wilkinson, Claiborne added, had "joined the popular party previous to his departure" from Louisiana and would act on behalf of the "popular party" in Washington.[62]

Two days after he reported that a public assembly had accepted Livingston's *Remonstrance*, Claiborne wrote to Madison that a new group of protesters had begun to organize for the purpose of drafting a memorial to Congress. According to Claiborne, the "free people of Colour manifested some dissatisfaction at not receiving an invitation to the meeting of citizens who adopted the memorial to Congress." An invitation to a meeting to address "*their* rights and, the propriety on their part of drafting a memorial to Congress," was prepared and submitted to a printer. But the printer refused to reproduce it, and for this Claiborne "sincerely thanked him."[63]

The city council, however, considered the invitation "a provocation to rebellion to demand equal citizenship with the white" and asked Claiborne to take measures to prevent any further organization of the "free people of Colour."[64] Specifically, the city council demanded that Claiborne "punish the Mulatto man who handed the Letters to the printer with great Severity, and to banish the author (when known) from the province." Claiborne, however, rejected these suggestions because he believed that "the events" that "spread blood and desolation in St. Domingo, originated in a dispute between the white and Mulatto inhabitants, and that the too rigid treatment of the former induced the latter to seek the support and the assistance of the Negroes."[65]

Claiborne chose to advise rather than to order corporal punishment and banishment. In the presence of Mayor James Pitot, Claiborne spoke with "nine of the most discreet and most influential free men of Colour" in order to tell them that he disapproved of their letter and their proposed meeting. Claiborne reported that after their conversation the men "seemed convinced of their error, and declared their intention to abandon the suggested project."[66]

While Claiborne believed that he had managed to quiet the protest of the "free people of Colour," he also expressed confidence that the protest movement based on Livingston's *Remonstrance* was about to dissolve. Claiborne wrote Madison that James Pitot, who had great influence as mayor of New Orleans, had assured him that there would be no public disturbance in the city. The governor believed that "many of the Citizens are now convinced of the impropriety of popular meetings at this particular period, and I should not be

The Organization of Protest against Territorial Government in Orleans

surprised if the contemplated one should ultimately fail." If the "African trade had been continued for a few years," Claiborne added, "no murmers against the Law of Congress would have been heard."[67]

The day after he reported that there would be no further protest from the "free people of color" Claiborne wrote Madison to update him on the identities of those who wrote and circulated Livingston's memorial. The governor admitted that he had "seen one sheet of the original manuscript," but that he had "no doubt" that Livingston wrote it "with the advice of Daniel Clark and Evan Jones." Claiborne also noted that the "highly inflammatory" *Remonstrance* had "obtained many signatures" and that it was his "fear" that it would "create a general Spirit of discontent, and perhaps render the temporary administration more arduous than it has hitherto been."[68]

The backgrounds and views of the three delegates chosen to present the *Remonstrance* to Congress caused Claiborne further anxiety. Claiborne characterized Derbigny as a man of "strict integrity" who was "pleased with the principles of our Government but much attached to his native country [France]." Sauvé was "an amiable good man, a wealthy planter universally esteemed by his neighbors," but Claiborne feared that he would "take little part in the agency." Destréhan was a "Frenchman in politics and affections" who was "one of the tools of M. Laussat and greatly mortified at the cession of Louisiana to the United States." Destréhan had no understanding of the English language, but this would not prevent him from an effort "to be the most prominent man on the mission." All of these men, Claiborne noted, were "warm advocates of the slave trade." This is, of course, was not surprising since Sauvé and Destréhan were prominent planters and Derbigny, considered a friend and associate of such men, supported the planter interest.[69]

Beyond his specific accusation that Derbigny and Destréhan were more attached to France than they were to the United States, Claiborne also claimed that many of those who signed Livingston's *Remonstrance* were nostalgic about the Spanish rule of Louisiana. Claiborne specifically accused the ex-Spanish governor, the Marquis de Casa Calvo, and the ex-intendant, Juan Ventura Morales, of having made an attempt "to excite and perpetuate in the district a grateful recollection of the former favours of his Catholic Majesty." Probable proof of a friendly relationship between Casa Calvo, Morales, and those who supported the *Remonstrance*, according to Claiborne, was that "the first meeting of the Memorialist was on the 1st of July, and the address to the Marquis" was "of the same date." This, Claiborne wrote, suggested that the "occasion of that assemblage was embraced to procure signatures to that adulatory address."[70]

As Claiborne anxiously observed the actions of his political opponents, he finally managed to obtain a copy of the *Remonstrance of the People of*

Louisiana printed in the *Louisiana Gazette* on July 24, 1804. He sent it along with a letter to Madison on July 26, 1804. In his letter, Claiborne reported that he had discovered that Daniel Clark was to set out the next day on a "mission" to the rural districts of the province in order to obtain more signatures for the *Remonstrance*. Clark proposed, according to Claiborne, to "go as far as Natchitoches."[71]

Claiborne also used the opportunity of sending the *Remonstrance* to Madison to defend himself against some of the complaints included in it. Claiborne stated that he had attempted to ensure that a language barrier did not hinder justice or government. Nearly all of the justices of the court of pleas spoke both languages, Claiborne indicated, and he employed an interpreter at the "Governor's Court." He also argued that the people of Louisiana had never suffered under "the evils of a military government," as was stated in the *Remonstrance*.[72]

The governor added that it was his belief that the ultimate demand for state government for Louisiana made in the *Remonstrance* "did not originate with any of the *ancient inhabitants* of Louisiana; they wanted the privilege of electing their Legislative Council, and the slave trade opened for a few years." Louisianans were "an amenable, well disposed people" but were "too easily influenced by the counsels of men who flatter them."[73] The Louisianans would be satisfied without statehood, Claiborne claimed, if they were granted the rights to elect the second Legislative Council and to import slaves to Louisiana. The latter right was extremely important, according to Claiborne, because Louisianans were under the impression that with statehood, they would be guaranteed control of their own slave trade until 1808.[74]

In closing his letter to Madison, Claiborne admitted that he faced a new problem with regard to public discontent and political strife. "I was particularly desirous to keep this city free from party disputes and party writings; but the introduction of newspapers among us, has opened the avenues to political discussion, and I see with concern that the spirit of party is daily acquiring nourishment."[75]

The publication of the *Remonstrance* in the *Louisiana Gazette* on July 24 began an editorial war between the *Gazette* and another newspaper, the *Union*, which Claiborne had selected to print the "Laws of the United States" and his own "ordinances." Immediately after the *Remonstrance* was published in the *Gazette*, an anonymous writer attacked it in the *Union*, and claimed that an increase in taxation on the people of Louisiana would be necessary to support statehood. Because Louisianans were "unaccustomed to the liberty of the press," Claiborne stated, they believed that the anonymous writer had the support of the governor since the editorial appeared in his newspaper. He denied that he had ever attempted to "exercise any influence or authority over the press," but he did admit that he had "taken the liberty" in his "character as a citizen" to "request the editors of the newspapers not to print any piece that might tend to irritate or divide our society." Claiborne's requests had little or no effect. On August 7, 1804, an anonymous writer in the *Gazette* returned fire on behalf of the supporters of the *Remonstrance* and attempted to disprove the claim that a state government would require more revenue than the current government.[76]

Etienne de Boré contributed to the newspaper debate on statehood and citizenship on August 9, 1804, when he published a letter that Congress had addressed to the inhabitants of Quebec in October 1774 in the *Moniteur de la Louisiane*. The *Letter to the Inhabitants of Quebec* urged the sending of delegates to the Continental Congress, and was designed to remind the people of Quebec of the rights due to them as British subjects.

The "first grand right" that the people of the British colonies were entitled to was "that of the people having a share of their government by their representatives chosen by themselves," and, "of being ruled by laws, which they themselves approve, not by the edicts of men over whom they have no control." According to Congress, however, the people of Quebec were denied this right, and the system of government established for them under the Quebec Act was tyrannical. "Your judges, and your Legislative Council, as it is called, are dependant on your Governor, and he is dependant on the servant of the crown in Great Britain. The legislative, executive and judging powers are all moved by the nods of a Minister."[77]

Boré, as president of a committee of Louisianans, wanted Congress's letter of October 26, 1774, to speak for itself. In a brief paragraph he introduced the document and suggested that Louisianans consider "what relation there is between the present situation of the Inhabitants of Louisiana, and that of Canada at that time when Congress put them in mind of their rights and privileges, which the agents of the English Government would not allow them."[78]

The New Orleans newspaper war over the *Remonstrance* in the summer of 1804 coincided with a devastating outbreak of yellow fever. By the middle of August both Claiborne and his wife were ill. Despite his illness, however, Claiborne attempted to manage the affairs of the government of Louisiana. He dictated a list of individuals whom he believed would be best suited to serve on the Legislative Council that was to be formed after the new government of the territory of Orleans was established on October 1, 1804, to his secretary, Joseph Briggs.[79] First on Claiborne's list was Benjamin Morgan, who was a natural choice because of his distrust of Clark. There was probably also another reason why he was selected. As Livingston's *Remonstrance* began to circulate, a group of English and American men prepared a memorial of their own that rejected the demands of the *Remonstrance* and demanded that English

The Organization of Protest against Territorial Government in Orleans

be made the language of the courts once statehood was obtained. The author or authors of this document are not known, but Benjamin Morgan displayed this memorial in his shop so that those who wanted to could sign it.[80] The remainder of Claiborne's recommendations for the Legislative Council included men who had proved their loyalty in the face of growing opposition, such as Dr. John Watkins, Julien Poydras, and Colonel Bellechasse.

On August 30 Claiborne struggled back to his writing desk and wrote to Jefferson to complain that it was difficult to find loyal Republicans who had professional talents to serve in the territorial government. It was his "misfortune" ever since "he had the honor to represent the General Government in the Western Country to have found the weight of at least professional talents on the federal side." Claiborne stated that out of thirty lawyers, he was only able to discover three Republicans: Lewis Kerr, appointed as sheriff of New Orleans; Edward Nichols, appointed as clerk of the Governor's Court; and Henry Brown, whom Claiborne made a notary public. The governor warned that "as federal influence declined in the States, the remote Territories" would "become Asylums for that Party; and particularly for men whose politicks embarrass them at home."[81]

Since he had discussed political opposition, Claiborne did not fail to mention Daniel Clark and Edward Livingston. Clark, Claiborne claimed, was "the first adventurer" to engage in Florida land speculation. Many others had followed his example, and Claiborne hopefully forecast that "the probable outcome of their rapacious Schemes is very just and will be a matter of Triumph to many worthy Citizens." Claiborne also claimed that Clark had acquired "a great influence" over Edward Livingston and that Clark had convinced Livingston to make remarks in the *Remonstrance* alluding to the contents of Claiborne's published letter of January 2, 1804. Claiborne was "enclined to think," however, "that Mr. Livingston now regrets the part he acted in this Business, but his pride will not permit him to acknowledge it."[82]

Claiborne concluded his letter to Jefferson of August 30 with the wish that the president "excuse this incorrect scrawl" as he was weakened by yellow fever. The disease took a serious toll on the Louisiana government. Claiborne and his family were ill; Hore Browse Trist, collector for New Orleans, was dead; and on September 16 Claiborne's secretary, Joseph Briggs, died.[83] It was then that Claiborne received a petition that requested him to take precautions against a possible slave insurrection.[84] He responded by increasing patrols and furnishing the city grenadiers with muskets and ammunition.[85]

In addition to these administrative difficulties, Claiborne was forced to deal with a personal tragedy. On September 27, three days before the Act for the Organization of Orleans Territory and the Louisiana District was to go into effect, yellow fever claimed the lives of his wife and his daughter.[86] Despite

The Organization of Protest against Territorial Government in Orleans

this "heavy burden," Claiborne worked on, and one of his last acts as temporary governor was to write a letter of introduction to Madison for Derbigny, Sauvé, and Destréhan, the *Remonstrance* envoys who were about to sail for Washington.[87]

CHAPTER FOUR

"Pestered with Intriguants"
Territorial Administration under Attack
in Orleans and Washington

On August 30, 1804, the same day that Claiborne wrote to President Thomas Jefferson to complain about the difficulty of finding suitable men to serve in government, Jefferson sent Claiborne a list of appointments to the Legislative Council. The president named Etienne de Boré, Benjamin Morgan, Daniel Clark, Dr. John Watkins, Evan Jones, Joseph Bellechasse, John Roman, and William Wykoff "absolutely" to the Legislative Council, but he also gave Claiborne limited power in appointment choices. Out of a pool of five others that Jefferson recommended for council that included "Derbigne, Detrehan, Dubuys, Cantarelle of the Acadian coast & Sauve," Claiborne was allowed to choose three. In addition, Claiborne was permitted to select either George Pollock or Dr. Robert Dow for the Legislative Council. Boré, Clark, and Jones, "appointed absolutely," were critics of Claiborne's administration, as were the envoys Derbigny, Destréhan, and Sauvé, whom Jefferson recommended for the Legislative Council. Why had Jefferson selected them?[1]

Jefferson informed Claiborne that he had hoped to base his choices for the Legislative Council on a few critical factors. First, he believed that the council should be composed of "a majority of Americans, say 7. Americans and 6. French, or persons of such long standing as to be considered as French." Second, Jefferson wanted the council to include "some mixture of the mercantile with the planting interest" and "a representation of the different settlements in the country, justly proportioned, as far as they can furnish proper materials, to that of the city." Between April and July Jefferson wrote two letters to Claiborne and asked him to provide recommendations for such a council. Claiborne did so on August 17, but Jefferson made his decision to make council appointments on August 30, before Claiborne's letter reached Washington.[2]

Although Jefferson did not receive Claiborne's list of recommendations for the Legislative Council, he had received information on prominent residents of Orleans from him in the past, and he received intelligence concerning them from another source. On July 1, 1804, General James Wilkinson wrote to Jefferson and submitted "Portraits of several prominent Characters in Louisiana, (the Territory of Orleans) from the Pens of two Gentlemen, strangers to each other, of different Nations & opposite prejudices—The one a French Man, the other an Atlantic American." Who were these men? According to Jefferson, the authors were Evan Jones and a Frenchman, La Bigarre. La Bigarre, Jefferson recorded, was "Frenchman by birth but an American in all his partialities" who "only visited the country for 6. or 9. months," married a Livingston, and sold antiseptic gas. In annotating the list, Jefferson wrote that "La Bigarre who wrote one of the lists of characters for W. is & always was totally unprincipled, & no confidence ought to be placed in what he says." Jones, on the other hand, according to the president, possessed "manners stiff" and an "integrity irreproachable" as well as "decent talents & a better knoledge of the province than any other American."[3]

The most interesting portraits on the list are of the individuals involved in the production and delivery of the *Remonstrance.* Neither of the descriptions of Daniel Clark was complimentary. The first of these, numbered 66, "such as Mess.' Clark Jones &c &c," described Clark as "rather an Englishman at heart" who was "unpopular and too assuming." Because of this, the author of this portrait concluded, "it might be unwise to countenance at present his cunning & overbearing pretensions." The second characterization of Clark, numbered 92, was somewhat milder than the first. "Mr. D. Clark possesses capacities to do more good or harm than any other individual in the province—He pants for power, and is mortified by disappointment."[4]

It seems most likely that Jones was not the author of the first portrait of Clark. In his analysis of the list, Jefferson made the same assumption based on the fact that the author listed Jones in his characterization of Clark. It also seems more likely that La Bigarre would characterize Clark as an "Englishman at heart." What is certain, and surprising, however, is that Jones, as the author of at least one of the portraits, presented Clark, his political ally, as an overly ambitious individual. Not surprising is the fact that the only description of Jones presents him in the best possible light. "*Evan Jones*—a man of education, an American by birth and by attachment, He is talented, proud high spirited, rich, ardent and decisive at sixty five years of age." Jones was described somewhat negatively in the portrait of John Prevost. It was mentioned that Evan Jones had married Prevost's sister and that Jones would "govern" Prevost's politics.[5]

Both La Bigarre and Jones had negative opinions of Etienne de Boré. In one portrait Boré was described as a man of fortune who had important connections but also as "a man of mean extraction, without abilities either natural or aquir'd" and "principally distinguishd by his vanity and blind attachment to the French Nation." The second portrait of Boré was even less flattering. Boré was estimated to be a "rich and enterprising" planter who was "ignorant & destitute of any knowledge or talents relative to political or Civil government; of an high & assuming temper pluming himself upon a certain influence which he claims from wealth; & is generally hated by his own countrymen."[6]

Pierre Derbigny and JeanNöel Destréhan, two of the *Remonstrance* envoys, were also portrait subjects. Derbigny, although described as having "decent morals," was the subject of the most negative portrait on the list. "*Pre Derbigny*, . . . a man of some information, but a crouching cunning and artful *Camleopard*, ungrateful to the Spanish Govt by which he was employ'd because a devoted Friend of Laussat & Boreé; in short dangerous & not to be trusted with any office." A second portrait of Derbigny was not as harsh, but it was critical. He was described as a young man "of talents but without fortune or connections Genteel. Sober and industrious, but not very generally esteemd—his principles not free from suspicion, & much attached to his native Country." Jefferson included his own comments on Derbigny and described him as "a native of France, of good information & strict integrity. pleased with the principles of our govmt.—but much attached to his native country—speaks English." This description is clearly based on the character sketch that Claiborne provided to Madison on July 13, 1804.[7]

The portraits of Destréhan by Jones and La Bigarre were positive. The first described Destréhan as sensible, rich, of good reputation, and "one of the most Respectable men in the Province." The second noted that Destréhan was a "well informed man, of mild & aimiable temper, possessed of the greatest share of influence among his countrymen, more energetick and pleasing than that of Mr. Boree." Jefferson also included Claiborne's description of Destréhan from his letter of July 13 on the portrait list. The governor had described Destréhan as "a native Frenchman in politics" who was "one of the tools of M. Laussat."[8]

Jones and La Bigarre did not write an evaluation of the third envoy to Congress, but Jefferson described Pierre Sauvé as "a native of France" and "an amiable good man, a wealthy planter universally esteemd by his neighbors & will be good citizen under our government, but probably take little part in the agency. Speaks English."[9] As in the case of Jefferson's notes on Derbigny, this sketch is from Claiborne's letter of July 13, 1804.

Jefferson appears to have recommended Sauvé and Derbigny based on Claiborne's characterizations of these two men. In appointing Bellechasse, Jefferson noted that Claiborne had recommended him. Jefferson, however,

Territorial Administration under Attack in Orleans and Washington appeared to dismiss Claiborne's advice on Destréhan and accepted the positive sketches of Destréhan provided by Jones and La Bigarre. While Jefferson had reservations about Boré's involvement in "disrespectful" protest against territorial government, he was impressed with Boré's "integrity, agricultural merits, the interests he had at stake & his zeal for liberty." In a way it seems as if Jefferson identified with Boré, an innovative, informed planter who attempted to convince Louisianans that they should organize to protect promised freedoms. It is also probable that Jefferson hoped that Boré might be flattered by his appointment and that he would support Claiborne. It is more difficult, however, to explain Jefferson's appointment of Clark and Jones, whom Claiborne had continuously described as unprincipled enemies in his letters to the president. While he did not explain his reasons for doing so, it seems most likely that Jefferson wanted to win their support.[10]

It is certain that Jefferson's wish for a majority of Americans on the Legislative Council influenced his appointments. In a letter dated August 16, 1804, Jefferson asked Madison to advise him on his choices for appointments to the government of Louisiana, including those of the Legislative Council. Jefferson listed these in "French" and "American" columns. The "French" recommendations included Destréhan, Cantarelle, Dubuys, Poydras, Bellechasse, and "Favre or Boré." The "American" recommendations included Morgan, Watkins, Clark, Jones, Roman, Wyckoff, and Dow or Pollock. This gave the Americans a seven-to-six majority. Madison apparently approved this list because it is essentially identical to the appointments Jefferson made on August 30.[11]

Claiborne commented on Jefferson's appointments during his first week as governor of the territory of Orleans, on October 5, 1804. He claimed that he was forced to omit the names of Derbigny, Destréhan, and Sauvé from the list of councilors "on account of the intended visit of those gentlemen to Washington as Bearers of the Memorial to Congress, & the certainty that neither could give attendance in Council during the ensuing winter." Claiborne also attempted to have Evan Jones's appointment to the Legislative Council rescinded. The governor wrote that "the Conduct of Mr. Jones (one of the Councillors)" in a "late transaction" would "not appear in a favorable light."[12]

While Claiborne attempted to ensure the exclusion of Derbigny, Destréhan, and Sauvé, he did not attempt to prevent Daniel Clark and Etienne de Boré from serving as well. Why did he not attack them as he had done in the past? Perhaps he believed that these two men alone could do little damage on the thirteen- member Legislative Council.

As it turned out, Claiborne's effort to convince Jefferson that Jones was unsuitable as a legislative councilor proved futile. Claiborne wrote to Jones on October 5 to notify him that the president had appointed him to the Legislative Council. Three days later, Jones wrote back to Claiborne to refuse the appointment. Jones's expressed reason for doing so was that he thought that accepting this appointment, made possible by the act of March 26, 1804, would be inconsistent with his position as a signer of the memorial for the repeal of that act and declared that his refusal was an act of patriotism. "I was born an American—I glory in that name—In defence of that happy land which gave me my birth; my life and fortune shall always be staked; but I cannot consent to, for any consideration, to do an act, which I think subversive of the rights and liberties of my fellow citizens."[13]

In an obvious attempt to win public support for his position, Jones sent his resignation letter to newspapers. On October 15, 1804, the *Union* published Jones's letter and an article by an author who wrote under the name of Fairplay. Fairplay accused Jones of using his resignation as a means "to put himself at the head of a party, which at any other moment he could not have hoped for." In addition, Fairplay insisted there was no inconsistency if a signer of the memorial served on the Legislative Council, especially if he agreed to serve for free. This, Fairplay argued, Jones would never agree to do. "I should not think he acted consistently if he accepted an appointment under any form of government, unless there was a good round salary annexed to it."[14]

Jones suffered an even more blistering attack on his character in a later issue of the *Union*. A writer who called himself Flagellus and who was clearly versed in Jones's past history criticized Jones's claim that he was a patriotic American. "Where did you imbibe the heroic principles protested in your letter? Was it with the British at Pensacola or the Spaniards?" Flagellus asked Jones how he dared to "boastingly" call himself an American when he was born "a subject of his British majesty in the colony of New York." Furthermore, Flagellus added, Jones kept his life and his fortune "safe in Pensacola" during the American Revolution and "left '*the happy land*' which gave you '*birth*' to fight her own battles as she could without you." Flagellus concluded Jones's patriotism was a recent phenomenon that originated in his "removal from the office of American Consul at this port by the present President, and the appointment of one whom you once detested, but who . . . is now your political friend and confidential associate." According to Flagellus, Jones's replacement by Clark was "the grand source of all the hostility" that he had "manifested against the government of the United States."[15]

As Fairplay and Flagellus attacked Jones in the newspapers, Claiborne did so in his correspondence with Madison. Claiborne suggested that the reasons that influenced Jones to refuse his appointment to the Legislative Council would "operate with all those who had signed the Memorial to Congress: Mr. Ed. Livingston has found that their acceptance would betray a *Dishonorable Inconsistency*." This meant that as many as eight councilors might refuse their appointments.[16]

Territorial Administration under Attack in Orleans and Washington

Claiborne believed that Jones was part of an effort to convince the signers of the memorial to refuse their appointments to the Legislative Council. On October 13 the governor reported that Jones had published his letter of resignation in the newspapers and that he was "using great exertion to induce the several councilors to follow his example." Still Claiborne hoped that Jones would fail because some believed he was dishonest and because his influence was "very limited." The governor admitted, however, that Jones, Clark, and Livingston had caused him "Trouble & Anxiety" and that he believed that Clark would "also decline acting as a Councillor."[17]

As Claiborne began to face the possibility of further resignations from the Legislative Council, a pamphlet attacking his administration and the structure of government established for Louisiana was published. The anonymous author of *View of the Political and Civil Situation of Louisiana; from the Thirtieth of November 1803 to the First of October, 1804 by a Native* charged that Claiborne followed orders to "leave the administration of Louisiana in the same state which he found it," and that this had resulted in chaos. "We have then at first a chief who unites the powers of the Spanish governor and intendant, a municipality organized in the French mode, and no tribunals." The fact that "Governor Claiborne fell as it were from the clouds, without knowledge of the country, its inhabitants, their manners, their customs, their very language, or their laws" made this bad administrative system worse.[18]

After these general criticisms, the author of the *View* listed some specific complaints. He first criticized Claiborne's decision "to create a court of pleas" that was "organized entirely after the American manner." This embarrassed Louisianans who could not understand English and the "judges themselves, who had no idea of those foreign forms, which they should follow and mix with Spanish laws."[19]

The author of the *View* also suggested that Claiborne further alienated Louisianans through his creation of American militia companies and by his appointment of Americans to government offices. The American militia companies were formed "by reducing the main body" in which the native Louisianans were enrolled. Government offices "were almost all distributed between the creatures of government, newly transplanted among us, and especially given to native Americans in preference to other citizens."[20]

It is clear that the author of the *View* thought that the introduction of English in the courts and English speakers in government office was designed to exclude French Louisianans from politics and commerce. The author defined the "use of our native language" as the "most dear property," and in a reference to the treaty of cession asked if the United States had at least "contracted the obligation of maintaining us in the enjoyment of our liberty and property." If

French Louisianans were not able to use French in their daily lives, the author continued, they would have a desperate future.

> Eleven twelfths of our population would be rendered incapable of public trans-actions, and shackled in the discharge of private affairs! A handful of men would have a humiliating preponderance to the mass of the inhabitants! What do I say! the Louisianians would become STRANGERS ON THEIR NATIVE SOIL!!! afflicting, hopeless prospect on which we dare not turn our languid eyes![21]

Claiborne reacted strongly to the *View*. On October 16 he reported the circulation of the pamphlet and wrote a lengthy defense against the charges made against him. First, Claiborne denied that "native Americans enjoy'd all the lucrative Employments under my late administration." He noted that Pierre Derbigny was appointed clerk to the court of pleas and that the mayor and the majority of the municipal council were Louisianans. Finally, Claiborne concluded that he could only "recollect but three native Americans" among the various district commandants that he appointed.[22]

The governor also declared that the American militia companies were vol-unteer associations, and that he had considered it his duty to accept their offer of service. As for the organization of the court system, Claiborne claimed that the "formation of a court system devolv'd upon the American administration" because there was "no regular Judiciary in existence" when he arrived. He ad-mitted that English was the language of the supreme court but stated that this was "unavoidable, as the Judge knew neither French nor Spanish." The gover-nor also confessed that "it certainly wou'd have been a great convenience to have been correctly acquainted with the French language" but that he used in-terpreters and did not believe that "the people sustained any injury" as a result of his lack of knowledge of that language.[23]

That Claiborne considered the *View* to be a serious problem is proved by the fact that he wrote Madison about it again on October 22 and requested that his letter of October 16 be published if the *View* was published at Wash-ington. The governor also informed Madison that there was no doubt that Pierre Derbigny had written the pamphlet. Claiborne added that he always knew that Derbigny "was in his Affections a Frenchman," but that he had al-ways had "a high opinion of his Talents, Integrity and discretion" and that as a result "no person in Louisiana" had benefited more from government patronage.[24]

Because he believed that Derbigny's patriotism was suspect, and that Des-tréhan was not considered "as friendly to the U. States," Claiborne advised

Madison to confide only in Sauvé when the three agents of the memorialists arrived in Washington. Sauvé, according to Claiborne, was "not a man of talents," but his views were honest. The governor predicted that the agents would declare that "the people generally wish for the African Trade," that they would ask for some alteration in the government, and that they might be satisfied with "an Elective Council and a Delegate to Congress."[25]

While Claiborne became increasingly concerned that the *View* and the memorialists' agents might damage the credibility of his administration, more appointed councilors resigned. Robert Dow cited "family concerns" as an excuse. Etienne de Boré also resigned, and Claiborne feared that the "opinion of Mr. Jones, in his relation to his political consistency," was "adopted by Mr. Boré," and that this opinion might be "embrac'd by other gentlemen named." Because of this problem, Claiborne doubted he would be able to form a quorum for the first meeting of the Legislative Council scheduled for November 12, 1804. As replacements for Jones, Dow, and Boré, Claiborne recommended George Mather, Eugene D' Onsiere, and William Donaldson.[26]

As Claiborne became increasingly anxious about councilors' resignations and the memorialists' agents mission to Washington, he received some support from Benjamin Morgan, who, along with Dr. John Watkins, had accepted an appointment to the Legislative Council. Morgan allowed a petition of support for the system of territorial government established for Louisiana to be kept at his store so that anyone interested could sign it. According to an anonymous article in the *Louisiana Gazette* of October 26, the petitioners declared that "the prescribed government of the Territory" had "excited no differences among them" and that "on the contrary" they would "remain devoted to the United States and determined to support its laws." The petitioners also believed that Orleans Territory would be granted representative government when it was considered consistent with the general good and "not opposed to the principles of the Constitution." This was essentially, then, a rejection of the demand for statehood made in Livingston's memorial. When Orleans did become a state, however, the petitioners requested, "they (*'whose language is English'*) may be indulged in having the Legislative and Judicial proceedings conducted in their 'mother tongue.'" The anonymous author of the *Gazette* article added, however, that he was sorry to observe that the terms of the petition excluded anyone else from signing it as "many respectable native Creoles whose language is French" supported it and wanted to sign.[27]

While probably grateful for Morgan's support, Claiborne, if he knew about it, did not acknowledge it in his communications with Madison; instead, he continued to express his fears about the *View* and Livingston's memorial. On the issue of the *View*, the governor expressed his hope that it "would not receive any attention to the Northward," but included a duplicate copy of his letter of October 16 in case it did.[28] As for the memorial, Claiborne down-played it and claimed that few supported it except with regard to the "African trade" and their wish for "an elected legislative council." Still, he feared some of those who supported it, especially Etienne de Boré. Claiborne informed Jefferson that he knew "but few violent men" who were Louisianans, but that "M. Boré" was "perhaps the most so," and that Boré had "the opinion that if the Memorial" was "not entirely granted, an appeal should be immediately made to Bonaparte."[29]

The problems of the *View* and Livingston's memorial were serious but did not compare for Claiborne with the continuous difficulties that he faced in his attempts to form the Legislative Council, without which the government of Louisiana was legislatively powerless. Claiborne sincerely wanted to convene the council because he believed that the "Good of the Territory" required "many Legislative Acts." On October 29, however, Claiborne again reported that he did not know whether he would be able to convene the council by November 12: Jones, Boré, and Dow had declined, and he feared that "Colonel Bellechasse's private affairs" would prevent him from accepting his appointment. He also expressed his frustration that "Messrs Jones, Boré and Clark were appointed Councillors" as they were "great supporters of the Memorial," and would "not only decline serving the Council" but would "induce others to do so likewise."[30]

On November 5, a week before the Legislative Council was to meet, Daniel Clark and Michael Cantarelle resigned their council appointments. This infuriated Claiborne, who accused Clark of making exertions to induce those appointed to the council to resign their office. Specifically, Claiborne accused Clark of intimidating those who owed him money. "I know *one Gentleman* who would have accepted, but being indebted to Mr. Clark, he was fearful, that the displeasure of his Creditor would ensue, & be productive of great injury *to him*." In addition, Claiborne noted that Clark was "particularly intimate with the Spanish ex-Intendant Moralis," was "Decidedly in the Spanish Interest," and was involved in land speculation schemes. In short, Claiborne warned Madison that "Mr. Clark" was "an Enemy to the Government of the United States."[31]

Claiborne's doubts about convening the Legislative Council proved realistic when the date that he set for its first meeting passed. On November 18 Claiborne reported that "only five of the gentlemen appointed by the President" had accepted: "Messrs. Poidrass, Watkins, Morgan, Wikoff and Kenner."[32] The next day Claiborne again blamed this situation on Daniel Clark. "Bellechasse and Dubuys feared that their acceptance would draw a resentment from their creditors . . . the greatest of whom is Daniel Clark."[33]

As December began Claiborne was still without a government and had not received any instructions from Washington on how to deal with this situation. On December 2, 1804, Jefferson wrote to Claiborne to acknowledge the resignations of Boré, Jones, and Dow and enclosed two blank commissions for the appointment of new legislative councilors. The president admitted that "most of whatever discontent among the French inhabitants" was caused by "the introduction of our language too suddenly & the awkwardness the inhabitants experience in being unable to do business with their government but thro' an interpreter." In order to solve this problem, Jefferson planned to appoint three bilingual judges to the superior court, and he hoped that the Legislative Council would pass laws in both languages and that the "two languages" would "be placed by law on an equal footing." Despite his sympathy for Louisianans' discontent, however, Jefferson urged Claiborne to move against those who continued to use it to undermine the governor's rule. "If particular individuals continue to excite insurrection with you," the president declared, "the energies of the law must lay hold of them."[34]

On the same day that Jefferson sent Claiborne new commissions for the Legislative Council, Claiborne wrote to Jefferson to inform the president that he could wait no longer to convene the council and that he had appointed Eugene Dorciere and George Pollock to it. Both men accepted their appointments, and with seven men appointed out of a possible thirteen, Claiborne reported that the quorum requirement for the council was satisfied and that the legislature would "proceed to business."[35]

While he recognized that he had made a unilateral decision, Claiborne explained that he would *have delayed still longer*, the filling of the two blank Commissions" until he received Jefferson's advice, but "Mr. Poidras and Mr. Wickoff talked of resigning and going home" because the council could not meet. Claiborne's decision to fill the commissions is understandable given that further delay and the resignation of Poydras, who possessed "great Wealth and influence in the Territory and a friendly disposition to the United States," would have seriously hindered administration of Orleans Territory.[36]

As Claiborne convened the Legislative Council, Jefferson noted that the memorial envoys had arrived in Washington. The president found that they conducted "themselves with approbation" and that they "would find a disposition in the great majority here to do whatever circumstances will admit for our new fellow citizens, to do as much for them as we do for our own brothers and children settling in new territories."[37]

The day after Jefferson informed Claiborne about the arrival of Derbigny, Destréhan, and Sauvé, Livingston's memorial was introduced to the House of Representatives by Joseph Nicholson, a Republican from Maryland. Nicholson observed that the "three gentlemen appointed from that country had requested him to state that a copy of the which appeared in our papers in the course of the last statement was by no means original." The envoys also told Nicholson to warn the House that the translation that accompanied the French original was correct but contained expressions of the feelings of the inhabitants that should not be considered as a lack of respect for the government of the United States. Nicholson then mentioned three specific complaints described in the memorial. Louisianans, he said, prayed for "an alteration of the law so far as to allow them to be their own legislators, not dividing the Territory into two governments, and not prohibiting the importation of slaves."[38]

After Nicholson introduced the bill to the House, it was referred to a committee chaired by John Randolph established by Jefferson through his annual message to Congress of November 13, 1804, for "an amelioration of the form of government of the Territory of Louisiana."[39] Randolph was not sympathetic to Louisianans who protested against American rule, and he had suggested in October 1804 that U.S. troops might be used to reconcile them to their situation and that the troops should distribute "a thousand copies of Tom Paine's answer to their remonstrance."[40]

In the address that Randolph referred to, entitled *To the French Inhabitants of Louisiana*, Paine argued that a reading of the memorial revealed that its author was not a Louisianan and that his attempt to compare the efforts of Louisianans to obtain rights from the American government to those of the American revolutionaries revealed that the author did not understand the Louisianans' situation. Paine reminded Louisianans that they would enjoy the benefits of living in the Union soon enough and chastised them for their demand to continue the slave trade and to govern a territory that did not belong to them. "You are arriving at freedom by the easiest means that people ever enjoyed it; without contest, without expense, and even without any contrivance of your own. And you so far mistake principles, that under the name of *rights* you ask for *powers; power to import and enslave Africans*; and to govern a territory that *we* have purchased."[41]

Paine did not trust the loyalty of the Louisianans and believed that their "aim" was "that of governing Louisiana *in the lump*." While the memorial envoys were in Washington, Paine advised Jefferson that to make Louisiana a state at that time would "be sending American settlers into exile," and that it would be best to flood Louisiana with Americans first. When the number of Americans was equal to the number of French inhabitants, Paine suggested, it might be possible "to erect such part where such equality exist[s] into a constitutional state."[42]

While they waited for news from Randolph's committee, the memorial deputies were invited to dine with different officials. At a Federalist dinner organized by Timothy Pickering held on February 15, Senator William Plumer recorded his impressions of Derbigny, Destréhan, and Sauvé. Plumer considered them as "men of talents, literature and general information" who were involved in business and "were acquainted with the world." Most of all Plumer was "gratified that" they had "little of the French frippery about them" and resembled "New England men more than Virginians."[43]

In speaking to the memorialists, Plumer discovered that nothing would satisfy them but an elective government and that they were unhappy with the duties on imports and exports that Louisianans paid to the United States as they were higher than those they had paid to Spain. In addition, the memorial envoys informed Plumer that under Spain their religion and government were protected, but under American rule they were "obliged to support their religion & internal government." Derbigny, Destréhan, and Sauvé also complained about Claiborne, who could "not speak a word of French" and was "incompetent to discharge the duties of Governor." That the court system was established "in a language that most do not understand" was another source of discontent. The envoys also informed Plumer that "no man" who wanted to "enjoy the friendship of the people" could accept an office in the government of Orleans Territory. Finally, the memorialists complained that Jefferson had "studiously avoided conversing with them upon every subject that had relation to the mission here."[44]

Senator John Quincy Adams also attended the dinner at the invitation of Pickering. He discovered that the memorial envoys did "not appear very sanguine in the success of their negotiation" and that they were dissatisfied "above all with Governor Claiborne, whom they most cordially detest." An additional "object of great discontent" of the memorial envoys was the prohibition of the slave trade. Adams believed that if Congress satisfied two points of the memorial—the demand for a more suitable governor and restoration of the slave trade—the envoys "would return home well pleased." But, Adams concluded, "it is not probable they will be gratified in either."[45]

After waiting for a month for news from Randolph's committee, Derbigny, Destréhan, and Sauvé became discontented and sent a report on their impressions of the receipt of the memorial by Congress to Etienne de Boré and the "standing committee." It was eventually published in the *Louisiana Gazette*.[46]

The report, entitled *Reflections on the Cause of Louisianians respectfully submitted by their agents*, was an attack on those who might oppose the demands expressed in the memorial. A lengthy introduction praised the "peace and tranquility" that Louisianans enjoyed under Spain and justified the memorial with the criticism of the "first steps of an administration totally inexperienced in that country," which included the establishment of unfamiliar laws and the abrupt introduction of English in the judiciary and government.[47]

Next, the memorialists challenged "a piece" that was presented to Congress under the title of "counter petition." This was undoubtedly a reference to the petition that was posted at Benjamin Morgan's store and presented to the Senate on November 29, 1804. Derbigny, Destréhan, and Sauvé dismissed the "counter petition" as "the effort of the few to maintain the preponderance which they now enjoy over the many."[48]

Finally, the memorial envoys focused on the arguments made by those who opposed statehood for Louisiana. They divided the opinions of these men into "three species": those who argued that because Louisianans had not signed the treaty of cession, the third article of that treaty was no guarantee that Louisiana should be incorporated into the United States as soon as possible; those who believed that the treaty of cession did not provide for Louisiana's "admission into the Union, *except at some future period to be determined by the United States*"; and those who agreed that the treaty of cession entitled Louisiana to be incorporated into the Union "without any delay other than the necessary preparations" but who also thought "it *unsafe* for the interest of the United States to admit Louisiana immediately as a member of the federation."[49]

The envoys condemned the first species of opinion as "ungenerous and illiberal" because it suggested that a Louisianan had no right to challenge the law established for the government of Louisiana and should "abide by his master's pleasure and to receive with submission what he might think fit to grant." The logical extension of this opinion, the envoys declared, was that Louisianans, "once silenced with that *imperious tone* must be governed in an *imperious* manner, and treated not like brothers, but like vassals, whose disaffection and discontent must be kept down with imperious means." This was not the administrative method of a "free and generous government."[50]

The second species of opinion, according to the envoys, was based on a "specious" argument that all Louisianans would have to go through the process of naturalization before they became U.S. citizens. The envoys rejected this on the basis that Louisianans had already been allowed to assume the responsibilities of citizens of the United States, including the holding of public offices, the ownership of vessels "under certificates of registry of the United States, *as citizens of the United States*," and, last but not least, the payment to the United States of "the same duties which *all the other citizens of the Union* are subject to." Furthermore, the envoys argued, when there was any doubt "on the true expression of a treaty," it was "an invariable and sacred rule to give it the fairest and most liberal construction." The envoys concluded that nothing could be more explicit than the third article of the treaty of cession, which affirmed that the inhabitants of Louisiana were to be incorporated into the Union and enjoy the rights of citizens "as soon as possible" and that Congress should have followed this stipulation and passed laws for incorporation and citizenship. Instead, one year had elapsed "before a single step" was taken to do this.[51]

The third species of "opinion," that it was not safe for the United States to admit Louisiana as a state, was not, according to the envoys, a justifiable argument to delay satisfaction of the requirements of the treaty of cession. Even if this were the case, the envoys explained there was no evidence to suggest that if Louisiana was granted statehood it would become a threat to national security. It was their opinion that Louisianans as territorial inhabitants were a greater threat to the United States than they would be if they were citizens. Louisianans, in their present state, had "no liberty to defend" and "no political rights to preserve" and therefore had little reason to favor attachment to the United States. Such "alienated hearts" could not be depended upon to defend Louisiana from a foreign aggressor or to refrain from insurrection.[52]

Because they were frustrated by the wait for a report from Randolph's committee, the envoys presented the memorial to the Senate through William Giles of Virginia on December 31, 1804. It was then referred to a committee composed of Senators Giles, Jesse Franklin, Joseph Anderson, and Uriah Tracy on January 4, 1805.[53] Derbigny, Destréhan, and Sauvé met with this committee on January 9 and listened to the senators' "observations on the third article of the treaty." The next day the envoys provided the committee with a written response.[54]

The envoys were adamant that the third article of the treaty stated that Louisiana was to be incorporated into the Union as soon as possible, according to the principles of the Constitution, and that this meant "without any possible delay." "We firmly believe that any interpretation, tending to procrastinate the incorporation of the 'present' inhabitants of Louisiana into the Union, is directly opposite to the spirit of the third article of the treaty." The envoys also made it clear that they believed that Louisiana could not be incorporated as a territory under the Northwest Ordinance of 1787, as suggested by the committee, because this law was "clearly and unquestionably limited to the Territory north west of the Ohio."[55]

Another argument made by the Senate committee was that incorporation of Louisiana into the Union could "not be executed without the consent of the three fourths of the several states." Derbigny, Destréhan, and Sauvé countered with the claim that the treaty of cession stipulated the incorporation of Louisiana into the Union and that the United States had accepted this and that "to place it, at the present period, in the power of the individual States to refuse that incorporation would be exposing the Federal Government to the danger of not fulfilling its promise."[56]

As they waited for the Senate committee to make its recommendation on the memorial, the House committee chaired by John Randolph stated its position on the demands of that document. The House committee members had obviously read the memorial and the envoys' response to the Senate committee's observations on the third article of the treaty of cession. Randolph's committee first downplayed the grievances of the memorialists as "inseparable from those sudden transitions of government to which late political events have subjected the inhabitants of Louisiana." Next the committee flatly rejected the memorialists' interpretation that the third article of the treaty of cession guaranteed Louisianans the rights of citizens. "It is only under the torture that this article of the Treaty of Paris can be made to speak the language ascribed to it by the memorialists, or countenance for a moment that charge of a breach of faith, which they have conceived themselves justified in exhibiting against the government."[57]

In a more conciliatory tone, the committee suggested, however, that Congress not be prejudiced by the claims of the memorialists, and it did "earnestly recommend that every indulgence, not incompatible with the interests of the Union, may be extended to them." The specific "indulgence," which the committee then recommended as a resolution, was a law "for extending to the inhabitants of Louisiana the right of self-government." The committee members came to this decision after they had analyzed "forms of provincial government" established in the "remote territories of the United States" and "found nothing in them worthy of imitation."[58]

The committee members believed that if they gave "the Louisianans a government of their own choice, administered by officers of its own appointment: the voice of discontent would be hushed, faction (if it exist) disarmed, and the people bound to us by the strong ties of gratitude and interest." Still, it was not the members' intention that self-government "should be unaccompanied by wise and salutary restrictions." Recommended restrictions included prohibition of the importation of foreign slaves, establishment of a representative government only, guarantees of freedom of the press and trial by jury, a prohibition against taxation of U.S. lands, and a guarantee that any laws passed by the government of Louisiana that Congress disapproved of could be declared null and void within a certain time after their passage.[59]

Three days after Randolph's committee presented its recommendations to the House, Senator William Giles, chair of the Senate committee, presented a bill for the "government of the Territory of Orleans." The bill was modeled on the law established for the government of Mississippi Territory by the Northwest Ordinance. The governor of the territory was to divide it into twenty-five electoral districts. The inhabitants of each district would then elect a representative for a general assembly that was to meet annually. When the population of the territory reached at least "___ thousand" (later set at 60,000), Louisianans would be allowed "to form for themselves a constitution and State government and be admitted into the Union upon the footing of the original states," provided that the constitution established was republican and not inconsistent with the U.S. Constitution or the Northwest Ordinance.[60] The envoys were not pleased and supported an amendment to reduce the population requirement from 60,000 to 33,000. This effort failed, however, and the Senate passed the bill on February 18, 1805.[61]

As Derbigny, Destréhan, and Sauvé waited to learn about the final outcome of the bill for the government of Louisiana, they met with James Wilkinson, who, along with his acquaintance Aaron Burr, had spent the winter "copying maps of West Florida, Orleans and Louisiana Territories." Wilkinson introduced Burr to the envoys as "the first gentleman in Louisiana," and informed them that Burr intended to go to Louisiana "as soon as his term as Vice-President expired" to undertake "certain projects." In light of this, Wilkinson asked Derbigny to supply Burr with all of the information he possessed on that region. Derbigny was apparently "mystified" by this request.[62]

As it turned out, the envoys did not have long to linger around Washington and discuss Louisiana with Wilkinson and Burr. On February 28 the House resolved itself into a Committee of the Whole to consider the bill sent from the Senate providing for the government of the territory of Orleans. An amendment was proposed to allow for the Legislative Council and the "Representatives" to nominate candidates for governor. According to this proposal, the president would select the governor from among these nominees. This proposed amendment was defeated, however, in a close vote, fifty-seven to forty-six. This was the last attempt to alter the bill. The Senate passed it on March 1. On March 2 it was passed by the House and signed by Jefferson.[63]

The envoys had failed to secure statehood, or the power for Louisianans to nominate candidates for governor, but a government in "all respects similar," with certain exceptions to that "exercised in the Mississippi Territory," was established for Orleans Territory. This meant that the people of Orleans were to have an elected representative assembly giving them a voice in territorial government, but that body was subordinate to Jefferson's appointed Legislative Council and his appointed governor.[64]

While the memorial envoys carried out their mission, the people of Louisiana waited nervously for news about their efforts. As early as December 31 Claiborne reported the "great anxiety" of Louisianans "to learn the fate of the memorial to Congress." This anxiety, however, did not prevent the envoys' counterparts in Louisiana from constant attacks on Claiborne's administration. Evan Jones's brother-in-law, Judge John Prevost, who lived in the same house as Edward Livingston, wrote Madison to inform him that he had made an effort to persuade the Legislative Council to draft a code of laws.[65] Prevost indicated that the council was prepared to appoint Edward Livingston and James Brown, whom Jefferson had appointed as a judge of the superior court, on December 1, 1804.[66] Unfortunately, according to Prevost, Claiborne would refuse to allow this "either from an enmity to the[se] gentlemen or from a persuasion that the laws of Tennessee are fit for every state of Society in every clime." Because of this, Prevost informed Madison that he considered the governor as "wholly incompetent" and that he feared that "federal influence" was in operation in Louisiana as a result of "the imbecility of Mr. Claiborne."[67]

Like Prevost, James Brown was highly critical of Claiborne's administration. In a letter to John Breckinridge, he discussed his possible role in the drafting of a law code, and surmised that "the unfortunate dislike of the Governor" for Livingston, the council's choice for an assistant to Brown, would paralyze the process; then it was "widely believed that the Country be left without any laws except a few unimportant ones which relate to the Militia &c &c." Brown also concluded that Claiborne was unsuited for the office of governor, and noted that even Claiborne's friends admitted that he lacked "capacity and firmness" and that he was "totally ignorant of the Language of the Country." Overall, like Prevost, Brown concluded that "the unpopularity" of Claiborne's administration might occasion a "prevalence of the detestable doctrines of Yankee federalists among us." The similarity of the specific complaints about Claiborne made by Brown and Prevost, especially their warnings of Federalist machinations, suggests that if they had not both agreed to write letters, they had at least discussed the governor's shortcomings and his attitude toward Livingston.[68]

In addition to penning private letters on Claiborne's conduct, the governor's opponents also openly challenged his authority. In early January Claiborne observed that Livingston, Jones, and Clark attempted to reestablish the Louisiana Bank eliminated on Jefferson's order. These men, Claiborne wrote, had an obvious vested interest in the bank because they would be large stockholders, and he added that Livingston's interest too was clear as he had "speculated to great advantage since his arrival." Claiborne, however, blamed the actions of Clark, Jones, and Livingston on the delay of the establishment of a branch of the Bank of the United States for New Orleans. According to Claiborne, the lack of a bank had "greatly assisted the friends of the Louisiana Bank."[69]

By January 13 Claiborne witnessed the establishment of the new Louisiana Bank, despite his warnings to the people "of the doubts which existed as to the validity of its charter." According to Claiborne, the reason for public support of the bank was that the inhabitants had "received an opinion that a Bank would be of great public utility" and "were determined to make the

experiment." This, and the fact that some whom Claiborne considered political allies such as Julien Poydras and James Pitot were elected as directors,
probably encouraged Claiborne's support of the Louisiana Bank.[70]

While the founding of the Louisiana Bank caused Claiborne some concern, he was most anxious about the impact of a hostile press on the public.
The governor described the press as "an object of terror" and complained that
"the Livingston and Clark party" had attacked his administration with "great
malevolence."[71] Some of the editorial attacks on Claiborne were indeed very
personal and provocative. An anonymous author who called himself Fidelis
wrote a piece for the *Louisiana Gazette* in which he described a dream that
he had. In this dream, Fidelis walked past the governor's mansion on a night
five months after the death of Mrs. Claiborne. He noticed that it was lit for a
ball. The convent bell sounded, and suddenly the ghost of Mrs. Claiborne appeared and noticed the revels at the house. "She clasped her hands in agony,
she turned her eyes to heaven.—Then meek, resigned, sorrowful and lovely,
she bent her willing steps toward the graves of Louisiana."[72] This article greatly
disturbed Claiborne, but he was not provoked to action. It "excited greatly the
sensibility," however, of Micah G. Lewis, Claiborne's brother-in-law and private secretary.[73] Lewis discovered that the author was a certain Mr. Sterry and
challenged him. In the ensuing duel, Lewis received a fatal wound in the left
side, near his heart.[74] In writing to Jefferson to report this, Claiborne bitterly
complained that his "misfortunes became the Sport of party spirit" and that
the ashes of Lewis's "beloved sister were not suffered to repose in the Grave."[75]

Like Lewis, Claiborne and the Jefferson administration made efforts to discover the identities of their most prolific newspaper antagonists. Isaac Briggs,
who was appointed by Jefferson as a surveyor of lands south of Tennessee,
informed the president that he believed that Clark, Livingston, and Prevost
were Claiborne's primary newspaper enemies who wrote under the names
"An Inhabitant" and "Public Accuser."[76]

The "Public Accuser" was well known to Claiborne, who complained about
his attacks in January and February 1804. On February 21 Claiborne reported
that he knew that "Mr. Livingston" was "the author of the piece signed the
public accuser." The "Public Accuser" criticized Claiborne for his recognition
of "the Battalion of free people of colour," for the use of a "guard stationed at
government house," and for sanctioning the wedding of a couple who did not
ask their parents' permission to marry.[77]

Claiborne apologized to Madison for directing his attention "for one moment to News-paper Publications" but hoped that the secretary of state could
understand that the "malignity" of his opponents spurred him to "keep the
Executive advised" of his answers to accusations made in the press. In order
to demonstrate the types of attacks that were made upon him in editorials,

Claiborne forwarded copies of newspapers to Madison and Jefferson. The governor had no doubt that Clark and Livingston were the "Leaders of the opposition" who were behind these editorials, and he claimed their "ill-will" was excited by a knowledge of Claiborne's *dislike to them and all their measures.* Claiborne admitted, however, that both men possessed "Talents," and he feared that they would probably cause Claiborne "injury (by their writings) in the United States."[78]

Jefferson viewed the newspaper attacks on his appointed governor as a serious matter. On March 14 the president wrote Claiborne and informed him that he did not need to apologize to Madison for "troubling him with documents in confutation of the Accuser," and he commended Claiborne for doing so because it enabled them (Madison and Jefferson) "to understand the truth of the transaction." In order to reassure and encourage Claiborne, Jefferson also claimed that he and Madison understood and sympathized with his situation. "We perfectly understand the game which is playing against you, we know every man concerned in it."[79] Jefferson wrote to Madison and directed him to be severe with those who wrote scurrilous pieces about the governor of Orleans Territory: Claiborne was "pestered with intriguants," and because his conduct was above reproach, it was necessary to "shew that however thankfully we receive personal information as to our officers, we will not permit them to be written down by newspaper defamation."[80]

Jefferson's reassuring letter to Claiborne of March 14 reached Claiborne on May 4.[81] Around the time that Jefferson wrote this letter, however, Claiborne anxiously informed Madison that New Orleans had not received northern mail for five weeks and that he was "without any letters from the Department of State; or recent information from the Seat of Government."[82] The information that Claiborne was most eager to receive concerned the "issue of the Memorial to Congress." He did not yet know that the Act for the Government of Orleans Territory existed and that the memorial envoys were bound for home.[83] Jefferson also included this information in his letter of March 14 and added that he believed that one of the "deputies returned from hence" would probably join Claiborne's opponents actively but that the others were "dissatisfied" but "virtuous" men who would do nothing wicked.[84]

One of the reasons that Claiborne was so anxious to receive word on the memorial to Congress was that he believed public knowledge of the outcome of the memorial envoys' mission would allow him to fill the vacancies on the Legislative Council. The council had operated at a bare quorum since Claiborne convened it in early December 1804; there were times between December and March when a quorum could not be obtained. Despite this, Claiborne did not appoint more councilors. He was not willing to face another possible council appointment rejection, and he believed that such rejections would be unlikely after the issue of the memorial was resolved. "When the Memorial to Congress is decided there will be no difficulty in completing the Council, but I am unwilling at this time to offer a Commission to any citizen, lest my feelings should be subjected to the mortification of a refusal."[85]

By April 21, 1805, Claiborne had received news of the Act for the Government of Orleans Territory, and he bluntly predicted that the "Law of Congress for the Government of this Territory will not give general Satisfaction. The people have been taught to expect greater privileges and many are disappointed."[86] Claiborne added, however, that he believed that the act gave Louisianans as much power as they could be trusted with "until the limits of the Ceded Territory are acknowledged, the National attachments of our new brothers less wavering, and the views and characters of some influential men here are better ascertained." It is clear that Claiborne did not trust Louisianans to participate in government in any significant representative way, and this was primarily due to the activities of his political opponents. In the same letter to Madison, he confessed that "the opposition, the cruel opposition" had "harrow'd up" his "feelings excessively."[87]

A week after Claiborne made his prediction that Louisianans would be disappointed with the Act for the Government of Orleans Territory, Derbigny, Destréhan, and Sauvé arrived in New Orleans. On the morning of April 29 Sauvé visited Claiborne. The governor reported that the deputies were dissatisfied but that they would "not attempt to inflame the public mind."[88] Five days later, however, Claiborne reported that he met with Derbigny and was convinced that the envoys would "agitate and divide the public mind" through a pamphlet that they planned to publish. Claiborne found that Derbigny was "greatly disappointed and dissatisfied," that he considered "the Treaty [treaty of cession] as violated," and that he supposed "the Government was uncandid to the Agents and unjust to the Louisianans." While Derbigny also "expressed a hope that his fellow Citizens would be contented, and reconciled to the constitution which Congress had prescribed," Claiborne nevertheless feared that in a pamphlet written by the envoys "some imprudent observations" may be introduced.[89]

Early in June the pamphlet produced by the memorial envoys was published in *Moniteur de la Louisiane* and the *Louisiana Gazette*. In their *Report*, the envoys criticized the slow action of John Randolph's committee. This committee only took action, they complained, after some of the members "represented to their chairman, Mr. J. Randolph, the glaring impropriety, of neglecting an affair of so much importance, and earnestly solicited him to call a meeting of the committee in order to form some direction on the subject."[90]

When Randolph's committee finally met, the envoys reported, it unanimously recommended the extension of self-government, a "very satis-factory piece of intelligence." Their initial satisfaction disappeared, however, after they learned the committee had made little headway in writing a report of recommendations. The envoys again blamed Randolph for the delay. "The chairman whose business it was to draught it, had a thousand other avocations in which he felt an interest and neglected our affair in which he felt none." Again urged by other members of the committee, Randolph finally drafted the report, and by a unanimous vote the "committee was directed by the house to draw up a plan of government." Nothing came of this, however, and the envoys declared that this, too, was due to Randolph, "who did not once call a meet-ing of the committee" and so "the unanimous resolution of the representative body fell to the ground."[91]

The envoys were also very critical of the work of the Senate committee that was charged to design a plan for the government of Louisiana. They argued that they made every attempt to prove that the Senate committee plan, based on the Northwest Ordinance, was not applicable to Louisiana. This was be-cause the ordinance was "a local law, totally unconnected with *the Principles of the Federal Constitution* and made exclusively for the Territory N.W. of the Ohio." This effort failed, the envoys admitted, as did their strategy to amend the Senate bill, especially their request that the population requirement for statehood be set at 33,000. "After some insignificant debates, the Bill was passed without any favorable amendment and the number of free inhabitants that was thought expedient to be required for our admission was definitively fixed at 60,000."[92]

In conclusion, the envoys described their mission as a failure. Their cause, they believed, had "fallen into a sort of oblivion" because Congress devoted its "whole time and attention" to the trial of Samuel P. Chase. The "able inten-tions of the many" were undermined by "the bad will of the few." One consola-tion, according to the envoys, was that they had gained "the most important of all powers, that of making the laws by which you are governed." The envoys admitted, however, that this right was limited because the U.S. government could restrict the operation of such laws.[93]

In writing to Madison, Claiborne enclosed the *Report* and dismissed it as an unimportant document. "You will find in this production, evidences of dis-content, a want of information and of prudence on the part of the agents." Clai-borne predicted that it would "excite but little Interest in the Territory, and be productive of no Mischief." Because of this, the governor recommended that it would "be best to permit it unnoticed to Sink into oblivion." While he noted that there were men in Orleans Territory who "would sacrifice the Interest of any Country, or the Happiness of any people, to the gratification of their personal ambition," he was persuaded that "the great body of the Citizens of Louisiana" could "not be shaken from their Allegiance or be made to think that they are not greatly benefited by their annexation to the United States."[94]

On July 3 Claiborne began his term as governor of the territory of Orleans under the Act for the Government of Orleans Territory passed on March 2, 1805.[95] On that same day, Claiborne prorogued the Legislative Council, which apart from a break between May 4 and June 21 had been in session since December 1804. The council had worked in relative harmony, probably due to the fact that Claiborne's opponents had refused to serve on it, to produce over fifty laws. The most important of these were laws dividing the territory into counties and those for the creation of interior courts.[96]

In his speech proroguing the council, Claiborne thanked those who had "remained with firmness at the Post assigned to them by their Country" and attacked his opponents.

> The Best of Men may occasionally differ in political sentiments, and the investigation of their opinion leads to truth, and may be considered one of the salutary incidents of Political freedom. But unfortunately society is sometimes infested with members who argue not to enlighten, but to mislead their fellow Citizens, and who from motives of disingenuous ambition, or from malice, labor incessantly to raise themselves on the ruin of others. That there have been and still are a few Individuals among us of that description is I fear, too true. Under their Patronage, calumny may recommence its efforts.[97]

Claiborne was correct in predicting that his opponents might continue their attacks on his administration and the government of the United States. While the governor was positive that the majority of Louisianans were loyal to his administration, Aaron Burr had arrived in New Orleans to evaluate the strength of Claiborne's enemies.

CHAPTER FIVE

"A Severe Shock to W. C. C. and His Gang"

The Opposition's Representatives
in Territorial and National Government

Aaron Burr enjoyed a pleasant stay in New Orleans in the first weeks of July 1805. He met many of the elite of New Orleans society and was especially friendly with Governor Claiborne's political opponents. He stayed with Edward Livingston and was "lavishly entertained by Daniel Clark." Claiborne noted that Burr, while he was in New Orleans, was in "habits of intimacy with Livingston, Clark and Jones," but the governor gave no hint of the reason for the amicable relations between these men.[1]

"Burr's visit to New Orleans in 1805 coincided with the activities of the 'Mexican Association.'" This organization of about 300 members was founded "shortly after the American occupation of Louisiana," and "its avowed purpose was to bring about the conquest—or liberation—as they put it of Mexico." Daniel Clark and Edward Livingston were said to be "leading spirits." Clark, however, denied that he was a member of the Mexican Association, "yet he consistently worked with it." Whatever Clark's status with the Mexican Association, it is clear that he was impressed with Burr's visit. He went as far as to advise Lieutenant William A. Murray, an American officer stationed at Fort Adams, to make preparations to secure the fort as a base of operations for an attack on Baton Rouge and an invasion of Mexico. When Burr left Orleans Territory on July 14, 1805, he did so with two horses and a servant provided by Daniel Clark. Burr appeared satisfied with his visit. He found that "the populace in general" was "sympathetic to the plan to revolutionize Mexico" and promised to return in October 1806.[2]

While Clark dreamed of the wealth that he might gain from the conquest of Mexican land, the U.S. government targeted some of his property in the territory of Orleans for an investigation under the Act for Ascertaining and Adjusting the Titles and Claims to Land within the Territory of Orleans (Act for the Adjustment of Land Titles) passed on March 2, 1805. On July 8, 1805, Secretary of the Treasury Gallatin commissioned Allan B. Magruder and James Brown to ascertain and adjust titles and claims to land within Orleans Territory. Brown was the agent for the Eastern District of Orleans Territory, and Magruder was assigned to the Western District of Orleans Territory. Along with his general instructions, Magruder was instructed that two tracts of land would "require particular investigation, especially in order to ascertain, what conditions were affixed to the grant, and whether they have been fulfilled." These were grants of land on the Ouachita River, "one twelve leagues square, in favor of Baron Bastrop, and another about twelve leagues in length by two leagues in breadth, originally granted to the Marquis de Grandmaison and now claimed by Daniel Clark."[3]

Why was Clark specifically targeted for an investigation under the Act for Adjustment of Land Titles? It was probably due in part to the size of the tract and the circumstances under which Clark acquired it. On March 17, 1795, the Spanish governor of Louisiana, the Baron de Carondelet, who hoped to halt American settlement in Louisiana through Spanish land grants, deeded the Marquis de Maison Rouge, "an emigrant French knight," 4,000 arpents of land on the Ouachita. The condition attached to this grant was the settlement of thirty families of farmers "to be composed of French, Hollanders, Flemish and German royalists." The Spanish Crown approved this contract on July 17, 1795. Within two years, however, through an updated contract, Maison Rouge came to own four large tracts of land that bordered on both sides of the Ouachita River. The total amount of land amounted to 208,344 superficial arpents, or thirty leagues.[4]

The Marquis de Maison Rouge had little time, however, to develop his new lands. In the summer of 1799 he became ill and traveled to New Orleans to stay at the home of a friend, Louis Bouligny. On August 26 he drafted his will and named Bouligny his "sole and universal heir." Maison Rouge "made no reference to any claim of a grant of land made to him by the Spanish Government of thirty leagues of land; nor was it included in the inventory of his estate which was made by Commandant Filhiol [of Ouachita District] shortly after his demise." Despite this, Louis Bouligny considered himself the owner of the land, and he in turn "conveyed his entire interest in the Maison Rouge grant to Daniel Clark by three acts of sale executed on July 16, 1803, June 1, 1804, and January 12, 1812."[5]

When Bouligny sold his land to Clark, the land commissioners of the U.S. government began to investigate whether Maison Rouge had satisfied the terms of his contract with the Spanish government. While this was not a basis for investigation under the Act for Adjustment of Land Titles of 1805 or an act of 1807 that supplemented it, the commissioners of the Western District justified a government investigation of the Maison Rouge grant, which continued even after Clark's death, as a *"Class B"* investigation: "claims which though not embraced within the provisions of said acts [of Congress] ought, nevertheless, in the opinion of the Commissioners, to be confirmed, in conformity with the laws, usages and customs of the Spanish Government."[6]

The U.S. government's investigation of the Maison Rouge grant could be explained simply by the fact that it contained a large amount of land and that there were questions as to its sale to Louis Bouligny and Daniel Clark. This might only partly explain, however, the commissioners' determined efforts to establish doubts concerning Clark's ownership. U.S. government officials were advised of Clark's activities as a land speculator from the date the United States took possession of Louisiana. On January 3, 1803, General James Wilkinson, possibly the greatest land speculator in the American West at this point, wrote to Secretary of War Henry Dearborn and reported that many Americans were engaged in land speculation and that "our ex-Consul stands at the head of the list." In August 1804, after Clark had participated in the drafting of the memorial to Congress, Claiborne contemptuously condemned Clark's activities as a land speculator in a letter to Jefferson. "The Number of those who are connected with Land Speculation in Florida, I fear is considerable; Mr. Daniel Clark was the first adventurer, & many others followed his example." Three months before the passage of the Act for the Adjustment of Land Titles, Claiborne informed Madison that the ex-intendant of Spanish Louisiana, Juan Ventura Morales, had received a decree from the king of Spain that sanctioned his sales of land in West Florida and that this information had "given great pleasure to our Land Speculators, and particularly to Mr. Daniel Clark." Claiborne repeated this accusation in August 1805. He provided Madison with a list of lands that "Mr. Daniel Clark and other adventurers" had received from the Spanish. The consistent attack on Clark for his land speculation activities by Claiborne and Wilkinson probably contributed to the zealous investigation of his ownership of the Maison Rouge tract. In addition, the fact that Clark was Claiborne's political nemesis would not have encouraged the commissioners employed by the U.S. government to build a case for ownership in Clark's favor.[7]

While Gallatin did not name Edward Livingston for investigation under the Act for the Adjustment of Land Titles, Livingston came under scrutiny because he had obtained land from the Baron de Bastrop. Bastrop described himself as a refugee from Holland who had arrived in Louisiana in September 1795. Governor Carondelet proposed that Bastrop establish a colony on the Ouachita River. On June 21 Carondelet granted Bastrop twelve square leagues of land on condition that he settle 500 families there. The Spanish government ultimately rejected this colonization project. On January 18, 1800, Gilberto Leonard, acting comptroller general of the Spanish Royal Treasury, declared that Bastrop's contract had expired "not only because it had not received royal sanction, but also because the terms of the contract had not been fulfilled by him." Even though his colony was "officially outlawed," Bastrop continued to bring settlers to the Ouachita. Many of these were Americans.[8]

As of September 1801 Americans were prohibited from settlement in Louisiana by Spanish law. Despite this, Bastrop continued to sell to Americans, but he apparently considered that Texas offered him a better opportunity for the future, and he began to dispose of all of his Louisiana land. On January 25, 1804, Bastrop deeded two-thirds of his grant to an American resident of Kentucky, Colonel Abraham Morhouse, and the remaining one-third was sold to Edward Livingston. Later in the spring of 1805, Livingston sold this property to Colonel Charles Lynch.[9]

Because the Spanish government revoked Bastrop's contract, there was legitimate reason for a U.S. government investigation of his title to the land under the Act for the Adjustment of Land Titles. Such an investigation had the potential to cause financial embarrassment to Edward Livingston. This would not disappoint Claiborne, who had informed Madison on January 4, 1805, that Livingston had "speculated to great advantage since his arrival;—In one speculation alone he is represented to have made a clear profit of thirty thousand dollars."[10]

While the specific Ouachita properties of Daniel Clark and Edward Livingston received special attention by the American commissioners assigned to investigate land claims, Louisianans in general became concerned about the security of their land claims and titles. In fact, the passage of the Act for the Adjustment of Land Titles became the focus of Louisianans' protest against the American government of Orleans Territory. John W. Gurley, register of lands for the Eastern District of Orleans Territory, informed Madison of this in July 1805:

> Indeed there Can be no doubt that this law is regarded by the enemies of ye Government as a powerfull engine by which to excite discontent in this Territory. Already it is represented as intended to rob the people of their rights to destroy the equitable titles which exist in the Country and finally become instrument of the most vexatious oppression.[11]

James Brown, appointed to investigate land claims in the Eastern District of Orleans Territory, echoed this belief when he informed John Breckinridge that the law concerning land titles "was a fruitful source of disquietude" that

Opposition's Representatives in Territorial and National Government demanded "the early attention of the National Legislature."[12] As discontent with the Act for the Adjustment of Land Titles grew, Claiborne followed his orders to establish the government for Orleans Territory outlined in the Act for the Government of Orleans Territory of March 2, 1805. On July 26 he divided the territory into twelve election districts. Each district was to elect a set number of men for a territorial House of Representatives.[13] The governor also ordered that the elections for the House of Representatives be held on the third Monday of September 1805 (September 16), and that the House would convene on the first Monday of November 1805.[14]

Nineteen representatives attended the first meeting of the House on November 4, 1805.[15] Claiborne personally administered the oath of allegiance for each representative and then instructed the House to elect a Speaker and to nominate ten residents of the territory who possessed at minimum a "freehold estate in five Hundred acres of land." Jefferson would then select five of the ten for the Legislative Council. The next day the House met and elected Jean Nöel Destréhan as Speaker. Destréhan, on behalf of the House, promised the "best exertions" of the representatives "to promote the interest and happiness of our common country," and he claimed that the House "was fully persuaded of the co-operation and support" of Claiborne "in all measures essential to the convenience of our Constituents, and the welfare of this Territory." Claiborne was pleased to inform Madison on November 8 of the friendly tone of Destréhan's address and that he was "happy to find that nothing of the party Spirit" had appeared. Based on this, the governor felt free to "indulge a hope that the members generally" would "pursue a Conduct which will be approved."[16]

Claiborne's hope of a harmonious relationship with the House of Representatives began to disappear after its members made their nominations of ten territorial residents for the Legislative Council on November 8. The elected nominees included Joseph Bellechasse, John W. Gurley, Pierre Derbigny, John Baptist McCarty, Jean Nöel Destréhan, Pierre Sauvé, Joseph Villars, Evan Jones, and Francois Dannemours.[17] Four of the ten nominees—Derbigny, Destréhan, Sauvé, and Jones—were consistent critics of Claiborne's administration and the territorial government. Bellechasse, who received the most votes, had not openly demonstrated any opposition to Claiborne, but it was known that he was a friend of Daniel Clark.

The possibility that the future Legislative Council might be hostile to his administration did not escape Claiborne. On November 13 he sent Jefferson the list of the ten nominees elected by the House of Representatives and his recommendations concerning the suitability of the candidates for positions on the Legislative Council, which he obviously hoped Jefferson would use a guide in making his five selections for the council. The governor described McCarty and Bellechasse as "very honest, good men" who were militia colonels and who, Claiborne believed, were "well disposed to the present Administration." John W. Gurley, register of lands for the Eastern District of Orleans Territory, was represented as "an honest man, and a zealous American." Sauvé and Destréhan held "large estates" in the territory and "deservedly" enjoyed the "esteem of their neighbors." The governor reasoned, however, that because Destréhan had a seat in the House of Representatives, Sauvé would be a better choice for the Legislative Council. Claiborne believed that "Darbigny" (Pierre Derbigny) was "well informed" and "honest" but doubted that he was "altogether an American in sentiment or attachment."[18]

The governor admitted that he had "little personal knowledge" of the other elected nominees, "except for Mr. Evan Jones," and Claiborne mentioned that he could not say anything to recommend Jones to the confidence of the secretary. Dannemour, Claiborne reported, was a former "Commercial Consul of France" who possessed talents, but was so "old and *very infirm*" that he could no longer conduct business. Elected to the House of Representatives, Dominique Bouligny was, according to Claiborne, "formerly an Ensign in the Spanish service." Bouligny, Claiborne added, was a "young man of promising Talents; a native of the Province, with numerous and respectable connections." The governor found "Mr. Villair pere" to be an "old man of Talents and respectability" but who "in his politics" was said to be "a violent Frenchman."[19]

In his descriptions of the Legislative Council nominees, Claiborne also noted each man's occupation, language ability, and place of residence. This is not surprising since Jefferson had previously asked that the council be fairly equally composed of French and English speakers (with preference to those who could speak both) who represented different occupations and resided in New Orleans or the countryside. McCarty, Bellechasse, Bouligny, Dannemour, and Villair were planters, and Gurley and Derbigny were lawyers. Evan Jones was a merchant, and Claiborne thought that it was necessary "to repeat" his belief that there was nothing to recommend Jones to the president's confidence.[20]

A quick examination of Claiborne's recommendations clearly demonstrates that he only wanted those whom he believed to be friendly to his administration to be selected for the Legislative Council. Bellechasse, McCarty, Gurley, Bouligny, and Sauvé were his choices. Bellechasse, McCarty, and Gurley held offices under the U.S. government, which was an incentive for loyalty to Claiborne. Bouligny was a native of Louisiana with good connections and ambition and could therefore serve the governor well. Finally, there was Sauvé, who had gone to Washington with Derbigny and Destréhan but who Claiborne and Jefferson both considered the least talented but most harmless of the three. Claiborne's argument that the people would be better satisfied if

Sauvé remained in the House of Representatives appears as an excuse to pass over the critical Destréhan.

In addition to their election of council nominees hostile to Claiborne, the members of the House of Representatives further indicated their opposition to the governor and territorial rule when they appointed a committee to draft a memorial of protest to Congress. On November 11 the House instructed this committee to ask for a repeal of the section of the Act for the Government of Orleans Territory that provided for the introduction of common law because this would cause "great confusion" in the courts of justice. The House decided to postpone this resolution, however, until it heard the opinion of the superior court on that issue. Before the House adjourned its brief first meeting, however, it did send a memorial of protest against the Act for the Adjustment of Land Titles.[21]

The members of the House of Representatives had several problems with the act and asked that it be amended. In general, they were unhappy with the fact that Congress would make titles dependent upon conditions that could not have been known to Louisianans at the time that they acquired the land. Specifically, the memorialists complained that confirmation of titles under the act required that grantees were at least twenty-one years of age and the head of a family before October 1, 1800, and had cleared, cultivated, and resided on their land by that date. The memorialists declared that many men who had received grants before October 1, 1800, had been minors at the time and that they were now "aged invalids." Furthermore, while the Spanish government required that land granted be settled in three years, it never rescinded grants as a result of "non-performance of conditions, unless the party claiming had evinced some disposition to emigrate from the province." Grantees also often owned several tracts of land because they had moved when necessary and so did not reside on some of the tracts that they owned. For all of these reasons, the memorialists requested that Congress dispense with the sections of the act that required cultivation and actual residence prior to October 1, 1800, for confirmation of land titles.[22]

The memorialists also attacked the provision of the act that set the time limit for acceptable Spanish land grants at October 1, 1800. Because the "Spanish retained actual possession of the land after 1800," the memorialists requested that Congress make a provision "to confirm titles dated since the 1st of October 1800." Finally, the memorialists begged Congress to consider that as a result of fire and political changes, "the title papers of numerous claims" had "been lost or entirely destroyed."[23]

Besides their complaints about the problems of the act, the memorialists also made requests regarding land ownership that Congress had not dealt with in the Act for the Adjustment of Land Titles. They reported that many inhabitants, especially sugar planters, had exhausted the timber stocks on their properties and asked that the U.S. government establish rights of common land usage for cypress swamps that contained valuable lumber. In addition, the memorialists asked Congress to consider that many Louisianans had taken a "single concession" from the Spanish government as their original grant even though the Spanish government allowed them to take a "double concession" because they were certain that they would get the other half from the Spanish government later. As a result, many settlers felt entitled to a "double concession."[24]

John Gurley informed Gallatin on December 11, 1805, that a memorial from the territorial House of Representatives was on its way to Washington. Gurley admitted that he did not know the contents of this memorial, as it had not been made public. He was certain, however, that one object of the memorialists was to "obtain a prolongation of the time for enregistering claims." Gurley was certain that it was "absolutely necessary" that this wish be satisfied. On the same date James Brown wrote to Gallatin and informed him that 370 claimants had registered in the Western District and that some claims were suspect but that Spanish land records pertaining to these were in Pensacola. Two months later, Gurley informed Gallatin that the March 1, 1806, deadline set for registering claims had passed, and only 160 persons had registered in the Eastern District. In addition, Gurley reported that he had read the memorial and believed that the memorialists had legitimate grounds for contesting the Act for the Adjustment of Land Titles. "My opinion is, from the best information which it has been in my power to acquire, that the facts Stated in the memorial are Correctly and fairly represented."[25]

Gallatin did not ignore the memorial or the advice of Brown and Gurley. On April 4, 1806, he informed Senator Joseph Anderson that he had "duly considered the memorial," and he believed that there were many instances where there was no legal evidence of grants. Because of this, and because "hardship would follow from exclusion of those who were granted lands as minors," Gallatin recommended that "quiet possession of three years" would be considered as "permission to settle." Furthermore, Gallatin recommended that after lands granted had been in quiet possession of the owners after ten years, the grant could "not be invalidated by reason of the grant having been made to a minor." Gallatin also echoed Gurley and declared that it "was absolutely necessary" to extend the deadline for registration of land claims in the territory of Orleans since only 150 claims had been registered in the Eastern District and less than 500 had been registered in the Western District.[26]

On the basis of Gallatin's recommendations, Congress amended the Act for the Adjustment of Land Titles. The amended act, approved on April 21,

1806, removed the age qualification for land ownership if "the claimant had inhabited his land for ten years prior to December 30, 1803." The act was further amended on March 3, 1807, and the age requirement for land ownership was entirely repealed, as was the head of family requirement. While not all of the memorialists' complaints were addressed by these amendments, their primary questions concerning age, family status, residency, and the date of settlement deadline were settled in favor of the Louisianans.[27]

While Louisianans challenged the federal government's law on land claims, they also continued to challenge its prohibition of the slave trade. In December James Brown, who in addition to his position as a register of lands was also U.S. district attorney for Orleans Territory, informed Gallatin that the lawyers of the territory had "unanimously expressed an opinion that the prohibitions against the importation of slaves contained in the Act of 1804 for the Government of this Territory, are repealed by the Act of 1805 [Act for the Government of Orleans Territory]." The clause of the act of 1805 that eliminated the ban on the importation of slaves was that which stated that Louisianans were granted the second grade of government and were "entitled to all the *rights, privileges and advantages* enjoyed by the inhabitants of Mississippi Territory." Because the inhabitants of Mississippi Territory were entitled to import slaves already legally introduced into any of the states, it followed that citizens of Orleans also possessed "the right of importing into this country any Slaves already legally introduced into any of the states."[28]

Apparently the lawyers Brown referred to came to the conclusion that the inhabitants of Orleans Territory could import slaves from within the United States through an interpretation of the Act for the Government of the Mississippi Territory passed on April 7, 1798. The seventh section of this act made it unlawful for "any person or persons to import or bring into the said Mississippi territory, from any port or place, without the limits of the United States, or to cause or procure to be so imported or brought, or knowingly to aid or assist in so importing or bringing any slave or slaves." This section of the Mississippi Government Act implied that the people of that territory had the right to import slaves from other states. This is certainly how the section was viewed during the House debates over the Mississippi government bill. Representative George Thatcher of Massachusetts, who wanted to prevent importation of slaves to Mississippi Territory altogether, introduced a motion, which was defeated, to strike out the words "without the limits of the United States."[29]

Brown did not entirely agree with the lawyers' interpretation of the Mississippi Government Act as it pertained to slavery. He believed that slaves born in the United States or imported before April 7, 1798, could be imported to Orleans Territory, "but that there was some doubt as to slaves imported from foreign countries after that date and the matter should be submitted to the courts for a decision." Attorney General John Breckinridge, however, allowed the lawyers' "interpretation to stand" and declared that "inhabitants of Orleans could legally import slaves from any port or place within the United States."[30]

As direct foreign importation to Louisiana remained illegal, South Carolina, which had reopened the foreign trade in 1803, supplied Louisianans with slaves. "A U.S. senate report of December 31, 1807, named New Orleans as one of the ports receiving re-exported slaves." Louisiana's slave population grew from 24,800 in 1806 to 34,660 by 1810. While it must be considered that part of this increase was due to natural increase, smuggling, and (especially in and after 1809) slaves imported from refugee planters of St. Domingue, it is clear that importation of slaves from Charleston contributed to the increase.[31] New Orleans newspapers advertised the trade openly after the Louisiana lawyers' decision that slave importation from other states was legal. "For example, the firm of Kenner and Henderson put the following notice in the *Louisiana Gazette* on July 4, 1806: For sale: 74 prime slaves of the Fantee nation on board the schooner *Reliance* . . . from Charleston."[32]

With the removal of the prohibition on domestic importation of slaves, a major source of discontent for Louisianans concerning the U.S. government's administration of Louisiana was eliminated. The popular demand for repeal of the federal government's slave laws for Louisiana, a core component of Livingston's *Remonstrance*, began to vanish. Daniel Clark, Evan Jones, and Etienne de Boré, who, along with Livingston, had vigorously protested the 1804 slave law, quietly engaged in the purchase and sale of slaves between 1806 and 1810 and were not challenged by the government.[33]

Louisianan slaveholders certainly did not have to fear that Governor Claiborne was motivated to suppress the trade. As mentioned earlier, while he publicly criticized the slave trade, he was reluctant to stop importations and repeatedly advised Madison and Jefferson to remove the ban instituted through the Act for the Organization of Orleans Territory and the Louisiana District that went into effect on October 1, 1804. Furthermore, Claiborne had demonstrated his own willingness to ignore the ban when he allowed "a few distressed French families" who were exiles from St. Domingue to import their slaves into Louisiana on October 16, 1804. The governor also supported planters when he approved a new slave code that was drafted by the territorial legislature in 1806. The code was "one of the most comprehensive and severe in the antebellum South." Slaves' recourse against their masters was all but eliminated by the statement that "the slave's subordination of his master" was "not susceptible to any modification or restriction." Finally, Claiborne was decisive in his actions to prevent slave revolts. He supported the territorial legislature's actions to block the immigration of free men of color, who many whites considered responsible for the revolution in St. Domingue. He also approved an act passed on June 7, 1806, that excluded free men of color who were fifteen years or older from immigration to Orleans Territory.[34]

Between 1805 and 1806 Claiborne passively supported measures taken by the legislature on slavery, and did not criticize the members of the House of Representatives for their efforts to convince Congress to repeal the Act for the Adjustment of Land Titles. He became increasingly anxious during this period, however, that the House of Representatives and Legislative Council would seriously challenge his authority. Jefferson was careful to follow Claiborne's advice of suitable candidates. He did not select Pierre Derbigny or Evan Jones for the Legislative Council. Instead, the president informed Claiborne on February 10, 1806, that he had chosen Bellechasse, Gurley, McCarty, Destréhan, and Sauvé. The Senate, however, rejected Gurley's nomination, and Jefferson was forced to ask the Orleans Territory House of Representatives to nominate two persons to fill the vacancy on the Legislative Council, and he would select one of the nominees.[35]

Claiborne received the Legislative Council commissions of Bellechasse, McCarty, Destréhan, and Sauvé on February 20, 1806, and did not complain about those choices. What concerned him was that a fifth legislative councilor was not nominated and that the possibility existed that Evan Jones would be selected. In an effort to make sure that this did not happen, Claiborne wrote a letter to Madison and declared "that there is nothing more certain in my mind, than that Mr. Evan Jones *does not merit the confidence of the American Government*." As insurance, the governor also wrote to Jefferson and essentially repeated this statement.[36]

As it turned out, Claiborne's letters condemning Jones proved unnecessary, since the House of Representatives nominated Dominique Bouligny and Julien Poydras for the fifth Legislative Council position on April 2, 1806. Bouligny had not demonstrated any ill will toward Claiborne, and Poydras, who had served on the first Legislative Council, was one of Claiborne's greatest supporters. Claiborne reported that he was delighted with these nominations and considered both men capable of a position on the council but that Poydras, by virtue of talent and experience, was the more suitable of the two candidates.[37]

Jefferson, acting on the advice of Claiborne, selected Poydras for the Legislative Council. It was not until June 13, however, that Claiborne received Poydras's commission and sent it on to him. Claiborne had convened the Legislative Council and the House of Representatives on March 24, so he did not have the services of his political ally for the first session of the territorial legislature, which lasted until June 7, 1806. This was unfortunate for Claiborne, because the majority of members of the legislature were not friends of the governor's administration. Claiborne himself recognized this and hinted about the possibility of dissent between him and the legislature two days after he convened it. "The general Assembly of this Territory is now in session.—I anticipate some difficulty with these young Legislators; but I trust we shall harmonize, and the result of our deliberations will not be unacceptable to the people."[38]

On April 2 the House of Representatives, through Speaker John Watkins, promised to work with Claiborne and expressed loyalty to the United States but also presented a clear legislative agenda that included revision of the judiciary system, development of a "black code," improvement of inland navigation, the building of schools, and an examination of the records of the treasury. While the House worked on bills to address these concerns, Claiborne noted that there was a division within the House, exacerbated by his opponents, that prevented the members from working efficiently: "The Ancient Louisianans are greatly jealous of the few Native Americans who are in the House of Representatives, nor are there wanting some designing mal-contents out of office and confidence who have recourse to every expedient, to disseminate the Seeds of distrust and discontent."[39] The "designing malcontents out of office" that Claiborne referred to were most probably Daniel Clark, Pierre Derbigny, and Evan Jones.

As Claiborne became convinced that his political enemies in Louisiana contributed to the divisions within the Orleans House of Representatives, he discovered in late April that John Randolph had launched an attack on his administration in the U.S. House of Representatives on March 5, 1806. Randolph had become increasingly critical of the Republican administration and particularly Jefferson after he had learned in December 1805 that the president planned to request $2 million to send to France for the arrangement of the purchase of the Spanish Floridas. Randolph bitterly opposed the appropriation, which he considered a bribe to France, but he was defeated in the House and fell out with the Republican Party. "On March 5, 1806, he began his long public career of opposition." One of the subjects that Randolph spoke about in his remarks to the House was Orleans Territory. Randolph claimed that the territory was not prepared for an attack from Spain. This was a concern because that nation and the United States contested the boundary between Texas and Louisiana in 1805 and 1806. Randolph blamed Orleans Territory's military weakness on the "miserable Governor" sent to rule Louisiana and credited Daniel Clark, "an enlightened member of that odious and imbecile government," with providing him information on the situation in Orleans Territory.[40]

On April 29 Claiborne defended himself in a letter to Madison. Claiborne's fury at Randolph's accusation is evident in the tone of the letter. He declared that his government was not an "imbecile one" and asked Randolph to produce "proof of its imbecility." The governor went on to defend his conduct by blaming others for the problems of his administration. He noted that "the difference in language" and the "Jealousy" that existed "between the Ancient and Modern Louisianans" were "Great Barriers to the Introduction of that harmony and mutual confidence" that he desired. Claiborne also made certain to mention "facts" of which he had "long since apprized" Madison: that Louisianans had a "partiality for France" and that "the intrigues of a few artful and designing men had promoted discontents."[41]

While Randolph attacked Claiborne, Jefferson attempted to replace his chosen governor for Orleans Territory. On May 4, 1806, Jefferson wrote to Monroe and offered him "the choice of the two governments of Orleans & Louisiana." In describing the positions, Jefferson was careful, however, to first mention that the salary for the office of the governor of Orleans was $5,000 while that of the governor of Louisiana was $2,000.[42]

It is not surprising that Jefferson continued to favor Monroe over Claiborne for the position of governor of Orleans. During his participation in the Jay-Gardoqui negotiations in 1785 and his service to ensure the purchase of Louisiana as envoy extraordinary to France, Monroe had gained an understanding of U.S. policy, and, more specifically in 1803, of Jefferson's policy on Louisiana. In addition, Monroe spoke French and had demonstrated his ability to socialize and negotiate in French society. Monroe, however, refused Jefferson's offer with the explanation that he was forced to improve his home in Virginia and attend to other private matters that he had neglected.[43]

The timing of Jefferson's offer to Monroe is also noteworthy. It was no secret either in Washington or west of the Appalachians that Aaron Burr, who talked of his plans to anyone who would listen, was involved in preparations for an expedition to separate the western states and territories from the Union or conquer Mexico or both.

At the same time, there were growing fears that Spain, which had reinforced its armies in Florida and Texas, planned to conquer Orleans Territory. Given the United States' weak military presence in Orleans, Claiborne would obviously need the full support of its inhabitants. Claiborne did not have this. In fact, his political opponents were more powerful in 1806 than ever before.

Prior to the first meeting of the new territorial House of Representatives in March 1806, Claiborne had governed along with a Legislative Council that caused him few problems. This was primarily because his political opponents on the council resigned their posts. Through the 1806 elections for the House of Representatives, however, and the nominations of the representatives for the Legislative Council, prominent critics of Claiborne's administration were placed in positions of power, including Representative Etienne de Boré and Legislative Councilors Jean Nöel Destréhan and Pierre Sauvé. It is not surprising that Claiborne experienced difficulties with this government. Obviously, Jefferson wanted a governor of Orleans Territory who could unite people in the face of crises. He expressed this belief in hindsight to the Marquis de Lafayette, whom he had also encouraged to take the position. "Your presence at New Orleans [during the Burr Conspiracy] would have been of value, as a point of union & confidence for the ancient inhabitants American as well as Creole." Jefferson clearly understood that the political struggle in Orleans was not simply a conflict between Louisianans of French origin and Americans who supported Claiborne.[44]

Prominent opposition leaders included men of French origin such as Boré, Derbigny, Destréhan, and Sauvé, but also Clark and Jones who had identified themselves as Americans before the United States purchased Louisiana. All of these men of wealth and influence considered Claiborne incompetent and, more important, the embodiment of the Jefferson administration's program for the government of Louisiana, which appeared to threaten their economic interests.

As Jefferson attempted to replace Claiborne, the governor of Orleans Territory faced further difficulties in dealing with the legislature. On May 6 Claiborne informed the members of the territorial House of Representatives and the Legislative Council that he had received a bill that they had passed entitled An Act to Establish Certain Conditions Necessary to Be a Member of Either House of Legislature of the Territory of Orleans.

According to this act, no one who held other offices under the government could be a member of the legislature. This act was obviously designed to undermine Claiborne's support in the territory, since most of his political allies were Americans who had arrived in the territory after the Louisiana Purchase, and some had held government posts. This bill, if passed, was to be effective immediately, which meant that some members would lose their seats. Not surprisingly, Claiborne vetoed this bill on the grounds that such an act could "not be constitutional, unless its operation" was "prospective and not permitted to affect the sitting members."[45]

Claiborne considered that the writing of the membership bill was the project of "ancient Louisianans in the Legislature" who were "jealous of control." He also believed that they would "illy receive a check from the Executive Authority." Both of these ideas were correct. Claiborne's political opponents were no longer simply government outsiders sniping at the governor from behind anonymous newspaper editorials or memorials of protest. In the spring of 1806 Claiborne's political opponents had come to dominate the legislature of the territory of Orleans and were prepared to challenge the governor through legislation. Claiborne recognized this fact by May 14. He wrote Madison and informed him that he expected that the territorial legislature would accomplish little because it was divided, "and one party, the strongest, seems greatly influenced by a few men in this City, whose politics and views are, in my opinion, contrary to those of the United States." If this was not enough bad news, Claiborne also conceded that the legislature would send one of his political rivals to Washington. "Those men, who are great adepts in the arts of Intrigue, are desirous that Evan Jones should be elected the delegate to Congress, and I am inclined to think they will accomplish their object."[46]

Claiborne's prediction that Evan Jones would be elected as the representative to Congress proved incorrect, but the result of the election held on May 19 was not at all pleasing to the governor. The Orleans territorial legislature selected Daniel Clark as its first delegate to Congress. That Claiborne had little support in the legislature was indicated by the election results. According to the governor, the "votes of the ancient Louisianans were divided between Daniel Clark and Evan Jones," while "native Citizens of the United States" supported Claiborne's candidate, Dr. John Watkins.[47]

In addition to their rejection of Claiborne's candidate for Congress, the territorial House of Representatives and Legislative Council continued to attack Claiborne in a legislative struggle. During this conflict, Pierre Sauvé and Jean Nöel Destréhan resigned from their positions on the Legislative Council. Their expressed reason for resigning was that they could no longer continue their duties because of ill health. There can be little doubt that Sauvé and Destréhan had calculated that their resignations would embarrass Claiborne. The timing of the resignations (Sauvé's on May 21 and Destréhan's on May 23) occurred shortly after the election of Daniel Clark and at a time when Claiborne's rejection of legislation approved by the territorial House of Representatives and Legislative Council provoked hostility from the governor's opponents. Claiborne was not swayed by the pleas of sickness of Sauvé and Destréhan. He refused to accept their resignations on the grounds that only the president could approve them and that until such time as he did so, both members should remain in their offices.[48]

Despite the hostile activities of his political opponents, Claiborne did not shy away from using his powers to veto legislation of which he disapproved. On May 22 the governor sent Madison a copy of another act passed by the legislature and informed the secretary of state that he would veto it. This piece of legislation, entitled An Act Declaratory of the Laws Which Continue to Be in Force in the Territory of Orleans, was designed to ensure that the old civil law was not completely replaced by American common law.[49]

Claiborne was convinced that the acts of the members of the legislature were "influenced by a few *Intriguers*," specifically Daniel Clark and Evan Jones, who "were actively employed in political concerns." The governor then attempted to suggest that Clark opposed his administration because he was "greatly soured with the General Administration" and that Jones was "from principle . . . inimical to the American government." In order to ensure that Madison did not think that there was any merit to the political positions of Clark and Jones, Claiborne suggested that the real reason for their opposition was personal, not political. When Clark realized that he could not control the opinions of the governor, he began to oppose him. Claiborne claimed that Jones's hostility to him stemmed from the government seizure of a prize cargo.[50]

On July 28, 1804, Jones purchased a cargo of 208 hogsheads and 50 barrels of sugar, 57 hogsheads of coffee, 10 boxes of cinnamon, and 457 bags of pimento from the French brig *Hector* for $20,000. The captains of this vessel stated that the vessel had come from St. Domingo, but further investigation of the papers revealed that they were forged. An investigation determined that the ship was the *Active*, built at St. Johns, New Brunswick, and that it was captured between Jamaica and London and sent to New Orleans under a prize crew. Because of this Claiborne ordered the cargo seized. Claiborne's personal involvement in this thorough investigation is interesting given that privateers constantly sold cargo from prizes with little difficulty and because the customs officials at New Orleans had admitted the French captains of the ship to land at New Orleans and dispose of their cargo.[51]

On May 26 Claiborne vetoed An Act Declaratory of the Laws Which Continue to Be in Force in the Territory of Orleans, and this provoked the legislature to mutiny. The Legislative Council, "in a unanimous and spontaneous movement," reacted to Claiborne's veto by threatening to dissolve the legislature. It also produced, on May 28, a "statement of motives" for this action, signed by a majority of representatives, designed to win popular support. The main reason for dissolution, according to those who supported it, was that taxpayers' money spent on the House and Legislative Council was wasted because "the most essential and salutary measures taken by the Legislature" were "successively rejected by the Governor of the Territory." Of greatest concern to those who signed the manifesto was the rejection of the Act Declaratory of the Laws. The supporters of the manifesto argued that "the most inestimable benefit for a people" was "the preservation of its laws, usages, and habits and that it was only by such preservation that transition from one government to another was possible." Congress, the statement supporters asserted, understood this, and through the fourth article of the act for the government of the territory of Orleans allowed the people of Orleans to keep those laws that did not conflict with the Constitution.[52]

The supporters conceded the necessity of the application of the Constitution and federal laws to all of the states and territories of the Union, but argued that they could not understand what difference it would make if the laws of contracts and wills should be governed under civil law in the territory of Orleans and under common law in other states. Differences in local law in England did not destroy the English's loyalty to the constitution of their country. On the contrary, the supporters of the statement warned the English would be alienated, discontented, and attracted to disorder if government disturbed "those customs to which each province was attached by the bonds of experience and long habit."[53]

Another argument made in support of An Act Declaratory of the Laws was that there should be no problem with the coexistence of the civil law in Orleans with common law in the states because common law codes of each state differed so much and that the Constitution allowed each state "the right to preserve or to modify that which it had seen fit to adopt of the common law and even to replace it with other laws according as it might judge to be the most suitable to its special situation."[54]

Finally, those who were in favor of An Act Declaratory of the Laws argued that the "wisdom of the civil law" was recognized by all of Europe, that it was the code that "nineteen-twentieths of the population of Louisiana" was accustomed to, and that replacement of the civil law would ruin commerce in Orleans. The ancient inhabitants would fear, out of ignorance of common law, to sign contracts or dispose of properties and would be forced to consult a jurist with expertise in common law for all transactions.[55]

The supporters of the statement then attacked Claiborne and those members of the House of Representatives who opposed An Act Declaratory of the Laws as conspirators who had a "secret intention" to throw Louisianans "into the frightful chaos of the common law." Ultimately, the supporters of the statement blamed Claiborne for the failure of the passage of An Act Declaratory of the Laws because "the majority of the Chamber of Representatives" passed it and the Legislative Council passed it as well; "nothing more was lacking to the act than the approval of the Governor in order to give the act the force of law, but such approval was refused!"[56]

The rejection of An Act Declaratory of the Laws was not the only reason that the Legislative Council gave for its call for the dissolution of the legislature, however. It was also because it had "seen rejected, one after the other, measures of no less importance." This was an exaggeration. In addition to An Act Declaratory of the Laws, Claiborne had only vetoed An Act to Establish Certain Conditions Necessary to be a Member of Either House of Legislature of the Territory of Orleans. This act, as mentioned earlier, ensured that those who held an office in the pay of the U.S. government could not serve in the legislature. The Legislative Council considered this necessary in order to render the deliberations of the legislature "as free and as independent" as possible and maintained that this act was "in accordance with a principle respected both by the Federal Government and by that of the individual states." A third act, an "act prescribing the formalities to be observed in the elections of the representatives of this Territory," was written, according to the Legislative Council, to prevent abuses in the electoral process and "to leave nothing to the arbitrary will of the executive." This bill, according to the Legislative Council, "encountered difficulties," but Claiborne had not vetoed it. Despite this, the Legislative Council based its decision to dissolve the legislature on what councilors perceived as Claiborne's arbitrary and extensive use of the veto.

> Without doubt the executive holds his absolute *veto* from the special Constitution applied to this Territory, but if by means of that *veto* his will and nothing but his will is to constitute the supreme rule, if he is to reign alone, and openly, the Legislature ought not to serve as a plaything to amuse people.[57]

The legislature's statement was published in the *Telegraph* on June 3, and a few days later it ceased to sit. Claiborne was more "relieved" than disappointed as the legislature prepared to conclude its first session. He informed Jefferson that he was less than satisfied with the introduction of the elected House of Representatives that was influenced by his political enemies. "I always thought that an early extension of the Representative system to this Territory was a hazardous experiment; and of this I am now convinced." The governor admitted that "the Executive and the two houses of assembly" did not "harmonize" but that "a stranger" arriving in Orleans "would not probably hear of the difference—unless he should fall in with Daniel Clark, Evan Jones, or Peter Derbigny."[58]

While Claiborne downplayed the significance of the division between the executive and the legislature and the influence of his political opponents, it is clear that the governor had faced a serious challenge from the Legislative Council and the majority of members in the territorial House of Representatives. This is proved by the fact that Claiborne's nemesis Daniel Clark was elected to Congress, giving the territorial opposition a voice in Washington. Certainly Clark could not contain his glee at this outcome as he wrote to James Wilkinson on June 16, "I have within these 3 or 4 weeks past found it necessary, in order to oppose Governor Claiborne's Creatures and schemes with success to accept the appointment of Delegate from this Country to Congress." After he had asked Wilkinson about "the part" he should "act in Washington" and the people he should "most see," Clark was satisfied to note the impact that his election to Congress had on Governor Claiborne. "My nomination has been a severe shock to W. C. C. and his Gang, they are much chop-fallen, and all the first Characters & best men have united against them."[59]

In June 1806 the faction opposed to Governor Claiborne's administration was a serious threat to executive control of the territory of Orleans. The Leg-islative Council and the majority of the House of Representatives had united against the governor. Worse still, their elected delegate to Congress, Daniel Clark, scheduled to depart for Washington in October, was in close contact with James Wilkinson, who schemed with his associate Aaron Burr to build a western and/or Mexican kingdom that threatened to end Jefferson's dream of an empire of liberty.

CHAPTER SIX

Folly and Failure

The Fall of the Opposition Faction

T hroughout the spring and early summer of 1806, Aaron Burr made final preparations to move a military expedition down the Mississippi
to capture New Orleans. Burr was certain that this object could be accomplished without spilling blood because Louisianans wanted to separate
from the United States and would welcome him as a liberator. At least this
is what Burr had told British minister Anthony Merry in his efforts to obtain
British financial and naval support for his attack. While Burr did not specifically name those who had provided him with intelligence on the sentiments
of Louisianans toward the United States, he did tell Merry that a British naval blockade of New Orleans should continue "until the commanding officer
should receive information from him or Mr. Daniel Clark of the country having declared itself independent." Following this revolution, Burr and Wilkinson would use money from New Orleans banks and Louisianan military support to conquer Mexico.[1]

Contrary to Burr's promises to Merry, few Louisianans, with the exception
of Clark, Livingston, and other Burr associates, were aware of the planned invasion of Orleans Territory. Governor Claiborne, who was touring the counties of the territory during the summer of 1806, wrote nothing of a possible
invasion. He was concerned, however, about the damage that Daniel Clark
would do to his administration as Orleans Territory's representative in the U.S.
Senate. On July 9 Claiborne informed Jefferson that he hoped to visit Washington in October to counter the critique of Orleans territorial government
that Clark was sure to make in Washington. "I have uniformly experienced in
this quarter, the opposition of a violent & if you will pardon the expression,
an unprincipled faction; of this faction Mr. D. Clarke is a conspicuous and
zealous member; I am apprized of his intention to injure me (if in his power)
at the Seat of Government." Claiborne expected that Clark would find allies
in his efforts to discredit the government of Orleans Territory. Specifically,

the governor suggested that Clark counted on the support of John Randolph, "whose unprovoked and cruel attack" had renewed opposition to Claiborne's administration within Orleans Territory.[2]

Claiborne was correct that opposition to his administration appeared to have grown during the spring and summer of 1806. Randolph's attack on Claiborne in the House of Representatives may have been one contributing factor, but the fact that Clark had won a victory over Claiborne with his election to Congress was probably more important. An additional essential feature of opposition to Claiborne's administration during the summer of 1806 was that two key figures in New Orleans, Daniel Clark and Edward Livingston, were associates of Aaron Burr.

During the planning stages of the "Burr Conspiracy," Clark had proven himself valuable to both Burr and Wilkinson. He had met with Burr in 1805 and treated him well while he visited New Orleans. Under the guise of business engagements, Clark also visited Vera Cruz, Mexico, in September 1805 and in February 1806, and reported the strength of the army and navy in and around that city and in the towns between it and Mexico City. Apparently the governing officials knew of Clark or had been alerted about his activities, since he also recorded that he was surprised to return from the "Land of Promise" safely "after being represented to the Vice Roy as a person dangerous to the Spanish government." Wilkinson and Burr had every reason to believe that Clark would act in accordance with their plans, but after his election to the Senate, Clark's support for Burr and Wilkinson cooled as he focused on preparations for his future role as a delegate to the Senate.[3]

In addition to Daniel Clark, Aaron Burr considered Edward Livingston, who was indebted to him, as one of his supporters. Livingston had come to know Burr when he studied law at Albany after his graduation from Princeton in 1781 and during the 1790s, when both were involved in New York politics. When Livingston experienced his financial embarrassment while serving as mayor of New York, Burr became one of his creditors. On July 26, 1806, as he prepared his expedition, Burr transferred Livingston's debt to his emissary, Dr. Erich Bollman. Bollman traveled to New Orleans and met with Livingston, who was forced to make arrangements to pay it.[4] This would have encouraged Livingston to support Burr's plans. Livingston, however, would not have been averse to joining Burr. Before Burr first arrived in Louisiana, both Livingston and Clark had become involved in or associated with the Mexican Association.[5]

Livingston, motivated by debt and the possibility of riches, assisted Burr in the purchase of 350,000 acres of land that was part of the Bastrop grant described earlier. Burr did not register this claim, however. This is significant, because it is clear that "Burr did not expect to make his claim good under the

The Fall of the Opposition Faction

government of the United States. The purchase was sheer speculation, the success of which was contingent upon the success of his other plans."[6]

By the end of July 1806, Burr committed himself to his plan to conquer Orleans Territory. He wrote to Wilkinson and informed him that he had sent an emissary to Jamaica to arrange for British naval support, and that he would start to move west on August 1. Burr declared that he would reach the falls of the Ohio with 500 to 1,000 men by mid-November, and that he would rendez-vous with Wilkinson at Natchez in December. The conquest of Orleans, Burr predicted, would be accomplished in three weeks because the people there were prepared to receive the invaders in return for promises to protect their religion and not subject them to a foreign power.[7]

Burr remained convinced that the people of Orleans would support his plans through September 1806. By that time he was on the move in the West and at Blennerhasset Island in the Ohio River. Burr told Harman Blennerhasset, a supporter, that the people of New Orleans were disgusted and that he expected to hear of the beginning of a revolt and of the seizure of the military stores and the revenue of the territory. By September 4, 1806, Burr had arrived in Cincinnati, Ohio, and was on his way to gather more recruits in Kentucky and Tennessee.

Four days later Wilkinson wrote to Daniel Clark and asked him to meet him at Fort Adams. Clark wrote back and stated that he would not meet with Wilkinson because he was getting ready to leave for Washington. With this letter Clark served notice that he would not participate in the execution of the plot. By mid-October, however, Clark decided that his disassociation from the plot was not enough and acted to frustrate Burr's plans. Before he left for Washington on October 22, he met with Derbigny and Bellechasse and other associates to advise them of Burr's project and told them to support the U.S. government. Clark also requested that members of the legislature not attend any meeting of the government if Burr gained control of New Orleans. The timing of Clark's decision to turn against Burr is interesting because it appears to coincide with his election as territorial delegate to Congress. It appears that Clark was satisfied with his new position and did not want to risk losing it as a result of involvement in Burr's scheme.[8]

Clark's defection was a serious blow to Burr's plan, because he was a leader of the faction opposed to Claiborne's administration. He was not the only conspirator, however, who turned against Burr as he moved toward New Orleans. Aaron Burr's agent Samuel Swartout arrived in James Wilkinson's camp at Natchitoches on October 8, with Burr's letter to Wilkinson of July 29. Over ten days Wilkinson learned from Swartout that 500 men were to proceed to Orleans Territory and would be joined by Louisianans. Together these men would start a revolution and seize all of the banks in New Orleans. The captured assets were to be used to fund an expedition that would sail for Vera Cruz on February 1, 1807. Wilkinson, however, believed that he was not in a position to support this plan. The government of Mexico had sued for peace and withdrawn troops across the Sabine River. Wilkinson could not cross that river to attack, and "if he remained idle at Natchitoches while Burr descended on New Orleans, he would get most of the blame and none of the booty." Because of this Wilkinson made the decision "to play the part of the patriot and save New Orleans."[9]

On October 21 Wilkinson wrote to Secretary of War Dearborn and President Jefferson and provided details about the plot. Jefferson, however, had already received numerous reports of Burr's activities in the West and began to organize a governmental response. Jefferson met with his cabinet on October 22, 24, and 25 and decided to send John Graham, who was secretary of Orleans Territory and happened to be in Washington, to alert the governors of the western states and territories and to arrest Burr. In addition, the decision was made to send marines to reinforce U.S. troops already at New Orleans.[10]

The actions taken by Clark, Wilkinson, and Jefferson in October 1806 doomed Burr's doubtful plans. Burr, meanwhile, unaware of what had occurred in Orleans Territory and Washington, continued his preparations to satisfy his dreams of conquest. On October 26 he wrote to architect Benjamin Latrobe and offered him 10,000 acres of his Bastrop purchase if he would plan a settlement there. It was obvious that this was to be a military settlement. Burr planned to send 40 to 50 men to clear the settlement, and then he would send 500 men there. These men would then move from this settlement to meet with Burr at Natchez, and together they would wait until the Orleans legislature declared the independence of the territory and invited Burr to take control of the government.[11]

Burr's dreams of conquest almost ended in mid-November 1806. John Graham arrived in Marietta, Ohio, and met with Harman Blennerhasset, who led him to conclude that Burr planned to take New Orleans. Graham next met with Ohio governor Edward Tiffin and convinced him of Burr's plans; Tiffin ordered the legislature to pass a bill for Burr's arrest. On December 2, 1806, a grand jury assembled, and on December 4 Burr appeared before it with his attorney, Henry Clay, to refute charges that he was organizing an expedition of conquest. The jury found insufficient evidence to indict Burr. After he was released he continued to make arrangements to move his expedition down the Mississippi despite the seizure of ten of his boats and 200 barrels of his provisions.

As Burr continued to organize his expedition in late October and through November, Wilkinson settled into his new role as protector of the Union. On November 5 he made peace with the Spanish along the Sabine River, and a

The Fall of the Opposition Faction

neutral zone along the Texas/Orleans frontier was established. Immediately after this was done, Wilkinson ordered his men to move toward Natchitoches. Arriving there the next day, he ordered more men to New Orleans to strengthen its defenses. By November 11 Wilkinson had arrived at Natchez. From there on November 12 he wrote to Jefferson and explained that the object of Burr's project was to start a revolution in Orleans and then send a force to conquer Mexico by way of Vera Cruz. Wilkinson further reported that he had been addressed by a "Gallo-American," Erich Bollman, and that he hoped to determine who was involved in Burr's plot.[12]

On the same date Wilkinson wrote to Jefferson, he also wrote a "sacredly confidential" letter to Claiborne and warned the governor that he was "surrounded by dangers" and that the "destruction of the American Union" was "Seriously menaced." In heroic terms he predicted that the "storm" would "probably burst upon New Orleans" and that he would "meet it & triumph or perish." Wilkinson promised to be in New Orleans in a few days and asked Claiborne to take steps to procure pickets, strengthen the fortifications of New Orleans, and obtain French artillery that remained in the city.[13]

Claiborne was not completely unaware that Burr was involved in some kind of project when Wilkinson wrote him on November 12, 1806. He had written Jefferson on November 5 to inform him that he had learned from "Western Papers" that Burr was in the western states and that he did not know Burr's views but feared that they were "political and of a kind the most injurious."[14]

It is clear from this letter that Claiborne had not yet received any intelligence from the federal government on Burr's plans. Claiborne had, however, received some information on the plot from Cowles Mead, who was the secretary and acting governor of Mississippi Territory, in the fall of 1806. In a letter to Mead written on November 18, Claiborne acknowledged that Mead's apprehensions about a revolution in the West had merit. In this same letter, Claiborne complained that his other major concern was that his enemies, and in particular Daniel Clark, were determined to ruin him. "Daniel Clark has pledged himself to have me dismissed, and he proposed to have complaints exhibited against me not only from this, but your Territory:—he boasts of his wealth, of his talent for intrigue, and of the numbers that are subservient to his will."[15]

Claiborne's greatest fear in November 1806 was that Clark had gone to Washington determined to destroy his political career. Therefore it is not surprising that Claiborne did not hesitate to take the opportunity to discredit Clark by implicating him as a leader in a conspiracy to separate the western states from the Union. On November 18 Claiborne informed Madison that if there was a plot to divide the Union, "the delegate to Congress from this Territory" was "one of the Leaders." According to Claiborne, Clark had "often said, that the Union could not last, and that had he Children he would impress early on their minds, the expediency of a separation between the Atlantic and Western States." As proof that Clark was involved in a conspiracy focused on that goal, Claiborne offered flimsy hearsay evidence. He noted that two of his most trusted political supporters, Dr. John Watkins, who had succeeded James Pitot as mayor of New Orleans, and J. W. Gurley, attorney for the territory of Orleans, had heard Clark express his belief that a separation of the Atlantic and western states was necessary.[16]

In another letter to Madison also dated November 18, 1806, Claiborne indicated that he had received a letter from a "Gentleman of *high rank*" who warned him that a storm was about to break on New Orleans and that the Union was menaced. This was Wilkinson's letter of November 12, and Claiborne borrowed directly from it to promise Madison that he would "perish or triumph over the enemies" of his country. Despite this show of bravado, however, Claiborne was obviously desperate for instructions or information from Washington as he complained that he had not received a letter from Madison since July 1806.[17]

On November 25 Wilkinson arrived in New Orleans, and he wasted little time in presenting the details of the conspiracy to Claiborne. Specifically, Wilkinson showed Claiborne the letter that Burr had written on July 29 describing the plan for conquest of Orleans Territory. Wilkinson also informed Claiborne about what Swartout, who had carried Burr's letter to Wilkinson, told him about the plot with regard to the instigation of revolution in Orleans Territory, the seizure of its banks, and the possibility of a British naval blockade.[18]

The day after Wilkinson's arrival, Burr's agents in New Orleans tried to introduce Wilkinson to Erich Bollman, who had news for the general from Burr. James Alexander, a New Orleans attorney and Burr recruit, attempted to have Wilkinson meet Bollman and failed. Edward Livingston made a second attempt and was also rebuffed by the general. On November 30, however, Wilkinson finally met with Bollman, who told him that Burr had the greatest confidence in Wilkinson and that Burr would arrive at Natchez on December 20 and wait for word from the general. Wilkinson listened to this and then informed Bollman that he would oppose the conspirators.

Following his declaration to Bollman, Wilkinson worked to set his trap for Burr. He and Claiborne addressed the New Orleans Chamber of Commerce on December 9 to request an embargo on trade so that every available seaman would be free to join a fleet that was assembling to defend New Orleans. The merchants agreed to this. Wilkinson was relieved to find that the people of New Orleans appeared cooperative, and he thanked Daniel Clark for advising Bellechasse to steer clear of involvement in Burr's plan. "He (Wilkinson) was

The Fall of the Opposition Faction

doubtless right in thinking that Clark's advice had helped to promote good relations, and it may have had something to do with the fact that not a single native Creole was involved in the conspiracy."[19]

By December 1806, then, it was apparent that Wilkinson believed that he had control of the situation in New Orleans, for Burr's associates in the city lacked popular support. Wilkinson was not aware, or ignored the fact, that Governor Claiborne did not completely trust him. On December 5 Claiborne had received a letter dated November 12 from Andrew Jackson, who had learned of the activities of the conspirators in Tennessee. In addition to advising Claiborne to organize his militia and put New Orleans in a state of defense, Jackson warned Claiborne that he would "meet with an attack from quarters" that he did "not at present expect" and that he should "keep a watchful eye on our General."[20] Claiborne probably took this warning seriously as he had his own reservations about Wilkinson's loyalty. He informed Jefferson in a later letter that "on the General's arrival in this City," he was "suspicious of his every movement."[21]

On the same day that Claiborne received Jackson's warning about Wilkinson, Claiborne indicated to Madison that he had changed his mind about Clark's involvement in the plot to conquer Orleans Territory and Mexico. Claiborne stated that upon "further enquiry" he found that he had "nothing to justify an opinion" that Clark was involved in the conspiracy and asked that his letter of November 18, which included his accusations against Clark based on information from Watkins and Gurley, "be considered confidential." Claiborne's "further enquiry" on Clark's association with the conspirators was limited to a conversation that he had with Dr. John Watkins. Claiborne wrote that Watkins had heard Clark "deliver some patriotic sentiments" since his election to Congress and that Watkins attributed Clark's former opinions "*more* to the impulse of some momentary passion, than to deliberate reflection."[22]

Why had Watkins changed his mind between November 18 and December 5 about Clark's involvement in the conspiracy? Certainly Watkins's claim that he had changed his mind because he had heard Clark utter patriotic sentiments after he was elected to Congress is false. Clark left the territory for Washington on October 20, and Claiborne made his accusation based on Watkins's information on November 18. A more likely explanation is that he feared that Clark would learn that Watkins had accused him of involvement in the conspiracy. Watkins was himself, as Claiborne would later learn, a key member of the New Orleans organization known as the Mexican Association, which supported plans for the conquest of Mexico. Because Clark himself had been involved in the planning of the conquest of Mexico, it would not be difficult for him to raise counteraccusations against Watkins. It is also possible that James Wilkinson, who arrived in New Orleans on November 25, had met with Watkins at some time before December 5. If Watkins told the general that he had convinced Claiborne to accuse Clark in the conspiracy, it is likely that Wilkinson would have told Watkins to rescind his accusations. Wilkinson had probably become increasingly anxious that Clark, who possessed letters about Wilkinson's plans, could ruin him, so Wilkinson did not include Clark in his arrests of Burr associates.[23]

As Wilkinson grew more confident that he had the cooperation of Claiborne and the people of New Orleans, he moved against the conspirators. In order to make this task easier, he pressured Claiborne to suspend habeas corpus and declare martial law. Claiborne refused because he believed that only the legislature could order this. Wilkinson, however, ignored Claiborne's refusal, and arrested Burr's emissary, Erich Bollman, on December 14. The next day Edward Livingston managed to secure a writ of habeas corpus for Bollman.[24]

On December 18 Wilkinson appeared before the superior court to "deliver in his return in person to the writ of habeas corpus in the case of Bollman." Wilkinson declared that as he was *"commanding the army of the United States"* and took full responsibility for the arrest of Bollman. He vowed to continue to make arrests because "the traitors in the city of New Orleans, were numerous" and that "even among the counselors of that court there were two, namely the two gentlemen who had applied for the writ in favor of Bollman." The general then asked that Alexander be sent for immediately in order that he might be charged with treason. Livingston, angered that Wilkinson had accused him, "urged strenuously" that Wilkinson should produce evidence of his accusation and further demanded that Wilkinson "should not leave the bar until he produced the evidence at least of his own oath in support of the charge." Wilkinson refused to do this in writing and left the court.[25]

After he was challenged in the superior court, Wilkinson made no further attempt to accuse Livingston of treason. The day after his court appearance, however, Wilkinson arrested Alexander and another Burr associate, Peter Ogden.[26] Livingston swore out writs for Alexander and Ogden, and when Wilkinson "failed to make sufficient return," Livingston applied for an attachment against Wilkinson. Judge James Workman, who presided over these court proceedings, wrote to Claiborne and stated that before he took action against a "a man who has all the regular force," he wanted to know whether Claiborne had "the ability to enforce the decrees of the court" and whether he would do so against Wilkinson. Claiborne did not respond to this letter, and on January 12 Workman wrote another letter to inform Claiborne that he had decided to adjourn the court of the county of Orleans because he took Claiborne's silence to mean that he supported the "lawless measures of the oppressor."[27]

While Wilkinson and other Burr associates were at each other's throats in

New Orleans, Burr moved down the Mississippi, and on January 10 he arrived at Bayou Pierre, thirty miles above Natchez. There he visited a friend, Judge Peter Bryan Bruin, who showed him a newspaper. From it Burr learned that Wilkinson had betrayed him, that Jefferson had condemned Burr's expedition, and that the acting governor of Mississippi, Cowles Mead, had ordered his arrest. The next day Burr decided to continue on to New Orleans, but he knew that the Mississippi militia was searching for him.[28]

Meanwhile, in New Orleans, Wilkinson engaged in a struggle with Burr's associates and the territorial legislature. On January 12 the general appeared before the legislature to demand suspension of habeas corpus. The legislature denied this request and debated a proposed memorial to Congress that sanctioned Wilkinson's conduct. This did not cow Wilkinson, who, on January 14, arrested Workman and Justice Lewis Kerr on charges that they had attempted to engage men to capture Baton Rouge, loot its banks, and invade Mexico.[29] On the same day Wilkinson arrested Colonel John Adair, whom Burr had sent ahead to New Orleans to announce his arrival.[30]

One anonymous New Orleans editorial writer recognized that Wilkinson had picked upon "only a few of the best known, most active, decided partisans of the arch-traitor." The general exiled Adair, Ogden, Alexander, and Swartout to eastern cities for trial. Workman and Kerr were released on a writ the day after Wilkinson arrested them because Claiborne interceded on Kerr's behalf. "Burr's two chief henchmen in the Crescent City, Edward Livingston and Daniel Clark," were never arrested. This is not surprising given that both men knew intimate details of Wilkinson's participation in the plot and that both possessed resources and connections that would allow them to challenge the general.[31]

A day after Wilkinson arrested Workman, Kerr, and Adair, Burr surrendered to a force of Mississippi militia under condition that he be tried in Mississippi Territory. This marked the end of Burr's dreams for the conquests of Orleans Territory and Mexico. His trial began in the Mississippi Superior Court on February 2 and ended on February 4. The jury cleared Burr of all charges, and he was released. Burr's freedom was short-lived, however. He fled in disguise toward West Florida, but was recognized and arrested by U.S. troops and taken to Fort Stoddert on February 19.[32]

While Burr waited to be tried in Mississippi, Wilkinson continued his effort to arrest those he considered Burr's associates or who challenged his authority. He convinced the superior court of Orleans Territory to assemble a grand jury "to inquire of all offenses against the United States, as well as those against the territory." On January 24 Evan Jones, the foreman, presented the court with a prepared statement. The jury had found that there was no justification for Wilkinson's arrests or his decision to ignore writs of habeas corpus.

The Fall of the Opposition Faction

The general's "unprecedented exercise of military power" was a "dangerous and alarming evil," and his arrests were based on "specious reasons." Finally, the jury dismissed Wilkinson's claim that the governor and two judges had advised him, because they considered such alleged advice as "a total dereliction of all regard to the constitution and laws of the United States, and as striking at the heart of liberty."[33]

In addition to coming under fire in the superior court, Wilkinson was criticized in the Orleans House of Representatives. In January John Watkins led those who designed a memorial to Congress protesting Wilkinson's abuse of powers. Supporters of the memorial condemned Wilkinson's actions as "too notorious to be denied, too illegal to be justified, too wanton to be excused." The memorial was submitted to the House on March 15, 1806, but after it was debated the House voted to reject it. This was a dramatic shift of opinion. One member noted that the House had been unanimous about sending a memorial to Congress protesting Wilkinson's conduct ten weeks prior to the debate on it.[34]

The majority of the representatives in the Orleans territorial House probably decided against a memorial critical of Wilkinson because the general showed more restraint in his self-serving efforts to identify and denounce conspirators after it was learned that Burr was arrested. In addition, the government and people of Orleans received confirmation about the existence of the conspiracy and those involved in it from sources other than Wilkinson. On February 12 Claiborne sent a message to the Legislative Council and the House of Representatives in which he stated that he had learned that Burr "was in the hands of the Civil Authority at Natchez" and that it was confirmed that one of Burr's "adherents" had proposed to "a Citizen" to "bring about the dissolution of the Union" and to seize New Orleans and use proceeds from its banks for an invasion of Mexico.[35]

At the beginning of May Claiborne was able to report with relief to Jefferson that "Burr's Conspiracy" was "at an end," but he added anxiously that the "intrigues of Burr and his Partisans" had "made great divisions in our Society, and tended to estrange from the Interests of the Government, Men who would not long since were viewed as its best supporters." Claiborne's mention of estranged men was a reference to Dr. John Watkins, mayor of New Orleans, and George Ross, sheriff of Orleans County. Claiborne had dismissed Watkins because he "was a member of the Mexican Association" and Ross because he had taken "an oath of Secrecy relative to the invasion of Mexico" and "some improper conduct" in settling his pubic accounts.[36]

As fear of Burr's conspiracy faded, the stormy struggle between Governor Claiborne's adherents and those who supported Daniel Clark continued unabated. Claiborne was soon complaining again about the actions of his

The Fall of the Opposition Faction

opponents. In particular, he was upset with Clark, who had tried to discredit the governor in Washington when he served as territorial delegate to Congress. Clark had arrived in Washington in early December and was apparently greeted with open arms by the Federalist Party. Its press compared him to the ancient heroes of Greece and Rome and declared that he was a sincere admirer of the Constitution. While it was obvious that Clark was friendly to the Federalists, he also made what was probably a futile effort to ingratiate himself with Jefferson. He gave Jefferson "a few maps and plans of remarkable places in the Orleans Territory and adjoining counties" and an "Indian axe found on his plantation in the County of Acadia," which Jefferson believed to be the "largest" he had ever seen.[37]

In his first months in the House of Representatives, in addition to his efforts to serve his constituents through bills for the establishment of post roads, a charity hospital, and settlement of land claims, Clark worked to discredit Claiborne and his administration.[38] On Christmas Eve, 1806, he made a speech critical of Claiborne's administration of the territory of Orleans. Specifically, Clark complained that Claiborne had neglected the organization of the militia and that he had preferred certain volunteers to others. "The people of the Territory had offered their services to the United States, and had been disregarded by the man put over them, and a preference given to another corps. The militia were in an unorganized state—there were indeed no militia in the Territory."[39]

Another subject that increasingly concerned Clark during his first months in Washington was the Burr Conspiracy. As newspapers across the nation uncovered more details about it, Clark became nervous that he would be implicated in the plot. He wrote to Edward Livingston on December 8, 1806, and informed him that he found that "Col. Burr occupied a great portion of the public attention" and that "among other objects imputed to him" was "settlement of Bastrop's Land which he is supposed to have purchased of Lynch." Clark warned that he had spoken to Albert Gallatin, secretary of the treasury, and believed that orders had been given to prevent settlement of the tract. To prevent further investigation of Livingston's Bastrop sales, Clark suggested that Livingston send him "a copy of the Grant to Bastrop, a Copy of the Contract, a Copy of the order to him to suspend the introduction of the families," and any other relevant papers. Clark promised to "translate, publish and spread them with a comment among the Members of both Houses."[40]

In a second letter on the subject of Burr and the Bastrop land, Clark notified Livingston that "the administration and those connected with it" considered the Bastrop grant "too large" and that "Burr's project bottomed on a supposed purchase of these lands makes the possession of them by an individual more unpopular." Clark warned Livingston that unless he came forward to

The Fall of the Opposition Faction

"convince the public" of his right to the property, he would have "a mountain of opposition to remove at a future date which would not now exist by manufacturing all the Papers respecting it." Finally, Clark wrote that he had written to Pierre Derbigny on the subject and "begged him" to see Livingston.[41]

On Christmas Day, 1806, Clark wrote his friend and old business partner Daniel Coxe and informed him of the seizure of some of Burr's boats at Marietta and that an "anonymous letter from Pittsburgh" had mentioned Clark as "the chief broker and paymaster to Burr." In an effort to defend himself against these allegations, Clark asked Coxe if he had heard of any of his "drafts for that purpose" or "of any funds" with which Clark was "to answer the demands."[42]

Clark soon found that his efforts to hide his association with Burr had failed. On January 11, 1807, Clark wrote Livingston and enclosed a copy of the *Aurora* that mentioned both men as conspirators. "As your name frequently figures in the ministerial papers as an Arch Conspirator you will have the Consolation of seeing mine joined with it and for that purpose I send you the last Aurora received here."[43]

In May 1807 Daniel Clark returned home to New Orleans. Those who had been involved in Burr's conspiracy and who opposed Claiborne's administration gave a warm reception to the territorial delegate to Congress. Edward Livingston presided over a "splendid Dinner" given in Clark's honor. He was "assisted by" Philip Jones, his protégé, and George Ross. Guests included John Watkins, James Alexander, James Workman, and William Brown, collector for the Port of New Orleans. Claiborne was convinced that this dinner was part of an effort to induce Clark to "take a violent part in the late proceedings here." This was clearly a reference to Livingston's opposition to Wilkinson's arrests and Claiborne's dismissals. The governor concluded that "The Faction" had spent "very unnecessarily their Money" because he had "no doubt that Mr. Clark from choice, would fall into their views."[44]

Claiborne's reaction to Clark's return to New Orleans was, not surprisingly, hostile. The governor had read about Clark's speech of December 24, 1806, in the *Orleans Gazette* and was stung by the criticism about the state of the militia in Orleans Territory. On May 23, 1807, the governor wrote to Clark and asked whether it was true that he had stated that the militia was unorganized and that Claiborne had favored some volunteers over others. On the next day Clark replied that the article describing his comments was correct. Claiborne then asked Clark to retract his criticism of Claiborne's management of the militia. He refused, and the governor demanded satisfaction. Seconds then arranged a time and a place for a duel.

On June 8 Claiborne and Clark faced each other at Fort Manchac, near Baton Rouge, in Spanish West Florida. When signaled, both men raised their pistols and fired simultaneously. Claiborne missed; Clark did not. The ball from Clark's pistol passed through Claiborne's right thigh and stopped in his left leg. Given the nature of the wound and medical knowledge of the day, it is surprising that Claiborne survived and kept his right leg. Nine days later, Claiborne wrote to notify Jefferson of his condition and assured him that he was in pain but that he would be able to walk in three weeks.[45]

Claiborne was not pleased with his decision to participate in a duel with Clark. On June 28 the governor confessed that his wound was "infinitely more painful" than he had anticipated but that this could be considered punishment for his "imprudence." While Claiborne suffered physical pain as a result of the duel, Clark suffered a loss of popular support. He had returned from Washington to a hero's welcome by men disgruntled with Claiborne's administration, some of whom were in key positions in the government and in the courts. Clark's opportunity to rally these individuals was lost, however, after he shot the governor. Perhaps one of the first of those to disassociate himself from the opposition faction was William Brown. In his letter to the president of June 17, Claiborne wrote that he "since had reason" to change his opinion about Brown, whom he noted "meddles not at all with the politics of the day" and was "a faithful" and "capable officer."[46]

Clark's shooting of Claiborne was only one factor in the decline of the opposition faction in Orleans Territory politics, however. Edward Livingston, perhaps second only to Clark as a leader of the opposition, also suffered a self-inflicted loss of influence in the territory of Orleans beginning in the spring of 1807. On May 20 Claiborne informed Jefferson that Livingston had won a superior court decision for a land claim "in front of the Fauxbourg of New Orleans" on the Mississippi River that was worth approximately $200,000.[47] This land was a section of the Batture St. Mary, part of an ancient land grant sold by the Jesuits and divided into lots when their order was suppressed in 1763. A man named Jean Pradel purchased the lot closest to New Orleans. The lot eventually passed through inheritance to Bertrand Gravier, who established a suburb on the Mississippi and sold sections of it in the 1790s. Gravier died intestate in 1797, and what was left of his property passed to his brother, Jean.[48]

The Batture was created from soil deposited along the suburban lots on the Mississippi River bank. The people of New Orleans used this soil to repair streets, build sidewalks, and construct levees. "The Batture itself, through long established custom, was used as a place for anchorage and wharfage." Over time, soil deposited by the Mississippi increased the size of the Batture. Traditionally owners of property on the Batture increased the size of their own property by moving the levee closer to the river. When Jean Gravier attempted to do this in 1804, however, the residents of New Orleans protested, and the city challenged Gravier's title to the land in the superior court. Gravier retained Edward Livingston as his attorney. Livingston won the case, on the grounds that "according to civil and Spanish law the right of alluvium was incident to the land which was formed by the river." Gravier paid Livingston with one- third of his land claim, which Claiborne estimated was worth $200,000.[49]

Livingston himself recognized the potential for profit from land sales, and along with Peter Delabigarre immediately purchased more Batture land at a cost of $77,000. In order to increase the value of his land, Livingston invested $13,000 in improvements, including "the building of a new levee, the digging of a canal, and the construction of a dwelling." During the spring and summer of 1807, however, residents of New Orleans, outraged at the decision of the superior court, assembled as mobs and repeatedly drove off the laborers Livingston had hired to make these improvements. Livingston sent these men back to work each time that they were dispersed. On September 14 he attempted to use constables to protect them, but they failed to stop the mob. The next day Livingston warned Claiborne that he planned to put his laborers to work at noon and that the increasingly violent mob would "change the insolence of riot into the crime of murder."[50]

As Livingston promised, his laborers resumed work at noon on September 15. At around four o'clock a crowd of approximately 400 moved on Livingston's property. Claiborne appeared and addressed them. He asked them to respect the decision of the superior court but said that it could be appealed and that he had sent information on Livingston's claim to Jefferson. The crowd, however, demanded that an agent be sent to collect evidence and affidavits as to the right of the public to use of the Batture and to present these in Washington. Claiborne agreed to this, and before they dispersed, the crowd selected John Baptiste McCarty, a popular militia colonel, for this task.

On October 21 the New Orleans City Council agreed to pay $3,000 for McCarty's trip to Washington. The city council also "initiated the legal maneuver of transferring its alleged title to the Batture to the U.S. government."[51] In December 1807 the city council asked Claiborne to inform Jefferson's administration that it wanted the public right to the Batture to be defended by the federal government.

In November Jefferson decided to review the case himself. After consultation with Secretary of the Treasury Gallatin and Attorney General Caesar Rodney, Jefferson met with his cabinet on November 27. Following this meeting he ordered Madison to evict Livingston from the Batture "in conformity with an act of March 3, 1807, which empowered the government to evict squatters from public lands." Madison then sent the order of eviction to the marshal of Orleans Territory on November 30, 1807.

Jefferson's decision to personally involve himself and his cabinet in a municipal case is extraordinary. Perhaps even more surprising is the fact that

Jefferson had not yet been asked to do this by the city of New Orleans. "Madison issued the instructions to the U.S. Marshal on November 30, two weeks prior to the city council's decision and a full month before any official request could have been received from New Orleans."[52]

Another interesting aspect of Jefferson's involvement is that he had received very little information on the Batture case when he made his decision. When he assembled his cabinet on November 27, Jefferson had read the argument presented by Pierre Derbigny, the city's attorney in the original suit against Livingston. After he had checked Derbigny's quotations from *Diderot's Encyclopedia*, Jefferson concluded that Derbigny's argument was "satisfactory." In soliciting Gallatin's advice, Jefferson sent him the "very able opinion of Derbigny's" and instructed him that it be returned after Attorney General Rodney had read it. Rodney, Jefferson informed Gallatin, was "in possession of the opinion of the court assigning their reasons." What Jefferson had not read, however, was Livingston's argument in the case. In December Livingston sent his information to Washington, but by that time Jefferson had already decided to evict him.[53]

Jefferson's uninvited personal involvement in a relatively uninformed decision suggests that he was eager for action against Livingston. What could explain this? Jefferson had no reason to favor Livingston, who had reluctantly supported him in the 1800 presidential election, damaged the reputation of his administration through his mismanagement of finances while mayor of New York, consistently opposed Claiborne, associated with Burr, and criticized Wilkinson in New Orleans. Despite all this, however, Jefferson's move against Livingston appears to be less of a snap decision based on a desire for vengeance for past wrongs than it does a shrewd political move. Jefferson knew that the Orleans Territory superior court's decision for Livingston was unpopular in Orleans Territory. On October 5, 1807, Claiborne had informed Madison of this while in Concordia, on a tour of the parishes.

> I left New Orleans on the 19th Instant, at which time Order was restored, and the agitation with respect to the Batture much subsided: I however, perceived on my Journey thro' several of the Parishes, but one sentiment with respect to the decision of the Court;—The long and uninterrupted use of the Batture by the City;—the sanction given by the Spanish authorities to the public Claim, and the heavy public expenditures in Maintaining the Levee, which fronts the alluvion, seem to have given rise to a very general opinion that *the Court has been in error in deciding the Batture to be private property.*[54]

Under these circumstances, Jefferson's decision to support the eviction of Livingston would be popular in Orleans Territory and therefore of political benefit to him and Claiborne. Certainly Jefferson could not have failed to notice that the two lawyers involved in the Batture case were both vocal opponents of Claiborne in the past. Jefferson's visible support for Derbigny's argument would ensure that close, amicable future cooperation between these two was unlikely. In addition, Livingston, one of Claiborne's most influential opponents, would suffer some major financial embarrassment and debt as a result of a decision against him.

On January 25, 1808, the U.S. marshal for Orleans Territory, Le Breton d' Orgenois, carried out Jefferson's order to evict Livingston. The city council thanked Claiborne for his effort to convince the federal government to take action against Livingston. The city also passed legislation prohibiting further construction and restored the traditional public rights for residents of Orleans to use this land.[55] Livingston wrote to his brother Robert that his eviction had "suspended" his "hopes for independence" because he had invested $12,000.[56]

As Livingston took stock of his financial losses, he engaged in a bitter pamphlet and newspaper battle with Derbigny and Jefferson. The *Orleans Gazette* took Livingston's side, while the *Louisiana Courier* defended the position of the city. It was Derbigny who first took the struggle against Livingston outside the courtroom. In a pamphlet published in the summer of 1807, Derbigny declared that the decision of the court for Livingston was a result of a flawed system of justice that did not work in a territory governed by civil law and that this was cause enough for the federal government to review it.[57]

> Will not the general government reflect that Louisiana, by the very nature of the Provisional government which rules it, is deprived of part of the advantages enjoyed by other citizens of the Union, in their judiciary contests, and the fate of their fortunes and their lives is definitely submitted to one sole tribunal, composed of three judges, who decide at once in the first instance, and in the last resort, in a country whose languages, manners, usages, and even sometimes whose laws are little familiar to them; and that the acknowledged integrity and information of those three judges are not always a solid security for the irrefragability of their judgment.[58]

This argument was well received by many in New Orleans who believed that Livingston's victory in the superior court was due to its reliance on an "alien legal system," that of common law, over French civil law. Derbigny further argued that the original sale of the Batture occurred when France governed Louisiana. "French municipal law clearly provided for battures and that, in the absence of written evidence of a grant to private owners, the Batture St. Mary continued to be in the possession of the sovereign power, which had now become the United States government." Jefferson was convinced by this argument, and he adhered to it despite the fact that Livingston challenged it for years.[59]

On December 10, 1807, Livingston's response to Derbigny's pamphlet, entitled *Examination of the Title of the United States to the land called the Batture*, was published. Livingston argued that in Paris all alluvial deposits that resulted in changes in the course of a river became the property of owners of riparian estates and that the decision of the superior court was based on Spanish law, which held soil deposited by a river belonged to the owners of riverfront property.[60]

Livingston carried on his pamphlet battle for years, enlisting the support of famous Philadelphia attorney Peter Duponceau. Duponceau contended that the civil law supported Livingston's ownership of the Batture and that "the decision of private right was not in violation of accepted customs, usages, and laws of the country, but rather derived from them." Moreau Lislet, "Louisiana's leading civil law authority," defended Derbigny's position. Lislet found that, according to Spanish law, "sand-banks or sandy tracts, (arenales) on the borders of rivers, make part of the commons of those towns."[61]

While Livingston's pamphlet effort generated much public discussion, it did not result in a review of his case. After he was evicted in January 1808, Livingston decided that he had no choice but to travel to Washington to see Jefferson. He arrived in Washington on the evening of May 5, and learning that Jefferson was soon to leave Washington, wrote to Jefferson to request "a short audience."[62]

The administration had been forewarned by Claiborne that the purpose of Livingston's trip was to present his arguments on the Batture case and the acts of General Wilkinson and the governor in 1806. Jefferson informed Livingston the next day that he was "pressed in finishing sundry articles of business" and found it "impossible to enter on any new subject" at that time. In concluding his brief note Jefferson added, "whatever the subject of Mr. Livingston's application, it goes in the first instance to the head of the department to which it belongs, from whom it will be communicated." From this note Livingston must have understood that the president was not willing to help him in any way. What Livingston did not know, however, was that Jefferson wanted to see him taken into custody. After Jefferson had learned of Livingston's arrival in Washington, he informed Secretary of the Treasury Albert Gallatin that if there was any possibility to arrest Livingston "for his public debt, the opportunity should not be lost."[63]

Livingston was not arrested, and when he failed to receive an audience he wrote a long petition but received no response. After he had returned to New Orleans empty-handed, Livingston wrote a pamphlet that was critical of Jefferson's involvement in the Batture case. In *Address to the People of the United*

States, published in December 1808, Livingston stated he was not surprised that Claiborne, "the most malevolent" of his enemies, was against him in the Batture case because Claiborne had staked his reputation on his public promise to influence the president to overturn the decision of the superior court. As for Jefferson, Livingston reported that he

> found it difficult to believe that the First Magistrate of a great people would quit the care of a nation to participate in the petty disputes of a corporate town; or, to secure the popularity of a favorite, that he would have set at defiance the very forms of law, braved the authority of the courts, and broken through the most important barriers of that constitution he had sworn to defend.[64]

Not content with merely publicizing his struggle with Jefferson, Livingston again left New Orleans to lobby congressmen to bring his case to the House of Representatives. Daniel Sheffey of Virginia introduced resolutions for a temporary restoration of Livingston's right to the Batture and for a compromise settlement. Congress debated the Batture case in the spring of 1810 but did nothing. Because of this, Livingston launched a suit of trespass against Jefferson in the federal circuit court in Virginia. Even though he was no longer in office, Jefferson worked to defend himself. He sought the advice of Virginia lawyers, prepared a brief for his defense counsel, and urged President Madison to appoint Governor John Tyler of Virginia to the district court. To block Livingston's efforts in Congress, Jefferson asked William Branch Giles, a Senate Republican, and Virginia congressman John Wayles Eppes "to stifle congressional action on the Batture question despite Livingston's repeated petitions."[65]

Jefferson was successful in his effort against Livingston. Tyler was appointed to the Virginia District Court and participated in its decision in *Livingston v. Jefferson* on December 5, 1811. The court concluded that a trespass was local and had to be tried where the land was located. This meant that the case of trespass would have to be tried in Orleans Territory, where it was most unlikely that a court would decide in favor of Livingston. Despite this defeat, Livingston continued his legal battle over the Batture for more than a decade and reached a compromise with the city of New Orleans in 1823.[66]

Livingston's legal struggle with Jefferson and the city of New Orleans cost him dearly, and not simply in terms of legal expenses. By challenging Jefferson and the city of New Orleans, Livingston temporarily lost whatever influence he had gained in Orleans Territory as a result of his authorship of the *Remonstrance* of 1804 and had little influence in Republican Washington. To a lesser degree, Daniel Clark had also managed to alienate residents of New Orleans through involvement in a dispute with the city council over real estate.

The Fall of the Opposition Faction

Along with a partner, Samuel Davis, Clark owned a ropewalk in the city. The city council wanted to connect the streets of old New Orleans with those in the suburb of St. Mary, but the ropewalk extended almost across the entire city and divided the two areas. The city attempted to negotiate for the dismantling of the ropewalk, but Clark refused to do so. When a fire destroyed the ropewalk on June 4, 1806, the city council met and attempted to persuade Clark to sell the property upon which it was built, but he refused and rebuilt it, despite the fact that this was unpopular with the public. The city, however, continued to attempt to persuade Clark to give up his ropewalk, and the matter continued before the courts until 1808.[67]

Between 1807 and 1808 Daniel Clark and Edward Livingston had seriously damaged their reputations as popular leaders of the party opposed to Governor Claiborne's territorial administration. Both were implicated in the Burr Conspiracy, both had involved themselves in unpopular property disputes, and Clark had shot the governor in a duel. As these men were increasingly attacked in the press as treasonous and grasping, Claiborne's reputation improved when he was recognized for his loyal conduct during the Burr Conspiracy and for his support of Louisianans during the Batture controversy.

CHAPTER 7

Jefferson Triumphant

Republican Orleans and American Louisiana

Daniel Clark and Edward Livingston, already implicated in the Burr Conspiracy, further damaged their reputations when they participated in an effort to blame Wilkinson for the plot to conquer Orleans Territory and invade Mexico. When the U.S. District Court of Virginia convened in May 1807 to try Burr on charges of treason, his counsel decided to attempt to focus the court's attention on Wilkinson, and sent James Alexander to New Orleans to ask Livingston and John B. Prevost to collect evidence against the general. Livingston gathered depositions and subpoenaed Daniel Clark to appear in Richmond to testify about Wilkinson's past association with the Spanish government. Livingston and Prevost apologized to Clark for putting him in this position, but Clark did not resist. On September 3, 1807, he sailed for Richmond on his ship, the *Comet*.[1]

Wilkinson, who had narrowly escaped an indictment for misprision of treason (defined as the deliberate concealment of one's knowledge of treason) at the Richmond trial in June, learned that Clark was on his way and wrote to him on October 5. The general warned Clark that he was in possession of a letter sent to him by Burr that referred to a "communication from New Orleans" in which Clark had mentioned "a meditated Mexican expedition, and the revolt of the western states, etc. etc." When Clark arrived in Richmond on October 11, Wilkinson went to see Attorney General George Hay and, "terrified beyond description, declared that Clark could ruin him." Burr saved Wilkinson from "ruin," however. After Clark arrived in Richmond, Burr sent him a note and stated that he had not sent for Clark and did not want him to testify. Clark left for Philadelphia.[2]

On October 17, however, Thomas Power, a Spanish agent who had attempted to interest Wilkinson in a project to start a revolution in the American West in the 1790s, testified that Wilkinson had corresponded at that time with the Spanish governor of Louisiana, the Baron de Carondelet. Wilkinson responded to this charge by publishing Power's testimony ten days later along with a denial of involvement with Carondelet. Power, incensed, turned over papers connecting Wilkinson to Spain to Clark, who in turn gave them to John Randolph of Roanoke. Randolph, summoned to serve on a grand jury after Burr arrived in Richmond, "was brought in contact with a new object of intense aversion, the famous General Wilkinson." Randolph had no patience for Wilkinson; "perhaps his irritation was a little due to the fact that Wilkinson's vices had so much helped to cover what he believed to be Mr. Jefferson's blunders." Whatever his motives, Randolph focused on the destruction of Wilkinson, who had escaped an indictment for treason in June.[3]

What had induced Clark to give Power's papers to John Randolph? He could have walked away from the trial in Richmond and perhaps salvaged his reputation since it was apparent that neither Burr nor Wilkinson wanted Clark to speak about the plot. When he left Richmond, Clark showed no desire to challenge Wilkinson in court. After he reached Philadelphia, however, he decided to do so. Clark must have had some strong motive since it was a certainty that Wilkinson would respond and reveal Clark's involvement in the plot to conquer Mexico. Wilkinson suggested that Clark's opinion of him had changed after Clark had learned that the general had "questioned Clark's financial credit." It appears, however, that Clark decided to turn on Wilkinson after he learned or perhaps merely feared that Wilkinson had already denounced him. Shortly after his arrival in Philadelphia, Clark told his friend and business associate Daniel Coxe that Wilkinson "had denounced him and many others in a secret letter to the President." Wilkinson, however, indicated in his *Memoirs* that Clark's attitude toward him had changed after Clark had learned that Wilkinson had questioned Clark's financial credit in Baltimore and that Clark had learned of this and turned on him. If Clark had ever learned of this, he never mentioned it.[4]

On October 20, 1807, Burr's trial in Richmond ended. John Marshall, who had presided over it, judged that Burr's direct object, the conquest of Mexico, was "not a treasonous enterprise." With the Burr trial over, Randolph attempted to have Congress examine the conduct of Wilkinson and presented two of the letters provided by Clark to the House of Representatives. One of these was from Carondelet to Captain Thomas Portell, commandant at New Madrid, dated January 20, 1796, informing Portell that Carondelet had sent him $9,640 to be given to Wilkinson. After he had read this letter Randolph asked Clark, as representative for the territory of Orleans, to provide further information on Wilkinson's activities, but Clark, to save face, declined to testify unless he was forced to do so by the House. Randolph next presented a resolution to request the president to order an investigation of Wilkinson. The House tabled it.[5]

On January 7, 1808, the House asked Clark to submit a statement of his information on Wilkinson. Clark complied and declared that Wilkinson had plotted with the Spanish government to separate the western states and territories from the Union and that he had received a pension for his services. The House next voted in favor of a request by John Randolph that the president begin an investigation into the charge that Wilkinson had illegally received money from the Spanish government. Following this, John Wayles Eppes moved that the president should submit any letters that he possessed that were relevant to the case. The House also approved this request.[6]

Unknown to members of the House, Jefferson had already decided that Wilkinson should face a court-martial. On January 2, 1808, Secretary of War Henry Dearborn appointed the members of the court-martial. As both Jefferson and Dearborn had always supported Wilkinson, it was unlikely that this court, composed of Dearborn's subordinates, would seriously consider Randolph's accusations against the general. Certainly there would be no reason for Jefferson to favor Randolph and Clark, who had become increasingly irritating to him.[7]

The court-martial lasted from January 11 to June 28. Clark refused to testify to the court but enlisted his associate and friend Daniel Coxe to do so for him. After listening to testimony for more than six months, the court concluded that there was "no Evidence of Brigadier General James Wilkinson having received a Pension from the Government of Spain or any of its officers or agents for corrupt purposes." The court further added that as far as it was concerned, Wilkinson appeared to have "discharged the Duties of his Station with honor to himself and fidelity to his Country."[8]

In its vindication of Wilkinson it is clear that the court-martial made a strenuous effort to ignore the evidence that Clark, through Coxe, presented to it. While Wilkinson emerged as the victor, Clark was implicated in the Burr Conspiracy. Several of the witnesses that Wilkinson called testified that Daniel Clark had advised them to support Burr's scheme to conquer Mexico. John Graham, who had once acted as secretary of Orleans Territory, stated that Clark had declared that the object of the conquest of Mexico was to establish an independent empire and that Graham "might be made a duke" if he supported the expedition. Lieutenant W. A. Murray testified that he had met with Lewis Kerr and James Workman in the spring of 1806, and that he was informed of the existence of the Mexican Association and of the plan to conquer Mexico. Kerr and Workman also told Murray that this expedition would be financed and equipped through the seizure of banks and shipping at New Orleans. Murray further declared that he at first refused to participate but asked the advice of Daniel Clark, who encouraged him to join in on the plan. Lieutenant Robert T. Spence testified that he had sailed from Philadelphia to New

Orleans on a ship with Burr's emissaries, James Alexander and Erich Bollman, and that he had carried a letter of recommendation from Burr to Clark and had dined with Clark and Bollman.[9]

In addition to his effort to discredit Clark through the testimony of witnesses during the court-martial at Washington, Wilkinson also attacked Clark in the New Orleans press. In a letter addressed to the citizens of New Orleans published in the *Louisiana Gazette* on March 8, 1808, Wilkinson claimed that the Mexican Association was a "diabolical band" that threatened the residents of New Orleans and that he would "prove that Daniel Clark himself was a member." Clark defended himself, and the result was a newspaper war that lasted for more than two years. In general, the *Louisiana Gazette* published articles defending Clark while the *Louisiana Courier* acted as the voice of Wilkinson.[10]

Less than three days after the *Gazette* published Wilkinson's letter to the residents of New Orleans, a piece appeared in that paper entitled "Letter from a Creole." The anonymous author of this article declared that Louisianans should consider themselves fortunate that they had "a man of such talents, integrity, and undaunted perseverance on the floor of Congress." A few weeks later, the *Gazette* published a highly flattering "Sketch of his character," and in April Joseph Bellechasse wrote an article defending Clark's conduct for the newspaper.[11]

The New Orleans newspaper battle between Wilkinson and Clark continued on into 1810. In its report on an Independence Day celebration in that year, the *Louisiana Courier* listed a series of toasts that were made. These included toasts of praise for Wilkinson and Claiborne. Clark was honored with two toasts: "Burr and Clark, twin brothers in villainy—their own confessions cover them with ignominy." "The Territory of Orleans—may it never sink under the influence of Clark."[12]

Those who raised their glasses against Clark on July 4, 1810, had little to fear from Clark's supposed influence. Clark spent most of his time between 1808 and 1810 defending himself against Wilkinson's charge that he was involved with Burr in a conspiracy. This charge would have seemed reasonable to all those in New Orleans who had witnessed Clark's association with Burr in July 1805. Clark sent statements and letters on Wilkinson's activities to Edward Livingston in order to obtain legal advice on how to proceed against accusations leveled against him.[13] Beyond his effort to influence Dearborn's court-martial and the Orleans press, Clark also used time and money to produce a book to challenge Wilkinson, entitled *Proofs of the Corruption of James Wilkinson*. This work, published in 1809, included all the evidence that Clark had produced against Wilkinson for the court-martial. Wilkinson countered Clark's accusations and evidence in his *Memoirs of James Wilkinson*, published in 1816, after Clark's death.

Clark's battle with Wilkinson also had an impact on Livingston. Pieces appeared in the *Courier* throughout 1808 that linked Clark and Livingston in the Burr Conspiracy and connected Clark's loss to Wilkinson to Livingston's defeat in the Batture case. An article reprinted from the *Philadelphia Aurora* declared that Livingston's removal from the Batture had "spread dismay and confusion among the 'choice spirits.'" "Livingston, Clark, Watkins and Co.," the anonymous author reported, had "found that their efforts to excite commotion, and their rides through all the districts to asperse the Government, and stir up sedition, have at length turned out to their confusion, and to the honor of the General Government." In a May article, the editor of the *Courier*, Jean Baptiste Thierry, declared that Claiborne was still in office despite "all of the intrigues of Daniel Clark" and that the governor had demonstrated his devotion to the people by his efforts to restore the Batture to the city of New Orleans.[14]

Thierry and the anonymous author correctly predicted that the influence of the Clark-Livingston faction was damaged beyond repair by the spring of 1808. Claiborne had predicted their demise in July 1807, in the wake of Burr's trial and his duel with Clark. He noted that Louisianans had begun "to distinguish between the real and pretended Patriots" and that "the hitherto great influence of certain unprincipled Americans, will very soon be [at] an end." Claiborne was correct; the influence of the leaders of the opposition faction had declined. This was shown in the territorial government elections in 1807. On October 5 Claiborne reported that the results of this election were very satisfactory to him because the majority of those elected were "ancient Louisianans, of honest reputation and Supporters of the Government." The opposition had elected a minority of members to government. According to Claiborne, "Dr. Watkins and those of his Party were but partially supported."[15]

Claiborne never again faced a legislature that challenged him as the one of 1806 had. The fear of an insurrection led by those who had opposed Claiborne faded after 1808 as well. The Burr Conspiracy, however, had heightened awareness of such a possibility, and there were occasional false alarms. In late December 1808 James Mather informed Claiborne that he had learned from an unidentified informant of a plot that a "Mr. L (one of the leaders)" had organized along with others to raise a troop of cavalry and to seize artillery and the banks of New Orleans. Claiborne considered the possibility of the threat serious enough to send a request to Colonel Thomas Cushing that additional troops be sent to New Orleans. Cushing refused and explained that he would send troops only if an actual insurrection occurred. In a letter to Secretary of War Dearborn, Cushing explained his rationale for refusing Claiborne's request. Cushing claimed that while Mather's suspicions might be "well founded," it was "equally probable" that Mather was "the dupe of some unprincipled men in that city" who amused themselves "at the expence of his credulity, as they have often done with that of Governor Claiborne."[16]

The possibility that an insurrection led by Livingston or any other member of Claiborne's political opponents would receive popular support was nonexistent by early 1809. The opposition faction had lost most of the popular support it had between 1804 and 1807. In September 1808 Claiborne delightedly informed Madison of his political opponents' loss of influence:

> The faction, who have so long been opposed to me, in this quarter, have really made me popular in the Territory. I meet at the present period, with more general support from the Body of the People, than I ever before experienced. This change (so agreeable to me) has not arisen from any particular merits of mine, but is attributable to the despicable character of my opponents, and the vile arts to which they resort, to destroy those, whom they cannot influence.[17]

Proof that Claiborne's opponents had indeed lost support was their loss in the elections for the territorial delegate to Congress in 1809. John Watkins ran as the opposition candidate, while Julien Poydras supported Claiborne. Poydras easily defeated Watkins. Claiborne noted his satisfaction at this result in a letter to Madison on February 13, 1809. "Mr. Julian Poydras has been elected Delegate to Congress for the ensuing two years; Dr. Watkins, was the candidate in opposition & is understood here, to have received all the support, which Mr. Daniel Clark could give him; But on counting the votes there appeared 20 for Poydras, and five (only) for Watkins."[18]

The Madison administration was equally pleased with the election of Poydras. On March 20, 1809, Secretary of State Robert Smith informed Claiborne that it was satisfactory to learn that a "Gentleman so deeply interested in the prosperity of the Territory" and who was "avowedly friendly to the general & local administration" was chosen as representative to Congress.[19]

Claiborne now enjoyed support in Washington. When Livingston attempted to bring his Batture problems to Congress, Poydras was there to speak against him and consistently defended Claiborne's policies. In Orleans Territory, the opposition had no power within the legislature, and while Claiborne was still criticized in newspapers such as the *Gazette*, Clark was engaged in his bitter struggle with Wilkinson and Livingston focused on his Batture claim.

The election of Poydras also marked a political victory for Jefferson. The president had wanted the state to enter the Union under the control of an American administration. The Act for the Organization of Orleans Territory and the Louisiana District, which gave the president the power to appoint the governor and the Legislative Council, demonstrated Jefferson's willingness to sacrifice representative government for this purpose. While he was steadfast in this goal, however, he also made attempts to win the hearts and minds of Louisianans through small concessions. He had insisted that the Legislative Council be comprised of French and Americans—with the Americans in the majority, of course—and suggested that officials should know or at least attempt to learn both languages. In November 1804 he appointed a House committee for the amelioration of the government of Louisiana. Jefferson's Republican majority in the Senate and House passed the Act for the Government of Orleans Territory on March 2, 1805, which gave Orleans Territory an elected House of Representatives. While these measures did not completely satisfy Louisianans who protested against lack of representation in government, they suggested that the president would gradually, by his own timetable, grant self-government to Orleans Territory.

On the issue of slavery in Louisiana, like that of representation, Jefferson performed a balancing act between appearing to consider the grievances of Louisianans and ensuring that Orleans Territory became an American state. As Congress debated the possibility of a ban on the slave trade to Louisiana, Jefferson presented a letter from Claiborne in which the governor mentioned the long history of the trade and his fear of restricting it. At the same time, Jefferson voiced no opposition when Congress passed its ban on importation of slaves to Louisiana with the exception of slaves that settlers brought with them from American states to the territory. Because this law encouraged settlement by American planters, there was little reason for Jefferson to oppose it. In fact, it made more sense for Jefferson to support this law as it fit with his goal of ensuring that Orleans Territory would join the Union as an American state.

It was the American planter who ensured that Orleans Territory would become an American state. Attracted by rich soils and lands accessible to the Mississippi and overseas markets, Americans immigrated to Louisiana in the thousands. The total population of Louisiana was estimated at 43,000 in 1803 and 76,000 in 1810. The majority of these new arrivals were Americans.[20]

The reaction of Louisianan planters to the restriction on importation of slaves in the face of American immigration to Louisiana is understandable, but their fears of hardship never materialized. Slaves were imported to Louisiana by planters/merchants like Daniel Clark and by smugglers throughout the territorial period. The Jefferson administration made little concerted effort to enforce the short-lived territorial prohibition on the importation of slaves in 1804 or the national ban in 1808. No extraordinary measures were taken to blockade the Louisiana coast to prevent smuggling. Such enforcement was beyond the capabilities of the American navy anyway, given the number of bays that offered smugglers protection and access to the interior along the Louisiana coastline. Furthermore, Governor Claiborne did not support legislation to ban the importation of slaves and in at least one case managed to contravene the national prohibition of the slave trade. One such instance occurred in the spring and summer of 1809 when St. Domingue planter refugees from Cuba arrived in New Orleans with their slaves. According to Claiborne, "a number of respectful and humane citizens" had petitioned him to allow the introduction of the planters' slaves into the territory. Claiborne sympathized and wrote to Julien Poydras in Washington and suggested that he would be "well pleased if Congress would relax its law forbidding the importation of slaves." The St. Domingue planters were eventually allowed to land their slaves, and this earned Claiborne support of these planter refugees.[21]

Finally, the Jefferson administration had not moved to challenge the opinion presented by lawyers of Orleans Territory that the people of Orleans had the rights of the inhabitants of other U.S. territories and that the territorial citizens of Mississippi were legally allowed to import slaves. Because of the Jefferson administration's laissez-faire attitude regarding the slave trade, the success of smuggling, and the arguments of Orleans lawyers, the planters of Louisiana never faced ruin as a result of a lack of slave labor, as they had feared they would when the Act for the Organization of Orleans Territory and the Louisiana District was passed in 1804.

The Jefferson administration had also worked to address some of the grievances that Louisianans had regarding land claims. The Orleans legislature protested the federal government's passage of the Act for Ascertaining and Adjusting the Titles and Claims to Land within the Territory of Orleans. There was a general fear that the U.S. government would use this act to dispossess Louisianans of their land. This fear subsided, however, as the federal government amended the act and loosened restrictions on titles. For example, the rule that a legitimate title was restricted to those who were twenty-one years old and the head of a family by October 1, 1800, was dropped, and the deadline that Louisianans were given to register their land was extended.

The fear of an American justice system based solely on the English language common law was somewhat lessened when Jefferson attempted to appoint judges who spoke both French and English. A measure that went further to reconcile Louisianans with the American justice system, however, was Claiborne's approval of the adoption of the *Digest of the Civil Laws Now in Force in the Territory of Orleans* by the territorial government on March 2, 1808. This code, the work of James Brown and Louis Moreau Lislet, a refugee of St. Domingue, was modeled primarily on Napoleon's Code Civil and the Projet of 1800. Its adoption calmed French Louisianans who believed that the introduction of common law would ensure their inability to defend themselves and their interests in court. Claiborne was not entirely satisfied that the territorial government had not adopted a code based on common law, and he recognized that his "approbation of the Civil Code" was not well received by the "native Americans." Nevertheless, he admitted that he had no choice but to approve it as the "adoption of this Code was recommended by the strongest consideration of Justice and policy." It was within Jefferson's power to persuade Claiborne to reject the code, but the president did not do so.[22]

Finally, Jefferson's decision to involve himself in the Batture case in New Orleans beginning in November 1807 must be considered as an important move to win favor for himself and his governor. Livingston should not have been so astonished that the president involved himself in a court dispute over property on the New Orleans waterfront. As Claiborne reported, when the controversy over Livingston's claim to the land began, the Batture was considered throughout the territory as public land despite the fact that Livingston's claim to part of it was upheld in a New Orleans court. When Livingston's workers appeared on the Batture, they were repeatedly driven off by angry mobs. Claiborne won the favor of the people of the territory for his efforts to bring the matter of the Batture to the attention of the president. Jefferson, by his support of the argument that the Batture was public land, won the gratitude and support of the people of Orleans Territory for his administration and that of his governor.

While many questions of property and law had been resolved to the satisfaction of most Louisianans by 1809, one issue that Livingston had outlined in the *Remonstrance* of 1804 had not. Many still wished that Louisiana be granted statehood. The territorial legislature drew up a petition to Congress for admission into the Union in May 1809. The governor sent a copy to Secretary of State Robert Smith with his remarks. Claiborne declared that while he witnessed the Louisianans' "growing attachment to the American Govt.," they were not yet prepared for self-government because the "Mass of the Inhabitants" still held "strong prejudices in favor of their laws and usages." If the "immediate controul of the Gen. Govt." were withdrawn, Claiborne argued, "those great principles of Jurisprudence so much admired in the U.S., would not meet here that patronage, which the genl. Interest required." Claiborne added that the time for the submission of this memorial was "illy chosen" as it was believed that the Spanish possessions in America were on the verge of revolution and that the "Rights of the Citizens" were "not generally understood, & his duties (more particularly political) often neglected."[23]

Thomas Robertson, secretary of the territory of Orleans, echoed Claiborne's belief that Orleans Territory was not prepared for self-government because of the expected arrival of 2,000 St. Domingue refugees from Cuba.

Robertson believed that the addition of this population to that of Orleans would "rivet upon us a decided an irresistible preponderance of French influence and thus prevent us for many years to come from considering this in heart and sentiment as an American country."[24]

Claiborne and Robertson were obviously nervous about the possibility that a disloyal element would gain control of the state government. While such an argument was plausible between 1804 and 1807, when Claiborne's opponents had influence in the press, in the territorial government, and, through Clark, in Washington, it was not in 1809. The old opposition, openly hostile to Claiborne and territorial government, that had reached its peak in 1806 was dying, and key leaders such as Livingston and Clark were in disrepute. Louisianans had not joined in any effort to challenge the American government through insurrection, and neither had they supported Burr's plan to conquer Orleans Territory. The St. Domingue refugees who arrived in New Orleans were concerned about settlement and made no effort to challenge American control of Louisiana.

Between May 1809 and January 1810 approximately 2,731 St. Domingue planter refugees expelled from Cuba reached New Orleans, along with 3,102 free persons of color and 3,226 slaves. The municipal council of New Orleans made arrangements to house the refugees and formed a welfare committee that collected and distributed $5,000 in aid by August 1809. At first Claiborne detained the refugees aboard their ships in accordance with the federal law that had gone into effect in 1808 that prohibited the foreign importation of slaves. In response to protest over this decision, however, Claiborne forwarded a petition from the residents of New Orleans requesting that the federal government not apply the law of 1808 to the planter refugees' slaves. By July 1809 Claiborne, acting without authorization from Congress, allowed the refugees' slaves to land.[25]

Claiborne's expressed reason for his unilateral decision to admit the slaves was that the Orleans territorial government could not afford any other course of action. Imprisonment and expulsion were too costly. Imprisonment, Claiborne admitted, would also be "an inhuman act," and expulsion would have made the planters "as Paupers on this community, who are already sufficiently burthened with contributions for the poor, the sick and the aged Emigrants."[26]

Economic concerns were not the only reasons that Claiborne allowed the St. Domingue planters and their slaves to enter the territory, however. While Claiborne stated that he would "much rather that the Space" in Orleans society "had been preserved for native Citizens of the United States" and not French planter exiles and their slaves, he recognized that he might gain political support from the exiles and from French Louisianans in general. Edward

Livingston, who was always prepared to avail himself of an opportunity to gain support from the French Louisianan community, wrote a letter in support of a bill for repayment of any fines that the refugee planters had incurred as a result of importation of slaves to Orleans. Congress passed this bill, and the *Moniteur de la Louisiane* printed the law beside Livingston's letter on July 30, 1809. This upset Claiborne, who had also supported relief measures for the refugees. He sent a copy of this newspaper to Washington along with his own jealous comments. "In this way it is, that this man, [Livingston] feeds his popularity—he and his partisans here wish to make it believed to the French that to the influence of his Letter alone may be attributed the passage of the Law." It is clear that Claiborne believed that "he risked losing to another political rival the credit he had hoped to obtain in the Gallic community for his action on the slave issue."[27]

Jefferson's position on the arrival of St. Domingue planters and their slaves in Orleans Territory was clear. He was not pleased at the influx of so many foreigners because it threatened to delay the Americanization of the territory, but at the same time, however, he realized that the refugees were in severe distress and that Claiborne's decision to allow them to stay would make them loyal citizens.

> We should be monsters to shut the door against such sufferers. True, it is not a population we can desire, at that place because it retards the desired epoch of its becoming entirely American in spirit. no people on earth retain their national adherence longer or more warmly than the French. but such considerations are not to prevent us from taking up human beings from a wreck at sea. Gratitude will doubtless secure their fidelity to the country which has received them into its bosom.[28]

Jefferson was correct in his assessment. The planter refugees of St. Domingue were grateful, and "doubts regarding the loyalty of the French population in general and of the refugees in particular turned out to be groundless." The hostile political climate that Claiborne faced in the territory between 1804 and 1807 had vanished. This was proven by the actions of the territorial legislature in 1809. This legislature petitioned for admission to the Union as a state, but in making their case for statehood, the petitioners of 1809 were careful to dissociate themselves from those who had demanded statehood in 1804. They acknowledged that the federal government had reason to doubt the loyalty of Louisianans at that time, but said that Louisianans had demonstrated their patriotism to the United States since then, especially during the Burr Conspiracy, of which Edward Livingston and Daniel Clark, protest leaders in 1804, were a part.[29]

Republican Orleans and American Louisiana

A Considerable portion of the inhabitants of this territory thought Some years ago that they had a right to sollicit the incorporation of this Country into the Union. . . . Things are now materially altered The Legislature of this territory, come forward, several years after, to Sollicit that incorporation not so much as a right than as a favor. Whatever may have been the political considerations which induced your honorable body to reject the application which was made to you in 1804, those reasons exist no longer. The loyalty of the whole population of this Territory has since then been put to the trial in circumstances sufficiently critical for you now to be convinced that the inhabitants of Lower Louisiana are not undeserving of Confidence of the federal Government. The devoted spirit of our militia, when war with Spain was on the eve of breaking out Our unshaken fidelity in the midst of treasons and conspiracies, are irrefragable proofs of the incorruptibility of our honor and of the sincerity of our affection to our common Country.[30]

The memorialists went on to describe the "inconveniences" suffered under their present system of government. These were similar to those presented by Livingston in 1804 and included the governor's executive veto, "powers and functions imperfectly defined," public officers who did not understand the language of the majority, the inability to elect public officers, and "a complicated jurisprudence." Unlike the memorialists of 1804, however, those of 1809 did not attack Claiborne. In fact, they declared that their position under the territorial government "would be even more grievous, if the chief of our executive, to whom we owe the public testimony of our acknowledgement, had not united his efforts to ours, to better our situation."[31]

On March 12, 1810, the Orleans territorial legislature's petition for statehood was presented to the Senate, and in turn was sent to a select committee that prepared a bill to enable citizens of Orleans to form a constitution and a state government. On April 27 the Senate passed this bill by a margin of fifteen to eight, and it was sent to the House of Representatives. Because the House adjourned in May, nothing was done until it reconvened. Julien Poydras presented the bill to the House on December 17, 1810. It was referred to a committee that reported on it ten days later. On January 2, 1811, debate on the bill began in the House of Representatives. As in prior debates on the structure of territorial government, Federalist politicians opposed the passage of a bill that they believed would increase the political power of their rivals. Major issues of debate concerned the boundaries of the new state, specifically whether it should include West Florida. These were eventually established on the east at the original territorial boundary, except for a section east of the Iberville River. Debate on the western boundary, disputed by Spain, ended with an agreement to admit Louisiana as a state but to give Congress control over the eventual boundary location. The bill passed by a vote of seventy-seven to sixty-six. The majority of those who opposed it were New England Federalists.

On January 16, 1811, the bill to enable Louisianans to form a constitution and a state government was returned to the Senate and sent to a committee. The committee recommended several amendments on January 25. These included a stipulation that suffrage for the constitutional convention be limited to white male citizens of the United States, not simply white males; a provision that set the state's western and eastern boundaries; and the establishment of a percentage of revenue from sales of land to be used for roads and levees. As these were discussed, Federalist senator Samuel Dana of Connecticut made a last-ditch effort to block the bill with the introduction of an amendment to ensure that the admission of a new state could only occur with the consent of each state or by a constitutional amendment. This attempt failed, and the bill passed the Senate on February 7 and was returned to the House. On February 13 the House passed it, and the president signed it on February 16, 1811. Candidates were to be chosen from each of the parishes and districts but were not to exceed sixty in total. Free white males who were citizens of the United States and who had resided in the territory for one year and had paid taxes were eligible for election.

Residents of Orleans Territory, including Governor Claiborne, learned of the passage of the enabling law when the *Louisiana Gazette* printed it on April 9, 1811. Although he had received no official information, Claiborne informed the legislature of its passage the next day. The legislature set the total number of delegates at forty-five and scheduled the election for September 3.

Through the summer of 1811 Claiborne worried that his political opponents might be elected to the state convention. On July 18 he provided Julien Poydras with a list of those whom he feared in New Orleans. "Here Sir Intrigue is the order of the day! We have candidates innumerable! among many others, Livingston, Massero, Moreau Lislet, Fromentin, Dubigny, James Brown and Watkins have their partisans, & will I am told be warmly supported!"[32] Claiborne exaggerated the danger. Livingston ran, but as he was possibly next to Clark the most unpopular man in the territory at this time, he was not elected. The only men who could be considered to be the oldest opponents of the governor who were elected were Watkins, and Destréhan. On November 4, 1811, the convention met and elected a temporary president, Le Breton D'Orgenois, and then adjourned until November 18. On that date Poydras defeated Watkins to become president of the convention.

Jean Nöel Destréhan led the opposition to certain aspects of the enabling act, including possible separation of the new state from upper Louisiana, the publication of all laws for the U.S. government in English, and the loss of traditional privileges. Despite this opposition, however, the convention voted to form a constitution and state government on November 21. A committee framed a constitution modeled on that of Kentucky and presented it to the convention eight days later. After a ten-day recess during which the draft of the constitution was translated, the convention reconvened and began to examine each article. On January 22, 1812, the convention completed this work and unanimously voted to accept the constitution.

Madison submitted the constitution of Louisiana to Congress on March 3, 1812. The House debate on the bill was relatively short. An amendment was introduced to extend the eastern boundary of the state to the Pearl River, and the House passed the bill by a vote of seventy-nine to twenty-three. This was a clearly partisan vote, as twenty of the congressmen who voted against it were Federalists. On April 2, 1812, Louisiana became a state after the Senate passed the bill and Madison signed it.

Louisiana had entered the Union as Jefferson had hoped it would. The majority of the population was loyal to the United States. The territorial government was supportive, for the most part, of a Republican governor's administration. Claiborne's political opponents, so troublesome between 1804 and 1808, were crushed. The ever-suspicious Claiborne had tentatively reached this conclusion as he considered the possibility of running for governor.[33] In June 1811 he thought that "the Intriguers" would make "great exertions" at New Orleans "to prevent the election of any Native Citizen of the U. States" as governor, but that it was probable that they would fail. By December Claiborne was more confident and reported that information he received from his friends indicated that "*were the election now to come on*, the public Sentiment would be found favorable to my pretensions."[34]

Claiborne was not mistaken about his chances. He won the election for governor easily. On August 10, 1812, he noted that he had "obtained a majority in each and every county in the state." Claiborne received 2,757 votes; Jacques Villeré, a native of Louisiana who had served as a justice of the peace, as a colonel of militia, and as a member of the first state constitutional convention, received 945 votes; and Destréhan, who had been elected to carry Livingston's *Remonstrance* to Congress and had caused problems for Claiborne in the territorial government of 1806, received 145 votes.[35]

Jefferson's dream for Louisiana, the Federalists' nightmare, had come true. Louisianans had overwhelmingly elected a Republican governor. Louisiana was now part of a Republican empire and would help to support that party's national power in Washington.

Jefferson's plans succeeded for four reasons. First, he let nothing interfere with his plans for Louisiana. From the beginning until the end of his administration, Jefferson personally oversaw the process by which Louisiana was to be incorporated into the Union. He involved himself in the design of the structure of the government at every stage and had the powers of a king over the territory.

When Orleans Territory was organized according to Jefferson's wishes in 1804, it should have included a representative assembly, because the Northwest Ordinance stipulated that a U.S. territory was to have a representative assembly when 5,000 free white inhabitants lived there. Jefferson, however, believed that Louisianans were not yet capable of self-government and that the territory should become solidly settled by Americans before statehood could be considered.

Jefferson was not squeamish about bending the law if he thought circumstances demanded it. In defending Wilkinson's conduct in arresting suspected Burr associates in 1807, Jefferson had written that on "great occasions every good officer must be ready to risk himself in going beyond the strict line of the law, when the public preservation requires it."[36]

While he was steadfast in his goal for an American Republican Louisiana, Jefferson was wise enough to make small concessions that deflated the protest movement organized in 1804 before it became serious. This was the second reason for Jefferson's success. Jefferson advised Claiborne to appoint French Louisianans to the Legislative Council, in the minority of course, and also suggested that officers should know French and English if possible. He attempted to appoint judges who spoke both languages. The Jefferson administration also calmed fears about land titles by dropping certain restrictions and not seriously enforcing the prohibition against the slave trade or challenging the belief that the prohibition of the domestic slave trade to Louisiana was abolished in 1805.

Jefferson called for a House committee to examine the possibility of adjusting the Act for the Organization of Orleans Territory and the Louisiana District of 1804, and in 1805, through the Act for the Government of Orleans Territory, a representative assembly was established that had the power to nominate representatives for the Legislative Council. While this gave the citizens of Orleans a taste of representative government, it did not threaten the Jefferson administration's control over the territory because the governor still selected from the nominees and the president still appointed the governor, who had the power to veto any legislation passed by the territorial legislature, a power exercised in 1806.

At the national level, Jefferson's control of Louisiana between 1803 and 1809 was never threatened because his opponents could never muster enough votes to reject any of the legislation for Louisiana that he supported or designed. An Act Enabling the President to Take Possession of Louisiana, An Act for the Organization of Orleans Territory and the Louisiana District, and

An Act for the Government of Orleans Territory established the government structure for Orleans Territory. Although these acts were debated in their bill form, opponents of the bills, primarily Federalists and some western Republicans, were unable to block their passage or to alter them significantly.

Certainly the government of Orleans Territory was adjusted, as previously mentioned, through the three acts listed above, but this was done on Jefferson's terms. John Quincy Adams had described his effort to alter the bill for the organization of Orleans as a "feather against a whirlwind." The same might be said of the attempts made by others who organized and criticized the territorial government of Orleans in Washington during Jefferson's administration. Pierre Derbigny and Jean Nöel Destréhan left Washington disappointed in March 1805 because they were not able to muster enough support in either the Senate or the House for Livingston's *Remonstrance*. Even more futile were the later efforts of Daniel Clark and John Randolph of Roanoke to discredit Claiborne's administration of Orleans Territory. Jefferson, despite his reservations about Claiborne's abilities, supported his appointed governor against his critics, and Clark, Randolph, and their associates were unable to drum up enough support to seriously threaten Claiborne. With the support of a majority in Congress, then, Jefferson was able to ensure that Louisiana became part of his Republican empire.

The fourth and final reason for Jefferson's success was that some of the most prominent Louisianans involved in the protest movement against territorial government in 1804 lost popular support as a result of their activities in 1806 and 1807. Clark and Livingston were both associated with Aaron Burr in 1805 and 1806, and this involvement damaged their reputations. Clark's shooting of Claiborne in June 1807 did little to help his already flagging influence. His replacement as territorial delegate to Congress by Julien Poydras was almost inevitable. Livingston's public reputation was damaged when he defended his claim for New Orleans waterfront property. Jefferson involved himself in this local property dispute. In evicting Livingston from the Batture and ensuring that it was declared federal land, Jefferson won the praise of the majority of Louisianans and weakened the financial strength and influence of one of Claiborne's enemies. In the wake of the Burr Conspiracy and the Batture affair, the Claiborne and Jefferson administrations enjoyed a degree of popularity that they had never enjoyed in the territory of Orleans.

The Orleans Territory that James Madison inherited from Jefferson was loyal to the Union and Republican in its politics. This loyalty was demonstrated by the overwhelming victory of William Claiborne in Louisiana's first state gubernatorial election in 1812 and during the war with Great Britain that commenced during that year. In fact, Claiborne won election as Louisiana's first governor "in large part because the War of 1812 created new circumstances that fused foreign policy and domestic governance."[37]

"As Claiborne wrote to an anonymous correspondent in 1813, the war had created equally dangerous possibilities of 'insurrection, invasion, or eminent danger of invasion.'"[38] Claiborne and many other Americans in Louisiana were concerned about the possibility of an enemy within who might betray them and aid the British. The British hoped that this was true. Captain James Stirling of the British Royal Navy believed that the people of Louisiana were "unconnected by blood or long fellowships with the other states of America" and informed the first lord of the admiralty that a "considerable party might be informed of a separation from the United States." The British sent a broadside to the French and other Louisianans of foreign origin including the Spanish, British, and Italians, in 1814, stating that "the American *usurpation in this country must end.*" To further provoke Louisianans, the British threatened that they would welcome runaway slaves.[39]

Claiborne and the British misread the situation in Louisiana in 1814. There was no party or enemy within that could be organized to separate Louisiana from the United States. Louisianans were united in defense of their new state in 1815. "That the British faced a united opposition in Louisiana was in no small part their own doing. British planners vastly overestimated white dissatisfaction. White Louisianans saw distinct advantages to citizenship in the United States, and few had any love for the British. In addition, by threatening racial revolt, the British reinforced white solidarity."[40]

Even Frenchmen who were entitled to exemption marched. The French consul in New Orleans had seventy-five Frenchmen listed for exemption but declared that all but one waived exemption when Andrew Jackson called them to arms. St. Domingue refugees made up 28 percent of the Battalion of New Orleans, and refugee privateers in Barataria supplied Jackson with "800 soldiers and especially excellent gunners."[41] The participation of Louisianans of different national origins in the successful defense of that state during the Battle of New Orleans proved that Jefferson's vision for a Louisiana loyal to the United States was a reality, even if it was not yet entirely "American in spirit."

Conclusion

Protest against territorial government in Orleans Territory occurred in three stages. The first stage of organized protest against territorial government lasted from March 1804 until October 1805. Leaders organized supporters, and the territorial government administered by Claiborne was criticized in letters to officials in the Jefferson administration, in New Orleans newspapers, and in a petition to Congress.

In the second stage of protest, which lasted from approximately November 1805 until the final arrest of Aaron Burr in January 1807, opponents of territorial government were influential in the territorial House of Representatives established by an act of Congress in 1805. They also gained a foothold in the appointed Legislative Council and a voice in Washington, in the person of Daniel Clark, who won the election for territorial delegate to Congress in May 1806 over Claiborne's candidate. During this stage, opponents of territorial government became a political faction that challenged territorial government and, more specifically, Claiborne's administration of this government through legislation and speeches in the Orleans legislature and in the House of Representatives and Senate in Washington.

The last stage of the protest marks the decline of the faction. After they were implicated in the Burr Conspiracy, Daniel Clark and Edward Livingston, leaders of the party generally opposed to territorial government and specifically opposed to Governor Claiborne, lost influence in Orleans society. Clark's duel with Claiborne and Livingston's waterfront property acquisitions further contributed to the decline of the political fortunes of each man. The election of Julien Poydras, a French Louisianan planter and Claiborne's political ally, to Congress as territorial delegate marked the end of the real political influence of those who were involved in the original protest against territorial government that began in 1804.

The evolution of the three stages of the protest movement can only be understood, however, in the context of Jefferson's plan for Louisiana. Jefferson made small concessions to Louisianans on the issues of representation, slaves, land, and laws, but he let nothing interfere with his plan to see Louisiana incorporated as an American state in an "empire of liberty." It is clear that this was Jefferson's goal from the first day of American possession and that he considered the rights and privileges of Louisianans as subordinate to this goal. It is also equally clear, however, that Louisianans did not expect the author of the Declaration of Independence to rule over them as a king.[1]

In November 1803 Louisianans hoped that Pierre Clément Laussat's unauthorized promises of citizenship and statehood that were based on his embellished interpretation of the third article of the treaty of cession between France and the United States would be fulfilled immediately or soon after the United States took formal possession of the French colony. Citizenship and statehood would secure Louisianans' property and representation rights.

Jefferson's primary objective for Louisiana was not to satisfy Louisianans but to ensure that their home became an American state. Jefferson believed that Louisianans were incapable of self-government, and he was uncertain about their loyalty to the United States. Because he was not prepared to risk his project for an "empire of liberty" that included Louisiana, Jefferson supervised the establishment of a territorial government that was ultimately responsible to him. Under An Act Enabling the President to Take Possession of Louisiana, passed on October 31, 1803, the Republican-controlled Congress granted Jefferson the power to "vest all the Military, civil and judicial powers exercised by the officers existing government (under France) in such person and persons as the President of the United States shall direct." In effect, this act allowed Jefferson to rule Louisiana in the much the same manner as the French and Spanish had prior to the Louisiana Purchase. The president appointed one man, William Claiborne, to "exercise all the powers and authorities heretofore exercised by the Governor and Intendant."[2]

The act of October 31, 1803, was designed as a temporary measure to allow for American administration of Louisiana until Congress passed a new bill that clearly defined the structure and mechanics of government for the new territory. Etienne de Boré, mayor of New Orleans, wrote Jefferson and expressed his hope that Congress would at least grant Louisiana the "second stage" of territorial government. The Northwest Ordinance stipulated that when the population of a territory reached 5,000 free white males, a representative assembly would be established there. Jefferson, however, had already rejected the Northwest Ordinance as a model for the government of Orleans Territory with the expressed reason that it turned the laws of Louisiana "topsy-turvy."[3]

On March 26, 1804, Congress passed An Act for the Organization of Orleans Territory and the Louisiana District. Jefferson, who supported and helped to design this act, retained the powers that he was granted in the act of October 31, 1803. The president still appointed all government officials, and executive power would be vested in a governor, whom the president could remove at any time. The only real change was that the governor was to rule in concert with "thirteen of the most discreet individuals in the territory."[4] These men would be appointed by the president and would constitute the Legislative Council of the territory of Orleans.

Fears of political powerlessness and potential economic ruin motivated Louisianans of French and American origin to protest against the government established for Orleans Territory. The Jefferson administration ruled Orleans as a royal province. Jefferson selected and appointed fellow Virginian William Claiborne to rule within Orleans Territory. While he believed that Claiborne would loyally wield the almost absolute power entrusted to the governor of the territory of Orleans, Jefferson did not believe that Claiborne was ideal for the job. Between 1803 and 1807 Jefferson repeatedly but futilely asked James Monroe, who had served the American government in France and could speak French, to serve as governor. Jefferson clearly understood that Monroe would be more popular with French Louisianans than Claiborne, who could not speak their language.

Claiborne's inability to speak French made him instantly unpopular among Louisianans such as Etienne de Boré, the mayor of New Orleans, who believed that Louisiana should have a French-speaking governor. Boré, like many other Louisianans, was also disappointed that the act of March 26 did not grant a representative body to the inhabitants of Orleans. This, however, was not the only aspect of the act that upset Louisianans. Congress included a provision in this act that prohibited Louisianans from importing slaves from within and outside of the United States. Americans who planned to settle in Louisiana, however, were permitted to import their slaves into Louisiana, an obvious attempt to encourage American settlement of the territory.

Claiborne had tried to warn Secretary of State James Madison that Louisianans deemed the preservation of the slave trade essential. The governor based this conclusion on a report written to him by his agent Dr. John Watkins, who had toured the Louisiana parishes. Watkins had noted that "No Subject" was "so interesting to the minds of the inhabitants of all that part of the Country, which I have visited as that of the importation of brute Negroes from Africa" and that permission to import slaves would "better reconcile them to the Government of the United States than any other privilege which could be extended to the Country."[5]

Claiborne's letter of warning, written on March 1, 1804, was sent, with Watkins's report enclosed, too late to have any influence on Congress's deliberations about prohibition of the slave trade in Orleans Territory. On March 10 Claiborne reported that a paper from Washington describing the Senate's passage of a law prohibiting foreign importation of slaves to Orleans Territory had arrived, and that it had caused "great agitation" because the prohibition of this trade was considered a "serious blow at the Commercial and agricultural interest of the Province." The threat of the elimination of the slave trade, while not the only issue of concern that Louisianans had about territorial government, was the primary reason for the first meeting held to discuss grievances. Etienne de Boré, perhaps the most famous planter in Louisiana, presided over it and suggested that the assembly send representatives to Congress "to represent the grievances of Louisiana but especially the desire of the inhabitants for the continuation of the Slave trade, and their great Solicitude for Speedy relief from their present commercial embarrassments."[6]

Planters/merchants dominated the leadership of the protest movement against territorial government. The "key leaders" at a second meeting organized to protest grievances concerning the Act for the Organization of Orleans Territory and the Louisiana District were Etienne de Boré, Daniel Clark, Evan Jones, and Edward Livingston. Aside from Boré, Clark, and Jones, two other prominent planters played a major role in the protest movement. Jean Nöel Destréhan and Pierre Sauvé were elected to present the remonstrance that Edward Livingston had written for Congress.

The prohibition of the slave trade may have provoked Louisianan planters/merchants to protest the Act for the Organization of Orleans Territory and the Louisiana District, but there were other aspects of it that also caused anxiety about territorial government. In his *Remonstrance*, Livingston denied that there was any evidence to support the argument that Louisianans were incapable of self-government, as Claiborne and Jefferson had asserted.

Another subject of concern regarding the Act for the Organization of Orleans Territory and the Louisiana District was that Louisiana was not incorporated into the Union as a state, nor were Louisianans granted the rights of citizens. Livingston vainly argued that this was a violation of the third article of the treaty of cession. Furthermore, Congress had not even guaranteed a date for incorporation of Louisiana as a state. Livingston noted that Louisianans feared that Congress would delay statehood for years.

Along with Livingston, Boré attacked the lack of representation in the Act for the Organization of Orleans Territory and the Louisiana District in New Orleans newspapers in August 1804. For example, Boré cleverly referred to a letter that members of Congress had written to the inhabitants of Quebec in October 1774. To encourage the people of Quebec to resist British control, Congress reminded them that the first "grand right" of British colonies was "that of the people having a share of their government by their representatives chosen by themselves."[7]

The Act for the Organization of Orleans Territory and the Louisiana District went into effect on October 1, 1804. Protest against the act through newspaper editorials and Livingston's *Remonstrance* to Congress accomplished little. The *Remonstrance* envoys, Pierre Derbigny, Destréhan, and Sauvé, arrived in Washington in December 1804. They were bitterly disappointed that the Republican-dominated Congress failed to satisfy them on the issues of the slave trade, representation, and statehood. Jefferson's party had enough votes in Congress to ensure that the essential structure of territorial government in Orleans was maintained.

Despite the fact that he did not believe in immediate self-government for Louisianans, Jefferson recognized that the structure of territorial government might be adjusted to provide some measure of popular participation. The Act for the Organization of Orleans Territory and the Louisiana District was due to expire on October 1, 1805. Jefferson had at least appointed the House committee for the amelioration of the government of Louisiana on November 13, 1804. Jean Nöel Destréhan, Pierre Derbigny, and Pierre Sauvé had presented Livingston's *Remonstrance* to this committee but became upset with the chair of the committee, John Randolph, who appeared to have little interest in their cause.

In general, the envoys found little congressional support in their efforts to satisfy the grievances in the *Remonstrance*. This is not surprising since the Republicans controlled the Senate and the House. Randolph dismissed the grievances expressed in the *Remonstrance* as problems that were inevitable as a result of a sudden change of government. He did, however, recommend "every indulgence not incompatible with the interests of the Union . . . be extended to the inhabitants of the territory." This wording is significant, because it fits with Jefferson's view of Louisiana: the interests of the Union came before those of the people of Louisiana.[8]

While the envoys became impatient with Randolph's committee, they presented the *Remonstrance* to the Senate. A Senate committee presented a bill for the government of Orleans Territory that authorized Jefferson to "establish within the Territory of Orleans, a government in all respects similar (except as is herein otherwise provided) to that now exercised in Mississippi Territory." Congress passed An Act for the Government of Orleans Territory on March 2, 1805.[9]

Like Mississippi Territory, Orleans Territory was to be governed according to the Northwest Ordinance of 1787 and would therefore gain a "general assembly" of twenty-five elected white men and would be able to make nominations for the Legislative Council subject to the approval of the president. This at least satisfied Boré's earliest request to Jefferson for the "second stage" of territorial government. In addition to limited representation, An Act for the Government of Orleans Territory appeared to offer some satisfaction to Louisianans on another issue, or at least it did in the eyes of some Orleans lawyers, who declared that the total prohibition against the slave trade in force under Act for the Organization of Orleans Territory and the Louisiana District was eliminated. James Brown, district attorney for Orleans District, described the lawyers' argument in a letter to Albert Gallatin, secretary of the treasury, on December 11, 1805.

Brown claimed that the "prevailing anxiety for the importation of slaves has induced every man capable of reading the acts of Congress to examine the regulations in force on that subject" and that the lawyers of the territory had "unanimously expressed an opinion" that the "prohibitions against the importation of Slaves contained in the Act of 1804 for the Government of this Territory" were "repealed by the Act of 1805 extending to us the second grade of Government." The act of 1805 extended to the people of Orleans "all the *rights, privileges,* and *advantages* enjoyed by the inhabitants of Mississippi Territory, and consequently that our citizens possess the right of importing into this Country any slaves already legally introduced into any of the States." Brown was willing to stake his career on this interpretation of the 1805 act. He offered to resign his post if the opinion that he had "been pressed to give on this subject was deemed erroneous or thought to compromise the interests of the Government." Apparently neither Gallatin nor anyone else in the Jefferson administration challenged Brown's interpretation. He continued to serve as district attorney until December 23, 1807, when he resigned because of a "variety of personal circumstances."[10]

While the act of 1805 opened the possibility for the resumption at least of the domestic slave trade, it was also apparent by 1805 that the federal government could do little to stop the foreign importation of slaves into Orleans Territory. John Watkins, who had become mayor of New Orleans, explained why this was so to John Graham, secretary of the territory, in September 1805. Watkins argued that "public opinion of the necessity of more slaves" and "the high price of labor" ensured that "all the vigilance of the best organized Government upon earth" would "not be sufficient to prevent their introduction." Louisiana's proximity to the Caribbean, Watkins asserted, made it a certainty that slaves would be smuggled in from St. Domingue, Jamaica, and Martinique. "The people," Watkins concluded, "ask for new Negroes, you refuse them they say they must have Slaves of some kind and will and do therefore procure such as they can get."[11]

Watkins's prediction that Louisianans would get slaves in any way possible was correct. Smuggling along a relatively unguarded coastline was an avenue for the supply of slaves throughout the territorial period. In addition, Louisianan planters continued to receive slaves through "legal" domestic importation. Slaves smuggled from the Caribbean were brought into Orleans Territory through the bays and bayous along the coast, and South Carolina legally exported hundreds of slaves to Louisiana. The Jefferson administration's efforts to stop the illegal traffic were minimal at best, and the omission of

Conclusion

specific regulations concerning the slave trade under the act of 1805 indicated that the administration had either reconsidered or neglected to reinforce the total prohibition on the slave trade to Louisiana. Orleans planters' initial fears of ruin as a result of federal legislation prohibiting the slave trade began to subside.

While the Act for the Government of Orleans Territory gave Louisianans hope that the federal government had reconsidered a total elimination of the slave trade, another piece of federal legislation passed on the same day, March 2, 1805, renewed fears about Washington's territorial administration. Those in Orleans who owned property believed that they might lose it under the Act for the Adjustment of Land Titles. This act set conditions for ownership that many could not meet, such as a requirement that owners of land had to have been at least twenty-one years of age and the head of a family before 1800 and had cleared, cultivated, and resided on their land by that date. Not surprisingly, landowners in Orleans organized to protest the Act for the Adjustment of Land Titles.

John W. Gurley, register of lands for the Eastern District of Orleans Territory, warned Madison that the protest against the Act for Adjustment of Land Titles was a serious problem that contributed to general discontent about territorial government.

> Indeed there can be no doubt that the law is regarded by the enemies of ye Government as a powerfull engine by which to excite discontent in this territory. Already it is represented as intended to rob the people of their rights to destroy equitable titles which exist in the Country and finally become the instrument of the most vexatious oppression.[12]

Two men in particular who stood to lose a fortune under the Act for Adjustment of Land Titles were Daniel Clark and Edward Livingston, who had speculated in lands granted by the Spanish government to the Marquis de Maison Rouge and the Baron de Bastrop. Secretary of the Treasury Albert Gallatin singled Clark out for an investigation of one of his major land titles under the Act for Adjustment of Land Titles.[13]

When the elected territorial House of Representatives established by the Act for the Government of Orleans Territory first met in November 1805, it petitioned Congress for a repeal of the Act for Adjustment of Land Titles. Albert Gallatin took this petition and Gurley's warning seriously and recommended that Congress amend the act. An amended act passed by Congress on April 21, 1806, eliminated the age qualification for land ownership if the owner had inhabited his land ten years prior to December 30, 1803. The act was further amended on March 3, 1807, and the age requirement for

Conclusion

land ownership was entirely repealed, as was the head of family requirement. While the amendments did not satisfy all of the grievances of Orleans citizens concerning land titles, they did eliminate the greatest sources of unrest.

Limited concessions regarding land titles and the continuation of the slave trade provided some satisfaction to those engaged in protest against territorial government. The Jefferson administration also made limited attempts to satisfy the citizens of Orleans on their third major charge against territorial government: lack of representation. The Act for the Government of Orleans Territory established a representative body, the territorial House of Representatives. Jefferson made an attempt to satisfy the citizens of Orleans of French and American origins by ordering Claiborne to appoint French and American Louisianans to the Legislative Council. Of course in keeping with his plan for an American state, Americans were to hold the majority of seats.

It is also apparent that Jefferson wanted to win over those who were key figures in the protest movement against territorial government and political enemies of his governor, William Claiborne. In 1804 Jefferson recommended Daniel Clark, Evan Jones, Etienne de Boré, Jean Nöel Destréhan, and Pierre Sauvé to the Legislative Council. Jefferson's attempt to win over these men with council appointments was risky because these men could have caused Claiborne considerable trouble if they decided to oppose him on the Legislative Council. Fortunately for Jefferson and his appointed governor, Jones, Boré, Clark, and other appointees that they influenced, such as Robert Dow and Michael Cantarelle, decided to demonstrate their opposition to territorial government through resignation, and Claiborne was able to reject the appointments of Destréhan and Sauvé because they were to sail to Washington to present Livingston's *Remonstrance* to Congress. Claiborne was able to replace those who resigned from the Legislative Council with men of his own choice who would be loyal to his administration. Between October 1, 1804, and November 1, 1805, Claiborne ruled with his Legislative Council without opposition from within territorial government.

The decision of Boré, Clark, and Jones to resign from the Legislative Council, designed to embarrass Claiborne, was a political mistake. It limited their attacks on Claiborne's administration to newspapers and unofficial petitions. With the election of the territorial House of Representatives, however, the political tide turned against Claiborne. Etienne de Boré and Jean Nöel Destréhan were among the nineteen representatives chosen, and the majority of representatives revealed their sympathy for those engaged in protest against the territorial government through their election of Destréhan as president of the House of Representatives on November 5, 1805. In making their nominations for the Legislative Council, the representatives elected Joseph Bellechasse, Jean Nöel Destréhan, Pierre Derbigny, Pierre Sauvé, Evan Jones, John W.

Conclusion

Gurley, Jean Baptiste McCarty, Joseph Villars, and Francois Dannemours. Of these nominations, Claiborne recommended Gurley, McCarty, Bellechasse, and Sauvé to the president. Jefferson selected Gurley, McCarty, Bellechasse, Destréhan, and Sauvé for the Legislative Council. It is not surprising that the president decided not to appoint Derbigny and Jones because they had clearly demonstrated their hostility to Claiborne's territorial administration. To ensure that Derbigny was not selected, Claiborne informed the president that he had doubts Derbigny was "altogether an American in spirit or attachment." Of Jones, Claiborne could only write that "it was not in his power to say anything that would recommend him" to the president's confidence.[14]

The House of Representatives and Legislative Council of Orleans Territory made political life very difficult for Governor Claiborne in 1806. Claiborne's opponents were in the majority in the territorial House. In addition to the petition against the Act for the Adjustment of Land Titles, the House passed legislation to prohibit those who held any other office under the American government from serving in either the House of Representatives or the legislature. This was an obvious attempt to ensure that Claiborne would not have the support of appointed U.S. territorial government officials in government. Claiborne acknowledged that he had received this piece of legislation on May 6, 1806, and then vetoed it.

Claiborne's political situation further deteriorated when the Orleans territorial legislature elected Daniel Clark as territorial delegate to Congress on May 19, 1806. Claiborne's administration would now come under fire from a Louisianan in Washington. In Orleans Territory, Claiborne's political opponents within the territorial government continued to cause problems for him after Clark's election. The legislature approved An Act Declatory of the Laws Which Continue to Be in Force in the Territory of Orleans, an act designed to ensure that American common law would not entirely replace the system of laws that had existed under the French and Spanish governments.

On May 26, 1806, Claiborne vetoed the Act Declatory of the Laws. The Legislative Council responded by threatening to dissolve the legislature. Jean Nöel Destréhan and Pierre Sauvé had already resigned their positions for the expressed reason of poor health on May 21 and May 22, respectively, but it is clear that their resignations were motivated by the legislative clash with Claiborne. On May 28 the House of Representatives produced a "statement of motives" to declare that taxpayers' money spent on the territorial government was wasted because the governor had rejected "the most essential and salutary measures taken by the Legislature." Claiborne's veto of the Act Declatory of the Laws was unacceptable, the signers of the statement argued, since "the most inestimable benefit for a people" was "the preservation of its laws, usages, and habits and that it was only by such a preservation that transition from one government to another was possible." The signers concluded that opposition to passage of the law by Claiborne and some members of the House of Representatives could only be considered as a conspiracy designed to throw the people of Orleans "into the frightful chaos of the common law."[15]

For the signers of the statement, an alternative to common law was the civil law that "nineteen-twentieths of the population of Louisiana" understood. The "wisdom of the civil law" was recognized across Europe. Eventually the signers were satisfied in their wishes for protection of civil laws. In the face of popular support for a civil law code, Claiborne approved a law code on March 2, 1808, designed by James Brown and Moreau Lislet, modeled on Napoleon's Code Civil and the Projet of 1800. Claiborne was not entirely pleased to adopt the Digest of Civil Laws Now in Force in the Territory of Orleans. He would have preferred a code based on American common law but admitted that he was forced to do so "by the strongest consideration of Justice and policy."[16]

As the Jefferson administration and Governor Claiborne made limited concessions to the people of Orleans on issues of concern to them such as the slave trade, land titles, representation, and law, key leaders of the faction opposed to the territorial administration in Orleans damaged their own political careers through actions that proved unpopular with the citizens of the territory. Both Daniel Clark and Edward Livingston were implicated in the Burr Conspiracy. This taint of treason haunted Clark until his death in 1813, and his efforts to clear himself by turning on James Wilkinson made the situation worse for him as the Jefferson administration and later the Madison administration stood by the general. In addition to his association with Burr, Clark shot the governor of Orleans. These two actions ensured that few people would want to be associated with Clark.

Edward Livingston damaged the popularity that he had gained as writer of the remonstrance to Washington in 1804 through his widely unpopular decision to claim land on the New Orleans's waterfront in 1807. At the request of his governor, Jefferson personally involved himself in the case, and Livingston's claim was overturned. This caused Livingston some financial hardship, and he spent a good deal of time and energy in contesting the decision against him. Livingston would eventually recover from the Batture Affair but not during the territorial period.

By September 1808 Claiborne was able to report that the actions of the faction that had challenged him for so long had made him more popular than he ever had been as governor. Proof that the faction was in decline was demonstrated by the election of Julien Poydras, Claiborne's longtime political ally, in January 1809 as territorial delegate to Congress and the moderate tone of

Conclusion

a request made by the legislature for statehood in May 1809. The petitioners made a clear effort to differentiate themselves from those who had demanded statehood in 1804 and whose motives were suspect.

Finally, Claiborne's decision to allow St. Domingue refugees and their slaves into Orleans Territory probably also contributed to the loss of support among the ancient Louisianans for the faction that had opposed Claiborne. Claiborne had responded to their requests to support the refugees and their slaves. Furthermore, as Jefferson had recognized, this decision would earn the gratitude of the refugees. Livingston certainly realized this in his desperate effort, as his colleague Clark saw it, to regain some popularity through his support for a bill to repay any fines that the refugees had incurred as a result of landing and caring for their slaves.

In 1812 Louisiana became a state in the Union. William Claiborne, who was targeted as the incompetent administrator of territorial government by Louisianans in 1804, was overwhelmingly elected as the state's first governor. Louisianans, while possibly not completely as American as Jefferson and his governor would have liked, found that their interests in slaves, land, and representation were not destroyed under territorial government. By 1812 the majority of Louisianans considered that their interests were tied to those of the United States. Given this, it is not surprising that Louisianans of every national origin answered Andrew Jackson's call to arms and aided him in a successful effort to defend their country from British invasion at the Battle of New Orleans in January 1815.

Overall, Jefferson succeeded in his attempt to bring Orleans Territory into the Union under his own terms. This was due to the fact that those in Washington who opposed his plans for the administration of Louisiana were always in the minority. As those who presented Edward Livingston's *Remonstrance* to Congress discovered, Jefferson always had enough support to overcome resistance by Federalists, some western Republicans, and those Louisianans who were dissatisfied with his rule of the territory. Throughout his presidency, Jefferson was able to set the pace for incorporation of Orleans into the Union. He also did what he could to ensure that the majority of officers who served in the Orleans territorial legislature were loyal to the government of the United States. Jefferson clearly believed that Americans could be trusted to serve the nation's or Jefferson's interests. Because of this he favored American immigration to Louisiana and the involvement of Americans in territorial government, preferably in the majority. Jefferson's primary objective, after all, was to make sure that Louisiana became an American and not a French state in the union.

It is fair to describe Jefferson's control of Louisiana during his presidency as imperial. While under Jefferson's rule inhabitants of Orleans gained the ability to elect a House of Representatives and the Legislative Council, final executive power rested with his appointed governor, who was empowered to veto legislation passed by the territorial House of Representatives, whose members Jefferson could remove if he believed it necessary. Given Jefferson's dominance in Washington, the voting concessions that Jefferson granted Louisianans posed little or no risk to his administration of Orleans territorial government.

For the most part, the Republican Party followed Jefferson's lead on the administration of Louisiana. There were a few exceptions among western members of the party who saw the interests at least in terms of Mississippi trade and slavery as linked with those of Louisianans. If these western Republicans had united with Federalists over slavery and government and had opposed the Jefferson administration, the president might have had to make real compromises, but this was never to be because the majority of Federalists opposed democratic government and the slave trade for Orleans Territory.

Did Jefferson's virtually unchallenged control over the political fate of Orleans Territory set a precedent for future western expansion? Before Louisiana became a state, American territories were to be incorporated into the Union through a process outlined in the Northwest Ordinance of 1787. This ordinance granted rights of election for a representative body and statehood when the territorial population reached a certain number. Jefferson, without serious challenge from Republicans or Federalists, dismissed the ordinance as impracticable for Orleans Territory. He was not seriously challenged over the passage of the Act for the Organization of the Territory of Orleans in 1804, which he helped to design and which gave him the power to appoint his own governor and Legislative Council. This could be seen as an extension of presidential and federal power over territories. The inhabitants of Orleans who protested against the territorial government learned that Jefferson in such a position of power could do whatever he pleased to their territory. Future western settlers would learn the same lesson: that the rights of citizens did not necessarily apply to the inhabitants of a new territory. In each new territory, the federal government established the privileges that territorial inhabitants would have until they were granted rights of citizens of the United States.

Conclusion

Notes

Introduction

1. Joseph G. Dawson, *The Louisiana Governors* (Baton Rouge: Louisiana State University Press, 1990), 84.

2. Sarah Paradise Russell, "Cultural Conflicts and Common Interests: The Making of the Sugar Planter Class in Louisiana, 1759–1853" (Ph.D. diss., University of Maryland, 2000), 53–56.

3. Address of the Colonists of Louisiana to Pierre Clément de Laussat, December 1803, Pierre Clément Laussat Papers, Historic New Orleans Collection; Petition of the Inhabitants of Louisiana to the American Commissioners, New Orleans, December(?) 1803, Laussat Papers.

4. John Preston Moore, *Revolt in Louisiana: The Spanish Occupation, 1766–1770* (Baton Rouge: Louisiana State University Press, 1976), 103.

5. Ibid.

6. Ibid., 113.

7. Ibid., 141.

8. Ibid., 145.

9. Ibid., 184.

10. Daniel Usner, *Indians, Settlers and Slaves in a Frontier Exchange Economy* (Chapel Hill: University of North Carolina Press, 1992), 119.

11. Ibid.

12. Arthur P. Whitaker, "The Commerce of Louisiana and the Floridas at the End of the Eighteenth Century," *Hispanic American Review* 8(2) (May 1928): 192.

13. Ibid., 192–193.

14. Ibid.

15. Clinton N. Howard, *The British Development of West Florida* (Berkeley: University of California Press, 1947), 7–8.

16. Robert R. Rea, *Major Robert Farmar of Mobile* (Tuscaloosa: University of Alabama Press, 1990), 35.

17. Ibid.

18. Howard, *West Florida*, 12.

19. Ibid., 11–12.

20. Rea, *Major Robert Farmar*, 41.

21. Ibid.

22. Ibid.

23. Ibid.

24. Howard, *West Florida*, 28.

25. Ibid.

26. Ibid.

27. Andrew McMichael, *Atlantic Loyalties: Americans in Spanish West Florida, 1785–1810* (Athens: University of Georgia Press, 2008), 15

28. Ibid.

29. Eric Beerman, *Victory on the Mississippi, 1779*, ed. and trans. Gilbert C. Din, in *The Louisiana Purchase Bicentennial in Louisiana History*, Vol. 2, *The Spanish Presence in Louisiana, 1763–1803*, ed. Gilbert C. Din (Lafayette: Center for Louisiana Studies, University of Southwestern Louisiana, 1996), 198.

30. Ibid., 200.

31. McMichael, *Atlantic Loyalties*, 16.

32. Ibid.

33. Ibid.

34. Thomas Jefferson to Albert Gallatin, November 9, 1803, ibid., 100–101.

35. Thomas Jefferson to DeWitt Clinton, December 2, 1803, *Thomas Jefferson Papers* (Washington, D.C.: Library of Congress, 1974); Everett S. Brown, *The Constitutional History of the Louisiana Purchase* (Berkeley: University of California Press, 1920), 98.

36. Clarence Carter, ed., *The Territorial Papers of the United States*, Vol. 9, *The Territory of Orleans, 1803–1812* (Washington, D.C.: U.S. Government Printing Office, 1940), 89.

37. Glover Moore, *The Missouri Controversy, 1819–1821* (Louisville: University of Kentucky Press, 1953), 271.

Chapter 1

1. John G. Clark, *New Orleans, 1718–1812: An Economic History* (Baton Rouge: Louisiana State University Press, 1970), 58.

2. Usner, *Indians, Settlers and Slaves*, 108.

3. Alexander DeConde, *This Affair of Louisiana* (New York: Charles Scribner's Sons, 1976), 32.

4. Ibid., 33.

5. Lewis W. Newton, *The Americanization of French Louisiana: A Study of the Process of Adjustment Between the French and the Anglo-American Populations of Louisiana, 1803–1860* (New York: Arno Press, 1980), 12.

6. Ibid.

7. DeConde, *This Affair of Louisiana*, 34–35.

8. It is estimated that the value of the 1801 cotton crop at New Orleans surpassed $800,000. Sugar was first successfully mass-produced in Louisiana on the plantation of Etienne de Boré, in 1795. By the time of the Louisiana Purchase there were sixty to seventy sugar plantations on both banks of the Mississippi around New Orleans that produced roughly 5.3 million pounds of sugar. The cotton and sugar boom increased the need for agricultural goods from the western United States. The "upriver" trade, which brought flour and whiskey to New Orleans, was valued in excess of $1 million in 1799. Clark, *New Orleans*, 209–219; James Pitot, *Observations on the*

Colony of Louisiana, 1796–1802, trans. Henry C. Pitot (Baton Rouge: Louisiana State University Press, 1979), 60.

9. Clark, *New Orleans*, 209.

10. The elder Daniel Clark lived in West Florida before he established himself in New Orleans. Governor George Johnstone appointed him receiver general of quit-rents on the governing council. Cecil Johnson, *British West Florida, 1763–1783* (New Haven, Conn.: Yale University Press, 1943), 62, 72.

11. Nolan Harmon Jr., *The Famous Case of Myra Clark Gaines* (Baton Rouge: Louisiana State University Press, 1946), 10.

12. Daniel Coxe was the younger brother of Tench Coxe. Tench Coxe became Daniel Clark's "Philadelphia agent. . . . He negotiated the purchase of ships required for Daniel's voyages, took out insurance on the vessels and their cargoes and made arrangements for the dispatch of the large quantities of cotton and pelts purchased for Daniel's account by the latter's partner, Daniel Clark Jr." Jacob E. Cooke, *Tench Coxe and the Early Republic* (Chapel Hill: University of North Carolina Press, 1978), 336.

13. Samuel Flagg Bemis, *Pinckney's Treaty: America's Advantage from Europe's Distress, 1783–1800* (New Haven, Conn.: Yale University Press, 1960), 44.

14. Ibid., 71.

15. Ibid., 267.

16. Ibid., 276.

17. Ibid., 273–274.

18. Ibid., 280.

19. Ibid., 274–275.

20. Ibid., 280.

21. "Despatches from the United States Consulate in New Orleans, 1801–1803, I," *American Historical Review* 32(4) (July 1927): 802 (hereafter cited as "Despatches, New Orleans, 1801–1803").

22. Ibid., 802–803.

23. Clark, *New Orleans*, 220.

24. "Despatches, New Orleans, 1801–1803," 803.

25. Ibid., 804. Hulings had trained as a doctor but, according to Pickering, had resided in New Orleans for "a number of years . . . where he had acquired a decent fortune."

26. Daniel Clark to Timothy Pickering, June 14, 1798, *Despatches from the United States Consuls in New Orleans, 1798–1807* (Washington, D.C.: National Archives and Records Service, 1958).

27. "Despatches, New Orleans, 1801–1803," 805. In the late 1790s the government of Spain wanted to halt American immigration to Louisiana. Because a U.S. consul would protect and assist Americans in Louisiana, the Spanish government considered this official as a danger to its interests and therefore refused to recognize him.

28. Ibid.

29. Johnson, *British West Florida*, 70–72.

NOTES

30. Ibid., 72.

31. Ibid., 72, 140.

32. Clark, *New Orleans*, 234.

33. Ibid., 272.

34. "Despatches, New Orleans, 1801–1803," 805.

35. Timothy Pickering to William Empson Hulings, May 18, 1799, *Diplomatic and Consular Instructions of the Department of State, 1791–1801* (Washington, D.C.: National Archives, 1945).

36. On August 15, 1799, Jones formally resigned his commission in the Louisiana militia. He seemed to believe that this made him an American citizen. On November 14, 1799, however, Pickering informed Jones that citizenship required that he become naturalized. "Despatches, New Orleans, 1801–1803," 806, 812.

37. Ibid., 806.

38. Pickering to Jones, December 20, 1799, *Diplomatic and Consular Instructions*. Jones continued to act as consul on the orders of Pickering. "Altho the Governor (de Casa Calvo) refuses to receive you as Consul of the United States yet as he knows that you have that office confided to you by the American government . . . I hope you will interpose by representation otherwise to prevent any of our citizens from being oppressed and injured until you shall be formally received in your Consular character."

39. "Despatches, New Orleans, 1801–1803," 812. In this same letter Jones mentioned that Hulings received a letter "forbidding him . . . from performing any Consular act whatever."

40. Ibid., 809.

41. Ibid., 810, 814.

42. Ibid., 814–815.

43. Ibid., 807. Jones continued to be active in matters of American interest in Louisiana. On August 10, 1801, he wrote to Jefferson to report that many American seamen died in New Orleans annually as a result of their inability to obtain medical care. Jefferson "recommended a bill for the establishment of a marine hospital in New Orleans because he believed the number of suffering Americans was larger than Jones reported and because it was necessary for a large part of the West to trade through the city." William E. Rooney, "Thomas Jefferson and the Marine Hospital," *Journal of Southern History* 22(2) (May 1956): 168–169.

44. Daniel Clark, *Proofs of the Corruption of General James Wilkinson* (1809; repr., Freeport, N.Y.: Books for Libraries Free Press, 1970), 142.

45. "Despatches, New Orleans, 1801–1803," 817.

46. George Dangerfield, *Chancellor Robert R. Livingston of New York* (New York: Harcourt, Brace, 1960), 317.

47. Ibid.

48. Ibid.

49. Ibid., 326.

50. Ibid., 330.

51. Ibid., 337.

52. DeConde, *This Affair of Louisiana*, 103.

53. Harmon, *Famous Case of Myra Clark Gaines*, 42.

54. Laussat to Pichon, August 24, 1803, in Arthur P. Whitaker, *The Mississippi Question, 1795–1803* (New York: D. Appleton-Century, 1934), 32 n.5.

55. Clark to Madison, March 8, 1803, "Despatches, New Orleans, 1801–1803," 332.

56. Ibid., 334.

57. Ibid.

58. Dangerfield, *Chancellor Robert R. Livingston*, 354.

59. Ibid., 327, 354–355.

60. Clark to Daniel Coxe, January 31, 1807, *Transcript of Record, The City of New Orleans Appellant, vs. Myra Clark Gaines, Appeal from the Circuit Court of the U.S. for the Eastern District of Louisiana, Filed October 19, 1883* (New Orleans: Tulane University Special Collections), 1528–1529.

61. Clark to Madison, April 27, 1803, "Despatches, New Orleans, 1801–1803," 336.

62. Ibid., 338.

63. Ibid.

64. Ibid.

65. Dangerfield, *Chancellor Robert R. Livingston*, 359.

66. Ibid.

67. Albert H. Bowman, "Pichon, the United States and Louisiana," *Diplomatic History* 1(3) (Summer 1977): 257–270.

68. Ibid., 261.

69. Ibid., 265.

70. Dangerfield, *Chancellor Robert R. Livingston*, 359.

71. Ibid., 362.

72. After the cession, Clark complained less about the actions of Laussat, who began to cooperate with the American government, but it is clear that he still regarded the prefect as an enemy. In a letter to Madison, Clark considered it necessary to note that Laussat had allowed the officers of a "French national Cutter," the *Terreur*, to impress a number of French sailors so that the secretary of state could "know the real Character of a man, who has on all occasions shewn himself the implacable Enemy of the Americans and the American Government." Clark to Madison, October 4, 1803, Carter, *Territorial Papers*, 9:70.

73. Clark to Madison, August 12, 1803, "Despatches, New Orleans, 1801–1803," 346.

74. Ibid.

75. Thomas Jefferson to William Claiborne, July 17, 1803, *Jefferson Papers*; Thomas Jefferson to Daniel Clark, July 17, 1804, ibid. Jefferson believed that Clark would be able to answer some of his questions but declared that "it would doubtless be necessary" to "distribute them among the best qualified to answer them." Jefferson left it to Clark to select those best qualified.

76. Report enclosed with Clark to Madison, September 8, 1803, Carter, *Territorial Papers*, 9:3.

77. Ibid., 38–44.

78. Clark to Madison, September 20, 1803, ibid., 54–55.

79. [Endorsed] Daniel Clark, September 29, 1803, ibid., 63–64.

NOTES

80. Clark to Madison, October 21, 1803, ibid., 82.

81. Carter, *Territorial Papers*, 9:82.

82. Ibid., 84.

83. Ibid.

84. Madison to Clark, September 16, 1803, ibid., 55.

85. Ibid.

86. Clark to Madison, October 20, 1803, "Despatches, New Orleans, 1801–1803," 350.

87. Ibid., 347.

88. Ibid., 348.

89. Ibid., 349–350.

90. Ibid.

91. Carter, *Territorial Papers*, 9:89–90.

92. Madison to Claiborne, October 31, 1803, ibid., 91.

93. Ibid., 93.

94. Ibid., 96.

95. DeConde, *This Affair of Louisiana*, 204.

96. Ibid.; Pierre Clément de Laussat, *Memoirs of My Life*, ed. Robert Bush; trans. Agnes-Josephine Pastawa (Baton Rouge: Louisiana State University Press, 1978), 78–79.

97. Carter, *Territorial Papers*, 9:130.

98. Laussat, *Memoirs of My Life*, 75.

99. Ibid. This is the same Etienne de Boré who was the first to mass-produce sugar in Louisiana.

100. Ibid.

101. Ibid., 60.

102. Ibid.

103. Ibid., 75

104. Clark to Madison, November 29, 1803, "Despatches, New Orleans, 1801–1803," 355.

105. Ibid., 354.

106. Ibid.

107. "Despatches, New Orleans, 1801–1803," 356, n.43.

108. Laussat, *Memoirs of My Life*, 78.

109. Ibid., 126 n.19.

110. Daniel Clark to James Madison, December 3, 1803, Arthur Whitaker, ed., "Another Dispatch from the United States Consulate in New Orleans," *American Historical Review* 38(2) (January 1933): 291–295.

111. Clark to Madison, December 13, 1803, "Despatches, New Orleans, 1801–1803," 354.

112. Wilkinson to Madison, December 20, 1803, Clark, *Territorial Papers*, 9:138.

113. DeConde, *This Affair of Louisiana*, 208.

114. Wilkinson to Henry Dearborn, December 21, 1803, Carter, *Territorial Papers*, 9:139.

Chapter 2

1. James Morton Smith, ed., *The Republic of Letters: The Correspondence between Thomas Jefferson and James Madison 1776–1826*, Vol. 2, *1790–1804* (New York: W. W. Norton, 1995), 1287; "An Act Enabling the President to Take Possession of Louisiana," Carter, *Territorial Papers*, 9:89. Jefferson had presented a draft of this act to Secretary of the Treasury Albert Gallatin, who in turn sent it to Republican senator John Breckinridge of Kentucky. Breckinridge and his friends apparently approved of Jefferson's bill since the bill that they submitted to the Senate on October 22, 1803, was a "verbatim copy except for a slightly different enacting preface" of the Jefferson draft Gallatin sent to Breckinridge. James Scanlon, "A Sudden Conceit: Jefferson and the Louisiana Government Bill of 1804," *Louisiana History* 9(2) (1968): 141–142; "Commission of William C. C. Claiborne as Temporary Governor," Carter, *Territorial Papers*, 9:143.

2. Madison to Claiborne, October 31, 1803, Carter, *Territorial Papers*, 9:92.

3. Ibid.; Brown, *Constitutional History of the Louisiana Purchase*, 101. The Senate committee was appointed to write a bill for the temporary government of Louisiana on December 5, 1803. Breckinridge presented the bill to the Senate on December 30, 1803.

4. Claiborne to Madison, January 2, 1804, *The Official Letter Books of W. C. C. Claiborne, 1801–1816*, ed. Dunbar Rowland (Freeport, N.Y.: AMS Press, 1972), 1:322.

5. In addition to the advice received from Daniel Clark on making a selection for governor, the Jefferson administration received information from John Pintard, who had lost his fortune in Alexander Hamilton's scheme to fund the national debt and who moved to New Orleans in 1803 in the hopes of rebuilding his fortune. Pintard asserted that the governor should know the French language "as the medium of an interpreter will render his situation extremely awkward and irksome." John Pintard to Albert Gallatin, September 14, 1803, Carter, *Territorial Papers*, 9:51.

6. Monroe to Jefferson, March 15, 1804, *Jefferson Papers*.

7. Benjamin Morgan to Chandler Price, August 11, 1803, Carter, *Territorial Papers*, 9:8.

8. Walter Prichard, "Selecting a Governor for the Territory of Orleans," *Louisiana Historical Quarterly* 27(4) (1948): 312–313.

9. Ibid., 378; Joseph Hatfield, *William Claiborne: Jeffersonian Centurion in the American Southwest* (Lafayette: University of Southwestern Louisiana, 1976), 123.

10. Claiborne to Madison, December 27, 1804, Rowland, *Letter Books of W. C. C. Claiborne*, 1:313; Claiborne to Madison, January 2, 1804, ibid., 327.

11. Claiborne to Madison, January 2, 1804, ibid., 326–327.

12. Ibid.; Deposition of George W. Morgan, January 28, 1804, Carter, *Territorial Papers*, 9:182.

13. Carter, *Territorial Papers*, 9:182.

14. Claiborne to Madison, February 7, 1804, ibid., 178.

15. Etienne de Boré to Thomas Jefferson, February 20, 1804, *Jefferson Papers*; Translation Duplicate, Boré to Jefferson, February 20, 1804, Carter, *Territorial Papers*, 9:185.

16. Carter, *Territorial Papers*, 9:185.

17. Ibid.

18. Ibid., 185–186.

19. Ibid.

20. Jack Ericson Eblen, *The First and Second United States Empires, Governors and Territorial Government, 1784–1912* (Pittsburgh: University of Pittsburgh Press, 1968), 33–40; Harry Ammon, *James Monroe: The Quest for National Identity* (New York: McGraw-Hill, 1971), 54.

21. Eblen, *First and Second United States Empires*, 42.

22. Thomas Jefferson to Albert Gallatin, November 9, 1803, *Jefferson Papers*; Carter, *Territorial Papers*, 9:100; Jefferson to Breckinridge, November 24, 1803, *Jefferson Papers*; Lowell Harrison, *John Breckinridge, Jeffersonian Republican* (Louisville: Filson Club, 1969), 167.

23. Section 1 of the act divided Louisiana into two sections. The land ceded by France to the United States that was south of the thirty-third parallel became Orleans Territory, and the section of the purchase to the north of the thirty-third parallel became the Louisiana District.

24. Carter, *Territorial Papers*, 9:203.

25. Ibid., 204.

26. Ibid., 205–206.

27. Brown, *Constitutional History of the Louisiana Purchase*, 98.

28. Daniel Clark to James Madison, "Despatches, New Orleans, 1801–1803," 348; William Claiborne to James Madison, January 10, 1804, Carter, *Territorial Papers*, 9:329; William Claiborne to Thomas Jefferson, January 16, 1804, *Jefferson Papers*.

29. January 7–8, 1804, "John Quincy Adams Diary, 1 January 1803–4 August 1809," in *The Adams Papers Owned by the Adams Manuscript Trust and Deposited in the Massachusetts Historical Society* (Boston: Massachusetts Historical Society, 1954).

30. Everett S. Brown, ed., *William Plumer's Memorandum of the Proceedings in the United States Senate, 1803–1807* (New York: Macmillan, 1923), 103–104.

31. Brown, *Constitutional History of the Louisiana Purchase*, 45.

32. *Annals of the Congress of the United States*, 8th Congress, 1st Session (Washington, D.C.: Gales and Seaton, 1852), 13:234.

33. Lynn W. Turner, *William Plumer of New Hampshire, 1759–1850* (Chapel Hill: University of North Carolina Press, 1962), 115.

34. Oliver Wolcott Jr. to Roger Griswold, January 14, 1804, Oliver Wolcott Jr. Papers, Connecticut Historical Society, Hartford.

35. Aleine Austin, *Matthew Lyon, "New Man" of the Democratic Revolution, 1749–1822* (University Park: Pennsylvania State University Press, 1981), 133–138.

36. Hilda Neatby, *Quebec: The Revolutionary Age, 1760–1791* (Toronto: McClelland and Stewart, 1966), 136; Philip Lawson, *The Imperial Challenge: Quebec and Britain in the Age of the American Revolution* (Montreal: McGill-Queen's University Press, 1989), 134–135.

37. Neatby, *Quebec*, 136.

38. Ibid.

39. Ibid., 137.

40. Joseph J. Casino, "Anti-Popery in Colonial Pennsylvania," in *Early American Catholicism, 1634–1820*, ed. Timothy Walch (New York: Garland, 1988), 237–239.

41. Ibid., 239.

42. David Hackett Fischer defined Pickering as a Federalist of the "old school." These were the "most mature leaders of the federal cause in 1800." They were born between 1720 and 1760 and were involved in the American Revolution. By 1800, according to Fischer, they were losing influence and "stubbornly" clung to "traditional Whiggish principles." David Hackett Fischer, *The Revolution of American Conservatism: The Federalist Party in the Era of Jeffersonian Democracy* (New York: Harper and Row, 1965), 1–2.

43. Brown, *Plumer's Memorandum*, 107–108.

44. Ibid., 109.

45. Ibid., 108–109; *Annals of the Congress*, 8th Congress, 1st Session, 13:234.

46. Brown, *Plumer's Memorandum*, 110–111.

47. Ibid., 111.

48. *Annals of the Congress*, 8th Congress, 1st Session, 13:238.

49. Ibid., 239. Senator William Plumer saw the letter but does not mention its date. The date of the letter is not mentioned in the *Annals of the Congress*. The clue that this is Claiborne's letter of January 2 is that Plumer made notes on the passages of the letter that were read to the Senate, and these match Claiborne's letter of January 2, 1804. Brown, *Plumer's Memorandum*, 112.

50. *Minutes of the Ninth Convention for Promoting Abolition of Slavery and Improving the Condition of the African Race* (Philadelphia: Solomon Conrad, 1804), 40–41.

51. *Annals of the Congress*, 8th Congress, 1st Session, 13:238, 940. This petition was presented on January 23, 1804.

52. Ibid., 111–112.

53. Brown, *Plumer's Memorandum*, 130.

54. Ibid., 112, 117.

55. Ibid., 116, 114.

56. Ibid., 111–112. This was a reference to the slave revolution of 1791.

57. Ibid., 117–118.

58. Ibid., 120–121.

59. *Annals of the Congress*, 8th Congress, 1st Session, 13:240; Brown, *Plumer's Memorandum*, 124, 127.

60. Brown, *Plumer's Memorandum*, 127.

61. Ibid., 127–129.

62. Ibid., 132.

63. *Annals of the Congress*, 8th Congress, 2nd Session, 13:244.

64. Ibid., 250.

65. Ibid.

66. Ibid., 251–252.

67. February 18, 1804, "John Quincy Adams Diary," *Adams Papers*; Brown, *Plumer's Memorandum*, 143–144.

68. Brown, *Plumer's Memorandum*, 144.

69. Ibid.

70. Ibid., 145.

71. Ibid., 146; Charles Adams, ed., *Memoirs of John Quincy Adams* (Philadelphia: J. B. Lippincott, 1874), 295.

72. *Annals of the Congress*, 8th Congress, 1st Session, 13:1054.

73. Ibid., 1058–1059, 1061.

74. Ibid., 1063.

75. Ibid., 1059–1060

76. Ibid., 1054–1055, 1060.

77. Ibid., 1069–1071.

78. Ibid., 1073.

79. Ibid., 1074–1075.

80. Ibid.

81. Ibid., 1186.

82. Ibid., 1187; Claiborne to Madison, January 31, 1804, Carter, *Territorial Papers*, 9:352–353.

83. *Annals of the Congress*, 8th Congress, 1st Session, 13:1188; Brown, *Constitutional History of the Louisiana Purchase*, 143.

84. *Annals of the Congress*, 8th Congress, 1st Session, 13:1193–1194.

85. Ibid., 1207.

86. Ibid., 1229.

87. Ibid., 1229–1230.

88. Seth Ames, ed., *Works of Fisher Ames* (Boston: Little Brown, 1854), 2:249.

Chapter 3

1. Claiborne to Madison, March 1, 1804, Rowland, *Letter Books of W. C. C. Claiborne*, 2:13–14.

2. Carl Brasseaux, *Acadian to Cajun: The Transformation of a People, 1803–1877* (Jackson: University Press of Mississippi, 1992), 4–5.

3. "Dr. Watkins's Report," Rowland, *Letterbooks of W. C. C. Claiborne*, 2:10. Claiborne had already informed Madison of his view that "a Complete Representative Government would be most pleasing to the French Inhabitants—they have been encouraged by Mr. Laussat to expect similar political privileges to the Citizens of the United States." Claiborne to Madison, February 25, 1804, Carter, *Territorial Papers*, 9:191.

4. Claiborne to Madison, March 2, 1804, Rowland, *Letterbooks of W. C. C. Claiborne*, 2:14.

5. Claiborne to Madison, March 10, 1804, ibid., 25. It is likely that this is Benjamin Tupper, who, along with other "subscribers, merchants, traders and others of the City of New Orleans," signed a recommendation for William Brown as collector of customs. John M. Geltson to Thomas Jefferson, September 1, 1804, Carter, *Territorial Papers*, 9:289–290.

6. Claiborne to Madison, March 10, 1804, Rowland, *Letter Books of W. C. C. Claiborne*, 2:25; Claiborne to Madison, March 16, 1804, ibid., 25, 46. This Benjamin Tupper was not the one who served in the American Revolution in Massachusetts and moved west with the Ohio Company. See William Chaffin, *Brigadier Benjamin Tupper of the Revolutionary Army and of the Ohio*

Company (Marietta, Ohio: Leader Print,1880). Albert Gallatin confirmed this in a letter to Jonathan Russell written on September 24, 1804: "I had no doubt that Benjamin Tupper who was appointed Receiver of public monies at Marietta was different from the Benjamin Tupper whom you had known in France. There is now at New Orleans another Tupper who arrived there from France last winter or spring, who is said to be a man of talents but unprincipled. He does not hold any office under Government, unless the Government of New Orleans has given him one, which is not probable. From the time of his arrival, he has been very troublesome, and is considered as the first promoter of the popular meetings and subsequent memorial of the inhabitants of Louisiana, whose prejudices in favor of the slave trade he artfully excited for that purpose." Albert Gallatin to Jonathan Russell, September 25, 1804, "Letters of Jonathan Russell, 1801–1822," ed. Worthington C. Ford, *Massachusetts Historical Proceedings* 47 (1913–1914): 294–295.

7. Claiborne to Madison, March 16, 1804, Rowland, *Letter Books of W. C. C. Claiborne*, 2:25

8. *Ordinance Providing for the Establishment of a Bank*, March 12, 1804, Rowland, *Letter Books of W. C. C. Claiborne*, 2:29–30.

9. Claiborne to Madison, March 16, 1804, ibid., 42.

10. Ibid., 25. Claiborne probably received this account from Dr. John Watkins, who, according to the governor, "had attended the meeting with a view of using his best efforts to give a proper direction to their deliberations." Because Watkins had acted as Claiborne's agent in the parishes of Louisiana in January 1804, it is likely that he attended the meeting on Claiborne's behalf or by his instruction. Claiborne to Madison, March 16, 1804, ibid., 42–43.

11. Ibid. Mr. Detrion was Jean Nöel Destréhan, who was a prominent sugar planter selected by Laussat to serve on his Conseil de Ville. Claiborne to Madison, July 13, 1804, Carter, *Territorial Papers*, 9:261.

12. Ibid., 44.

13. Ibid., 44–45.

14. Ibid.

15. Mr. Mericult is probably John F. Merieult, and Mr. Pitot is probably James Pitot. Both merchants signed the "Memorial to Congress of the Merchants of New Orleans" of January 9, 1804. Carter, *Territorial Papers*, 9:158. James Pitot was a "bosom friend of Boree [sic]." "Characterization of New Orleans Residents," July 1, 1804, Carter, *Territorial Papers*, 9:252; Claiborne to Madison, March 16, 1804, Rowland, *Letter Books of W. C. C. Claiborne*, 2:46.

16. Rowland, *Letter Books of W. C. C. Claiborne*, 2:46.

17. Ibid.

18. Ibid., 47.

19. Ibid.

20. Ibid., 85, 221.

21. Claiborne to Jefferson, April 15, 1804, Carter, *Territorial Papers*, 9:222.

22. Claiborne to Madison, May 3, 1804, Rowland, *Letter Books of W. C. C. Claiborne*, 2:124. For Madison's letter to Claiborne of February 6, 1804, see Carter, *Territorial Papers*, 9:176–177.

23. Rowland, *Letter Books of W. C. C. Claiborne*, 2:124–125.

24. Claiborne to Madison, May 8, 1804, ibid., 134.

NOTES

25. Brown, *Constitutional History of the Louisiana Purchase,* 149.

26. Derbigny to Claiborne, March 13, 1804, Rowland, *Letter Books of W. C. C. Claiborne,* 2:48–49; Bellechasse to Claiborne, March 13, 1804, ibid., 48; Claiborne to Bellechasse, March 17, 1804, ibid., 49.

27. Claiborne to Madison, May 23, 1804, ibid., 160; Jefferson to Claiborne, April 17, 1804, Carter, *Territorial Papers,* 9:225.

28. Claiborne to Gallatin, May 23, 1804, Rowland, *Letter Books of W. C. C. Claiborne,* 2:160–161.

29. Claiborne to Jefferson, June 3, 1804, *Jefferson Papers;* Jefferson to William Duane, February 7, 1808, ibid.; Jefferson to William Claiborne, April 17, 1806, ibid.

30. Claiborne to Jefferson, May 29, 1804, ibid.; Claiborne to Poydras, February 25, 1804, Rowland, *Letter Books of W. C. C. Claiborne,* 2:175–176.

31. Claiborne to Jefferson, May 29, 1804, *Jefferson Papers.* As Clark worked to have himself appointed governor, Morgan declared that it was his wish that Clark "not be appointed to this important office" because he was "deficient in dignity of character & sterling veracity to fill the office of governor" and because Clark was "liked by few Americans here but those dependant upon him." Benjamin Morgan to Chandler Price, August 18, 1803, Carter, *Territorial Papers,* 9:9; Claiborne to Madison, May 29, 1804, Rowland, *Letter Books of W. C. C. Claiborne,* 2:176; Prichard, "Selecting a Governor," 312.

32. William B. Hatcher, *Edward Livingston: Jeffersonian Republican and Jacksonian Democrat* (Baton Rouge: Louisiana State University Press, 1940), 76, 106.

33. Ibid., 76–77, 93–94.

34. Ibid., 96–97.

35. Ibid., 99.

36. Ibid., 109.

37. Claiborne to Madison, March 10, 1804, Rowland, *Letter Books of W. C. C. Claiborne,* 2:26.

38. George Dargo, *Jefferson's Louisiana: Politics and the Clash of Legal Traditions* (Cambridge, Mass.: Harvard University Press, 1975), 31.

39. Claiborne to Madison, June 3, 1804, Rowland, *Letter Books of W. C. C. Claiborne,* 2:191; James Pitot and Edward Livingston to Governor Claiborne, June 1, 1804, Carter, *Territorial Papers,* 9:241–242. The historians Charles Gayarre and William B. Hatcher state that the public meeting took place on June 1. Charles Gayarre, *History of Louisiana: The American Domination* (New York: William J. Widdleton, 1866), 17; Hatcher, *Edward Livingston,* 111. Because Pitot and Livingston state in their letter of June 1 that the planters assembled "yesterday," the meeting must have occurred on May 31, 1804. James Pitot and Edward Livingston to Governor Claiborne, June 1, 1804, Carter, *Territorial Papers,* 9:241–242.

40. Claiborne to Madison, June 3, 1804, Rowland, *Letter Books of W. C. C. Claiborne,* 2:190–191.

41. Claiborne to Madison, June 3, 1804, Carter, *Territorial Papers,* 9:242.

42. Ibid.

43. Gayarre, *History of Louisiana,* 17; Everett S. Brown, "The Orleans Territory Memorialists

to Congress, 1804," *Louisiana Historical Quarterly* 1 (January 1917): 99–102. Marietta Le Breton indicates, however, that Brown mistakenly believed that Petit, Pitot, Jones, and Livingston were chosen to draft the memorial in the March meeting called by Tupper. Marietta Le Breton, "A History of the Territory of Orleans" (Ph.D. diss., Louisiana State University, 1969), 121 n.61. Pierre Petit was an English-born merchant said to "be perfectly acquainted with all the Resources and Interests of the Province, friendly to the American Government active & energetick, in short a man of very influential character." "Characterization of New Orleans Residents," July 1, 1804, Carter, *Territorial Papers*, 9:252.

44. After Claiborne had seen the *Remonstrance* he stated that it was "generally acknowledged that Mr. Edward Livingston is the author of this production, and indeed he himself avows it." Claiborne to Madison, July 26, 1804, Rowland, *Letter Books of W. C. C. Claiborne*, 2:269–270. An examination of the handwriting of the memorial proves that Claiborne was correct. *Memorial to Congress from the Planters Merchants and Other Inhabitants of Louisiana*, Edward Livingston Papers, Princeton University.

45. Claiborne to Madison, July 26, 1804, Rowland, *Letter Books of W. C. C. Claiborne*, 2:270.

46. Hatcher, *Edward Livingston*, 113.

47. *Annals of the Congress*, 8th Congress, 2nd Session, 14:1598.

48. Ibid.

49. Ibid., 1600–1601.

50. Ibid., 1602–1603.

51. Ibid., 1604.

52. Ibid., 1605.

53. Ibid., 1605–1606. The territorial population requirement for statehood was 60,000.

54. Ibid., 1606.

55. Ibid., 1607.

56. Ibid., 1607–1608.

57. Hatch Dent to James McCulloch, July 14, 1804, Carter, *Territorial Papers*, 9:265.

58. Claiborne to Madison, July 1, 1804, Rowland, *Letter Books of W. C. C.* Claiborne, 2:233–234. Dent stated that the election of the remonstrance envoys to Congress occurred at the meeting of July 1. He described this meeting of Sunday, July 1, as a "larger meeting" that had been called for at a previous meeting, which would have been that of May 31, described earlier. There is no record of the meeting that Claiborne declared was scheduled for "Sunday next" in his letter to Madison of July 1. Dent to McCulloch, July 14, 1804, Carter, *Territorial Papers*, 9:265; Claiborne to Madison, July 13, 1804, ibid., 261.

59. Claiborne to Jefferson, July 1, 1804, *Jefferson Papers*, 246.

60. Ibid.

61. Claiborne to Madison, June 29, 1804, ibid., 245.

62. Ibid., 247. There is no report previous to this to indicate that Wilkinson was involved with "the popular party." Wilkinson sailed for New York on April 25, 1804. Claiborne to Madison, April 25, 1804, ibid., 234.

63. Claiborne to Madison, July 3, 1804, Rowland, *Letter Books of W. C. C. Claiborne*, 2:235

64. *Proceedings of City Council Meetings*, July 7, 1804, City Archives, New Orleans Public Library.

65. Claiborne to Madison, July 12, 1804, Rowland, *Letter Books of W. C. C. Claiborne*, 2:244–245. The identity of these nine men has never been established. Some of them may have served Spain in the militia formed by the "free people of color." Their names might be included among fifty-five of those militiamen who petitioned Claiborne to be allowed to continue to serve the American government in January 1804. Carter, *Territorial Papers*, 9:174–175.

66. Claiborne to Madison, July 5, 1804, Rowland, *Letter Books of W. C. C. Claiborne*, 2:236; Claiborne to Madison, July 12, 1804, ibid., 2:244–245; Marcus Christian, "Demand By Men of Color for Rights in Orleans Territory," *Negro History Bulletin* 36(3) (1973): 54–57.

67. Rowland, *Letter Books of W. C. C. Claiborne*, 2:238.

68. Claiborne to Madison, July 13, 1804, Carter, *Territorial Papers*, 9:261.

69. Ibid.

70. Claiborne to Madison, July 14, 1804, Rowland, *Letter Books of W. C. C. Claiborne*, 2:249.

71. *Louisiana Gazette*, July 24, 1804.

72. Claiborne to Madison, July 26, 1804, Rowland, *Letter Books of W. C. C. Claiborne*, 2:270–271.

73. This is an obvious reference to Clark, Jones, and Livingston.

74. Claiborne to Madison, July 26, 1804, Rowland, *Letter Books of W. C. C. Claiborne*, 2:270–271.

75. Ibid.

76. *Louisiana Gazette*, August 7, 1804. Claiborne had supporters writing in newspapers whom he never mentioned. Even before the *Remonstrance* was published, anonymous authors who called themselves the "Friends of the Laws" wrote that those who joined with the "few persons" who had "lost by the change of their situation" to "make representation for reform of the laws" were "acting against reason, even the interest of this country." Louisianans enjoyed profitable commerce, paid "no taxes," and would soon enjoy the blessings of "the law of *Habeas Corpus*," which would secure property and trial by jury. "You never have been so happy," the "Friends" informed Louisianans. "Believe us, be quiet!" *Le Telegraphe*, June 27, 1804, *Jefferson Papers*.

77. *Moniteur de la Louisiane*, August 9, 1804; Worthington Chauncey Ford, ed., *Journals of the Continental Congress, 1784–1789*, Vol. 1, *1774* (Washington, D.C.: Government Printing Office, 1904), 104–113.

78. *Moniteur de la Louisiane*, August 9, 1804; *Louisiana Gazette*, August 14, 1804.

79. Joseph Briggs to Jefferson, August 17, 1804, Carter, *Territorial Papers*, 9:276–278.

80. Le Breton, "History of the Territory of Orleans," 122.

81. Claiborne to Jefferson, August 30, 1804, *Jefferson Papers*.

82. Ibid.

83. Claiborne to Madison, September 17, 1804, Rowland, *Letter Books of W. C. C. Claiborne*, 2:336–337.

84. *Petition of the Inhabitants & Colonists of Louisiana*, September 17, 1804, Carter, *Territorial Papers*, 9:297.

85. Claiborne to Madison, September 20, 1804, Rowland, *Letter Books of W. C. C. Claiborne*, 2:337–338.

86. Claiborne to Madison, September 27, 1804, Carter, *Territorial Papers*, 9:299.

87. Claiborne to Madison, October 1, 1804, ibid., 344–345.

Chapter 4

1. Jefferson to Claiborne August 30, 1804, *Jefferson Papers*. John Roman was John Romain, an influential planter of Attakapas. William Wykoff was an early American settler of Opelousas. Dubuys was Gaspard Dubuys, a merchant and magistrate. Canatarelle was Michael Cantarelle, commandant of the Acadian Coast. George Pollock was a wealthy New Orleans merchant originally from Ireland. Dr. Robert Dow was born in Scotland but had resided in Louisiana for thirty years. "Orleans Characters," *Letters of Application and Recommendation during the Administration of Thomas Jefferson, 1801–1809* (Washington, D.C.: National Archives, 1962).

2. Claiborne to Jefferson, August 30, 1804, *Jefferson Papers*.

3. "Orleans Characters." Carter suggests that this list "was drawn up by Evan Jones for Wilkinson and supplemented by a second list by La Bigarre; Wilkinson then sent them on to Jefferson, who annotated and indexed them as one document." Carter, *Territorial Papers*, 9:257, 258 n.12. Jefferson's annotations to the list included comments on Derbigny, Destréhan, Sauvé, Jones, and La Bigarre. His comments on Derbigny, Destréhan, and Sauvé were based on those made in the letter that Claiborne wrote to Jefferson on July 13, 1804.

4. Carter, *Territorial Papers*, 9:253, 255.

5. Ibid., 255, 258.

6. Ibid., 248, 251

7. See ibid., 138.

8. Ibid., 249, 252.

9. Ibid., 257.

10. Jefferson to Claiborne, August 30, 1804, ibid., 283.

11. Jefferson to Madison, August 16, 1804, *Madison Papers* (Washington, D.C.: Library of Congress, 1964).

12. The details of this "transaction" are not known. Claiborne stated that he had sent papers on this subject to the secretary of state. Carter states that this communication has not been found. Carter, *Territorial Papers*, 9:308. It is most likely that Claiborne is referring to Jones's speculation in West Florida lands. Spanish land sale records indicated that Jones owned 40,000 arpents of land. *State Department Territorial Papers, Orleans Series*, August 15, 1805 (Washington, D.C.: National Archives, 1958).

13. Jones to Claiborne, October 8, 1804, *State Department Territorial Papers, 1764–1813*.

14. In this issue of the *Union*, it was also reported that Benjamin Tupper, "of the firm of Tupper and Foley, Merchant in this City, late of Boston," had died on October 13 (probably of

yellow fever). Tupper had called the first meeting to protest the system of government established for Louisiana by the U.S. government. *Union*, October 15, 1804.

15. Ibid., October 20, 1804.

16. Claiborne to Madison, October 8, 1804, Rowland, *Letter Books of W. C. C. Claiborne*, 2:349.

17. Claiborne to Madison, October 13, 1804, Carter, *Territorial Papers*, 9:310.

18. *View of the Political and Civil Situation of Louisiana; from the Thirtieth of November 1803 to the First of October, 1804 by a Native* (Philadelphia, 1804), 16.

19. Ibid., 17.

20. Ibid., 18–19.

21. Ibid., 22.

22. Claiborne to Madison, October 16, 1804, Rowland, *Letter Books of W. C. C. Claiborne*, 2:352–353.

23. Ibid., 354–358.

24. Claiborne to Madison, October 22, 1804, Carter, *Territorial Papers*, 9:312–313.

25. Ibid., 312.

26. Rowland, *Letter Books of W. C. C. Claiborne*, 2:374. George Mather was described in 1803 as a resident of the colony, probably born a British subject. Eugene Dorcier, according to Claiborne, was born in Switzerland, served in the American Revolution, and then immigrated to Louisiana, where he acquired "a handsome little property." La Bigarre or Jones characterized him as a former "dancing master in Philadelphia" and who was "of good disposition and fair character; tho destitute of influence." William Donaldson was born in England. He spoke French and was considered a "merchant of respectability and property." Carter, *Territorial Papers*, 9:10, 255, 277.

27. *Louisiana Gazette*, October 26, 1804.

28. Claiborne to Madison, October 26, 1804, Rowland, *Letter Books of W. C. C. Claiborne*, 2:375–376.

29. Claiborne to Madison, October 27, 1804, Carter, *Territorial Papers*, 9:314–315.

30. Claiborne to Madison, October 29, 1804, ibid., 317.

31. Claiborne to Madison, November 5, 1805, ibid., 320.

32. Claiborne to Madison, November 18, 1804, Rowland, *Letter Books of W. C. C. Claiborne*, 2:393. William Kenner, according to Claiborne, was "an American merchant possessing Considerable property in the City [New Orleans]" and was "a man of good understanding" who spoke French. Claiborne was relieved that Poydras accepted his appointment and considered it "a happy contrast to the part acted by Mr. Jones, Clarke & others." Carter, *Territorial Papers*, 9:277; Rowland, *Letter Books of W. C. C. Claiborne*, 2:390–391.

33. Claiborne to Madison, November 19, 1804, Carter, *Territorial Papers*, 9:334.

34. Jefferson to Claiborne, December 2, 1804, *Jefferson Papers*.

35. Claiborne to Jefferson, December 2, 1804, ibid.

36. Ibid.

37. Jefferson to Claiborne, December 2, 1804, ibid.

38. *Annals of the Congress*, 8th Congress, 2nd Session, 14:727–728.

39. Ibid., 1014.

40. Henry Adams, *John Randolph* (Boston: Houghton, Mifflin, 1894), 119.

41. Thomas Paine, *To the French Inhabitants of Louisiana*, September 22, 1804, in *The Complete Writings of Thomas Paine*, ed. Philip S. Foner, 964–965 (New York: Citadel Press, 1945).

42. Thomas Paine to Jefferson, January 25, 1805, *Jefferson Papers*.

43. Brown, *Plumer's Memorandum*, 222.

44. Ibid., 222–223.

45. February 15, 1805, "John Quincy Adams Diary," *Adams Papers*.

46. This was first published as a pamphlet in 1804, and then in the *Louisiana Gazette*, March 15, 1804. The seventeen-page pamphlet version is in the *Early American Imprints Series*, No. 7163.

47. *Louisiana Gazette*, March 15, 1804.

48. Ibid.

49. Ibid.

50. Ibid.

51. Ibid.

52. Ibid.

53. *Annals of the Congress*, 8th Congress, 2nd Session, 14:28, 20.

54. *Louisiana Gazette*, March 26, 1804; *Annals of the Congress*, 8th Congress, 2nd Session, 14:1017–1019.

55. *Louisiana Gazette*, March 26, 1804; *Annals of the Congress*, 8th Congress, 1st Session, 13:1017–1019.

56. *Annals of the Congress*, 8th Congress, 1st Session, 13:1018.

57. *Annals of the Congress*, 8th Congress, 2nd Session, 14:1015.

58. Ibid.

59. Ibid., 1016–1017.

60. Ibid., 59–60; Brown, *Constitutional History of the Louisiana Purchase*, 160–161.

61. *Louisiana Gazette*, June 11, 1805; *Annals of the Congress*, 8th Congress, 2nd Session, 14:61.

62. Thomas Abernethy, *The Burr Conspiracy* (New York: Oxford University Press, 1954), 20–21. Burr's political career in the East was over because he had killed Alexander Hamilton in a duel on July 11, 1804.

63. *Annals of the Congress*, 8th Congress, 2nd Session, 14:1209, 69, 1215, 1676.

64. "An Act for the Government of Orleans Territory," March 2, 1805, Carter, *Territorial Papers*, 9:405–407.

65. In a letter to Madison, Claiborne reported that it was likely that "Mr. Livingston's intimacy with Mr. Prevost will prove injurious;—they lodge in the same House and have already purchased in co-partnership some property in this City of considerable value." Claiborne to Madison, December 10, 1804, ibid., 348. Prevost was a native of New York and Aaron Burr's stepson. After arriving in New Orleans he married Evan Jones's sister. When James Monroe was appointed minister to France, Burr requested that his stepson be selected to serve as Monroe's

secretary. Monroe agreed "but with misgivings about Prevost's character—which reflected his distrust of Burr more than any known shortcoming in the stepson." Ammon, *James Monroe*, 114.

66. Brown turned down his appointment as judge of the superior court on the grounds that it would subject him to the loss "of a moment peculiarly favorable to the advancement" of his "private interest" and was "more serious to a loss of 3000 Dollars Annually." Brown to Jefferson, January 8, 1805, Carter, *Territorial Papers*, 9:365.

67. John Prevost to Madison, December 19, 1804, ibid., 356–357.

68. James Brown to John Breckinridge, January 22, 1805, ibid., 378–380.

69. Claiborne to Madison, January 4, 1805, ibid., 362.

70. Claiborne to Madison, January 13, 1805, ibid., 368.

71. Claiborne to Madison, January 10, 1805, ibid., 367.

72. *Louisiana Gazette*, February 8, 1805.

73. Claiborne to Madison, February 17, 1805, Carter, *Territorial Papers*, 9:393–394.

74. *Louisiana Gazette*, February 15, 1805.

75. Claiborne to Madison, February 17, 1805, Carter, *Territorial Papers*, 9:393–394.

76. Isaac Briggs to Jefferson, February 9, 1805, *Jefferson Papers*.

77. Claiborne to Madison, January 26, 1804, ibid., 380.

78. Ibid., 380–381; Claiborne to Jefferson, January 29, 1804, ibid.

79. Jefferson to Claiborne, March 14, 1805, ibid.

80. Jefferson to Madison, March 23, 1805, Carter, *Territorial Papers*, 9:416 n.88.

81. Claiborne to Jefferson, May 4, 1805, Rowland, *Letter Books of W. C. C. Claiborne*, 3:37.

82. Claiborne to Madison, March 18, Carter, *Territorial Papers*, 9:420.

83. The *Louisiana Gazette* published news it received from Washington on the bill for the government of Orleans Territory, but this news was generally received two months after an event occurred. For example, on March 19 the *Gazette* published the bill that Giles introduced to the Senate on January 30.

84. Jefferson to Claiborne, March 14, 1805, Carter, *Territorial Papers*, 9:416. It is most probable that Derbigny was the deputy that Jefferson referred to; Jefferson already knew him through Claiborne's descriptions.

85. Ibid.

86. The "people" knew of the memorial to Congress, and on March 15, 1805, the *Louisiana Gazette* published the memorial envoys' *Reflections on the Cause of the Louisianans respectfully submitted by their agents*, so it was also public knowledge that the "agents" demanded statehood for Louisiana.

87. Claiborne to Madison, April 21, 1805, Carter, *Territorial Papers*, 9:438.

88. Claiborne to Madison, April 29, 1805, ibid., 445–446.

89. Claiborne to Madison, May 4, 1805, Rowland, *Letter Books of W. C. C. Claiborne*, 3:38–39.

90. *Louisiana Gazette*, June 11, 1805. Randolph may have deliberately delayed the committee's work on Livingston's memorial, but there is no direct evidence of this. What is certain is that Randolph became involved in other issues that were apparently of more interest to him. In January 1805 he began a personal crusade against speculation in the Yazoo Land Claim in the

House. Debate on this issue ended on February 2, but a week later Randolph became deeply involved in the impeachment proceedings against Federalist justice Samuel P. Chase. The trial lasted until March 1. Adams, *John Randolph*, 116–153.

91. *Louisiana Gazette*, June 11, 1805.

92. Ibid.

93. Ibid.

94. Claiborne to Madison, June 6, 1805, Rowland, *Letter Books of W. C. C. Claiborne*, 3:79.

95. Jefferson wrote a governor's commission for Claiborne on June 8, 1805. His commission and the act "further providing for the government of the Territory of Orleans" became effective on July 3, 1805. Carter, *Territorial Papers*, 9:467.

96. *Acts Passed at the First Session of the First Legislature of the Territory of Orleans* (New Orleans: James M. Bradford, 1805), 358–372.

97. Claiborne to the Legislative Council, July 5, 1805, Rowland, *Letter Books of W. C. C. Claiborne*, 3:111–113.

Chapter 5

1. Claiborne to Madison, August 6, 1805, Carter, *Territorial Papers*, 9:489.

2. Abernethy, *Burr Conspiracy*, 25–30; Hatcher, *Edward Livingston*, 126–127.

3. The Secretary of the Treasury to Allan B. Magruder, James Brown, and Felix Grundy, July 8, 1805, Carter, *Territorial Papers*, 9:469.

4. Jennie Mitchell and Robert Calhoun. "The Marquis de Mason Rouge, the Baron De Bastrop and Colonel Abraham Morhouse, Three Ouachita Valley Soldiers of Fortune: The Maison Rouge and Bastrop Spanish Land 'Grants,'" *Louisiana Historical Quarterly* 20 (April 1937): 301–307

5. Ibid., 334–335, 342.

6. Ibid., 340–342; An Act for the Adjustment of Land Titles, Carter, *Territorial Papers*, 9:408–414.

7. Wilkinson to Henry Dearborn, January 3, 1804, Carter, *Territorial Papers*, 9:151; Claiborne to Jefferson, August 30, 1804, ibid., 287; Claiborne to Madison, November 10, 1804, ibid., 333; Claiborne to Madison, August 15, 1805, *State Department Territorial Papers*. Evan Jones was also listed as having received Spanish land grants.

8. Mitchell and Calhoun, "Marquis de Mason Rouge," 370–372, 399–400; R. Woods Moore, "The Role of the Baron De Bastrop in the Anglo-American Settlement of the Spanish Southwest," *Louisiana Historical Quarterly* 31 (July 1948): 607–613, 625–628. Livingston's association with Bastrop apparently began in June 1804, when the baron petitioned the U.S. government for the preservation of his Spanish right of exclusive trade with the Native Americans on the Ouachita River. Livingston to Madison, September 15, 1804, Carter, *Territorial Papers*, 294–295.

9. Livingston to Madison, September 15, 1804, Carter, *Territorial Papers*, 9:294–295.

10. Claiborne to Madison, January 4, 1801, ibid., 362.

11. John W. Gurley to Claiborne, July 25, 1805, ibid., 477.

12. James Brown to John Breckinridge, September 25, 1805, ibid., 512.

13. The number of representatives for each district was divided as follows: Orleans County, seven representatives; German Coast, Acadia, La Fourche, Iberville, Attacapas, Point Coupee, two representatives each; Rapide, Natchitoches, Ouachita, Concordia, one representative each.

14. Proclamation by Governor Claiborne, Carter, *Territorial Papers*, 9:478.

15. John B. McCarty, Hazure Del' Orme, Dominique Bouligny, John Watkins, James Carrick, Robert Avart, and Etienne de Boré represented Orleans. Jean Nöel Destréhan and Joseph Andry represented German Coast. Joseph LeBlanc and Felix Bernard represented Iberville. Joseph Landry and William Conway represented Acadia. Nicholas Veratt and Henry Thibodeau represented La Fourche. Ebenezar Cooly and Simon Croizet represented Pointe Coupee. Louis Fontianeau and Luke Collins represented Opelousas. Joseph Sorrel and Martin Duralde represented Atakapas. Alexander Fulton represented Rapides. Emmanuel Prudhomme represented Natchitoches. Samuel Mahn represented Concordia. Abraham Morehouse represented Ouachita. *Louisiana Gazette*, November 5, 1805.

16. Claiborne to the House of Representatives of Orleans Territory, November 4, 1805, Rowland, *Letter Books of W. C. C. Claiborne*, 3:224; Destréhan to Claiborne, November 8, 1805, Carter, *Territorial Papers*, 9:520; Claiborne to Madison, November 8, 1805, Rowland, *Letter Books of W. C. C. Claiborne*, 3:229–230.

17. Bellechasse and Gurley each received nineteen votes; Derbigny and McCarty each received eighteen votes; Destréhan and Sauvé each received seventeen votes; Dominique Bouligny and Joseph Villars (pere) each received sixteen votes; Evan Jones received fifteen votes; and Francois Dannemours received thirteen votes. Jean Nöel Destréhan to Jefferson, November 11, 1804, Carter, *Territorial Papers*, 9:524.

18. Claiborne to Jefferson, November 13, 1805, ibid., 525–526.

19. Ibid.

20. Ibid.

21. *Louisiana Gazette*, November 19, 1805.

22. "Memorial to Congress by the Territorial House of Representatives," November 14, 1805, Carter, *Territorial Papers*, 9:526–529.

23. Ibid., 529–530. The reference to fire might be that which damaged New Orleans in 1788. The Spanish government held documents pertaining to land grants after the United States took possession of Louisiana in 1803. Many of these documents were sent to Pensacola. Madison ordered Claiborne to recover them on February 10, 1806. Madison to Claiborne, February 10, 1806, ibid., 580.

24. Ibid., 530–531.

25. Gurley to Gallatin, December 11, 1805, ibid., 549; Brown to Gallatin, December 11, 1805, ibid., 545–546; Gurley to Gallatin, March 6, 1806, ibid., 606.

26. Gallatin to Joseph Anderson, April 4, 1806, ibid., 624.

27. Carter, *Territorial Papers*, 9:408 n.74.

28. James Brown to Gallatin, December 11, 1805, ibid., 548.

29. Clarence Edwin Carter, comp., *The Territorial Papers of the United States*, Vol. 5, *The*

Territory of Mississippi, 1798–1817 (Washington, D.C.: U.S. Government Printing Office, 1937), 21–22; *Annals of the Congress*, 5th Congress, 1st Session, 1313.

30. Breckinridge had resigned as a senator on August 7, 1805, to accept Jefferson's appointment to serve as attorney general. Paul Lachance, "The Politics of Fear: French Louisianans and the Slave Trade, 1786–1809," *Plantation Society in the Americas* 1(2) (1979): 162–197.

31. Approximately 3,226 slaves, representing nearly 10 percent of the 1810 census count of 34,660 slaves for the territory of Orleans slaves, were imported by St. Domingue planters who had fled to Cuba and were expelled from there in 1809. Ibid., 187.

32. Ibid., 181.

33. Gwendolyn Midlo Hall, *Afro-Louisiana History and Genealogy, 1699–1860* (Baton Rouge: Louisiana State University Press, 2000).

34. Lachance, "Politics of Fear," 184, 187; "Black Code: An Act Prescribing the rules and conduct to be observed with respect to Negroes and other Slaves of this Territory," *Acts Passed at the First Session of the First Legislature of the Territory of Orleans*, 150–190; "An Act to Prevent the introduction of free people of Color from Hispaniola, and the other French islands of America into the Territory of Orleans," ibid., 126–130.

35. Jefferson to Claiborne, February 10, 1806, *Jefferson Papers*.

36. Claiborne to Madison, February 20, 1806, Carter, *Territorial Papers*, 9:604; Claiborne to Jefferson, March 4, 1806, *Jefferson Papers*.

37. John Watkins to Jefferson, April 4, 1806, *Jefferson Papers*; Claiborne to Jefferson, April 3, 1806, Rowland, *Letter Books of W. C. C. Claiborne*, 3:283–284.

38. Claiborne to Madison, March 26, 1806, Carter, *Territorial Papers*, 9:615–616.

39. Claiborne to Jefferson, May 10, 1806, Rowland, *Letter Books of W. C. C. Claiborne*, 3:288.

40. *Annals of the Congress*, 9th Congress, 1st Session, 15:570. Randolph had become more openly critical of Claiborne as he fell out with Jefferson. On December 6, 1805, Jefferson, in a secret message to Congress, requested $2 million for the purchase of the Floridas from Spain. Jefferson had secured his cabinet's permission to encourage France to arrange the sale. His plan was to send the money for the sale to France. Spain was in debt to that nation and was in no position to refuse a sale arranged by Napoleon's government. Randolph was outraged by this and considered that the money Jefferson requested was a bribe to one nation to rob another. He attacked the Jefferson administration for this in a series of House speeches between March 5 and April 21, 1806. This conduct ensured that Randolph was "left a political wreck." Adams, *John Randolph*, 163–190.

41. Claiborne to Madison, April 29, 1806, Rowland, *Letter Books of W. C. C. Claiborne*, 3:293–294.

42. Prichard, "Selecting a Governor," 340–341.

43. Ibid.

44. Ibid., 333.

45. "An Act to Establish Certain Conditions Necessary to Be a Member of Either House of Legislature of the Territory of Orleans," *Acts Passed at the First Session of the First Legislature of*

the Territory of Orleans, 76–78; Claiborne to the Gentlemen of the House of Representatives and the Legislative Council, May 6, 1806, Rowland, *Letter Books of W. C. C. Claiborne*, 3:296–297.

46. Claiborne to Madison, May 8, 1806, Rowland, *Letter Books of W. C. C. Claiborne*, 3:297–298; Claiborne to Madison, May 14, 1806, ibid.

47. *Louisiana Gazette*, May 20, 1806; Claiborne to Madison, May 21, 1806, Rowland, *Letter Books of W. C. C. Claiborne*, 3:303–304.

48. Sauvé to Claiborne, May 21, 1806, Carter, *Territorial Papers*, 9:641; Destréhan to Claiborne, May 23, 1806, ibid.; Claiborne to Sauvé, May 26, 1806, ibid.; Claiborne to Destréhan, May 26, 1806, Rowland, *Letter Books of W. C. C. Claiborne*, 3:308.

49. Claiborne to Madison, May 22, 1806, Rowland, *Letter Books of W. C. C. Claiborne*, 3:305–306, 642 n.82, 642.

50. Ibid.

51. "Customs Certificate of Inward Entry," signed by Evan Jones, July 28, 1804, *State Department Territorial Papers*; Claiborne to Lewis Kerr and Sheriffs of the City of New Orleans, July 30, 1804, Carter, *Territorial Papers*, 9:270. Claiborne to Madison, August 4, 1804, Rowland, *Letter Books of W. C. C. Claiborne*, 2:290–292.

52. Claiborne to Madison, May 26, 1806, Rowland, *Letter Books of W. C. C. Claiborne*, 3:309; Excerpt from the Session of the Legislative Council of May 26, 1806, Carter, *Territorial Papers*, 9:650–657.

53. Carter, *Territorial Papers*, 9:651.

54. Ibid., 652.

55. Ibid., 653.

56. Ibid., 655.

57. Ibid., 656.

58. Claiborne to Jefferson, June 4, 1806, *Jefferson Papers*.

59. Clark to Wilkinson, June 16, 1806, Carter, *Territorial Papers*, 9:660–661.

Chapter 6

1. Abernethy, *Burr Conspiracy*, 36–37.

2. Claiborne to Jefferson, July 9, 1806, *Jefferson Papers*.

3. Abernethy, *Burr Conspiracy*, 29–30.

4. Charles Haven Hunt, *Life of Edward Livingston* (New York: D. Appleton, 1864), 126; Dumas Malone, ed., *Dictionary of American Biography*, Vol. 6 (New York: Scribner, 1961), 310). Dr. Justus Erich Bollman was born near Bremen and studied medicine. He was in Paris during the 1790s and "made himself useful to both sides." Later he attempted to rescue Lafayette, who was imprisoned at Olmutz in Austria, and was himself imprisoned for eight months. After this he sailed to New York where, as a friend of Lafayette, he was well received. Bollman failed as a businessman, but he made the acquaintance of Burr. Because Bollman knew several languages, Burr engaged Bollman to raise money for him in Europe and as one of his emissaries to New Orleans. Abernethy, *Burr* Conspiracy, 57.

5. Abernethy, *Burr Conspiracy*, 24–25.

6. Ibid., 73–74.

7. Ibid., 59–60.

8. Ibid., 172; *Moniteur de la Louisiane*, October 22, 1806.

9. Abernethy, *Burr Conspiracy*, 148.

10. Ibid., 152–154.

11. Ibid., 79.

12. James Wilkinson, *Memoirs of My Own Times* (Philadelphia: printed by Abraham Small, 1816), Vol. 2, Appendix C.

13. Wilkinson to Claiborne, November 12, 1806, Rowland, *Letter Books of W. C. C. Claiborne*, 4:55–56.

14. Claiborne to Jefferson, November 5, 1806, ibid., 33.

15. Claiborne to Mead, November 18, 1806, ibid., 35–36.

16. Claiborne to Madison, November 18, 1806, ibid., 36. On February 5, 1806, when it was feared that the United States would soon be at war with Spain, Claiborne had appointed Gurley as his aide-de-camp and had given him the rank of major. Carter, *Territorial Papers*, 9:597.

17. Claiborne to Madison, November 18, 1806, Rowland, *Letter Books of W. C. C. Claiborne*, 4:37.

18. Statement by Governor Claiborne and Captain Shaw, ibid., 38–40.

19. Abernethy, *Burr Conspiracy*, 177. While there is no evidence to prove that Bellechasse was involved in the conspiracy, Claiborne apparently received information that he had been offered the position of "Commander in Chief of the Militia" if he agreed to support a revolution in Orleans Territory and a subsequent conquest of Mexico. Claiborne warned Bellechasse that he had received this information and called upon him to report whether these reports were true. Claiborne to Bellechasse, January 7, 1807, Rowland, *Letter Books of W. C. C. Claiborne*, 4:85.

20. Andrew Jackson to Claiborne, November 12, 1806, Rowland, *Letter Books of W. C. C. Claiborne*, 4:54.

21. Claiborne to Jefferson, May 3, 1807, Carter, *Territorial Papers*, 9:730.

22. Claiborne to Madison, December 5, 1806, Rowland, *Letter Books of W. C. C. Claiborne*, 4:43.

23. Claiborne notified Jefferson on May 3, 1807, that he had discovered that Watkins was a member of the Mexican Association and dismissed him from his position as mayor of New Orleans. Claiborne to Jefferson, May 3, 1807, Carter, *Territorial Papers*, 9:731.

24. Claiborne to Madison, December 9, 1806, Rowland, *Letter Books of W. C. C. Claiborne*, 4:50–51.

25. *A Faithful Picture of the Political Situation of New Orleans at the Close of the Last and the Beginning of the Present Year, 1807* (Boston: 1808, reprinted from the original New-Orleans edition). Historians have speculated about the identity of the author. James E. Winston discovered that Orleans judge James Workman wrote a pamphlet, "that one was contemplated by Livingston," and suggested that "internal evidence" pointed to Workman as the author. James E. Winston, ed., "A Faithful Picture of the Political Situation in New Orleans at the Close of the Last and the Beginning of the Present Year, 1807," *Louisiana Historical Quarterly* 11(3) (July

1928): 359–433. Abernethy tentatively acknowledged Livingston as the author. Abernethy, *Burr Conspiracy*, 279.

26. Wilkinson's persistent pursuit of Alexander is explained by the fact that the general had learned that Alexander had implicated him as an associate of Burr. On December 16 Wilkinson wrote Claiborne and insisted that Alexander be arrested because he had "said publicly at the Coffee House the other night, that if Burr was a traitor I was one too." Rowland, *Letter Books of W. C. C. Claiborne*, 4:62.

27. *Faithful Picture of the Political Situation*; Abernethy, *Burr Conspiracy*, 178–179.

28. Abernethy, *Burr Conspiracy*, 117–118.

29. These were not groundless charges. Workman and Kerr "had taken the lead in organizing the Mexican Association in New Orleans." Ibid., 25. Just as Wilkinson was selective about whom he arrested, Claiborne was apparently careful only to defend those who were his political allies. When he was arrested, Kerr was a colonel in the militia and "had been for several years in the habits of intimate friendship with Governor Claiborne, and was generally believed to been high in his confidence, and very serviceable to his government." A week prior to his arrest Claiborne had assigned Kerr the task of arming the militia. Kerr's opinions were "unfavorable to the measures of Wilkinson," and it was said that he offered to "arrest General Wilkinson on *his own responsibility*, and ship him for the City of Washington." *Faithful Picture of the Political Situation*, 409–410.

30. Abernethy, *Burr Conspiracy*, 180, 182.

31. Ibid., 227.

32. Ibid., 222–223.

33. *Faithful Picture of the Political Situation*, 416.

34. Ibid., 419.

35. Claiborne to the House of Representatives, February 12, 1807, Rowland, *Letter Books of W. C. C. Claiborne*, 4:117–118. On March 3 Claiborne reported that he had learned of Burr's arrest near Fort Stoddert and that the "objects" of Burr's conspiracy were "the destruction of our Government and the dismemberment of the union." Claiborne went on to defend Wilkinson. "Perhaps some of the measures of the General may be considered as exceptionable; but I give it as my decided opinion, that the general policy he pursued, was the best, that could (under all circumstances) have been resorted to, and that to him, this City and Territory are in a great measure indebted." Carter, *Territorial Papers*, 9:712. Claiborne's opinion would have carried weight with those in the House who supported him. On March 23 Claiborne reported with satisfaction that the memorial was defeated by a vote of fourteen to seven and that "rejection of the memorial and by such a large majority, will destroy the effect which it was intended to produce." Claiborne to Madison, March 23, 1807, ibid., 722.

36. Claiborne to Madison, May 3, 1807, ibid., 731.

37. *Moniteur de la Louisiane*, February 14, 1807; Clark to Jefferson, December 18, 1806, *Jefferson Papers*; Jefferson to Clark, December 21, 1806, ibid.

38. *Moniteur de la Louisiane*, April 11, 1807. This article was in the form of a letter from Daniel Clark to his constituents dated March 6, 1807. Clark was especially interested in a proposed

project that Jefferson supported for construction of a post road between Fort Stoddert and New Orleans. Clark to Jefferson, January 20, 1807, *Jefferson Papers*. The charity hospital Clark proposed for New Orleans was for sailors who could not afford to pay for care. Clark to Jefferson, February 6, 1807, ibid.

39. *Annals of the Congress*, 9th Congress, 2nd Session, 215.

40. Clark to Livingston, December 6, 1806, Edward Livingston Papers.

41. Clark to Livingston, January 5, 1807, ibid.

42. Clark to Coxe, December 25, 1806, *Transcript of Record, The City of New Orleans Appellant, vs. Myra Clark Gaines, Appeal from the Circuit Court of Louisiana Filed October 19, 1883*. This was a paternity suit against Daniel Clark. Many of Daniel Clark's letters were sequestered for evidence.

43. Clark to Livingston, January 11, 1807, Edward Livingston Papers.

44. Claiborne to Madison, June 1, 1807, Carter, *Territorial Papers*, 9:742–743. Philip Jones, a native of New York, was appointed register of wills at New Orleans on February 27, 1805. He married the widow of Hore Browse Trist. When Hore Browse Trist died of yellow fever in August 1804, Claiborne recommended William Brown to Jefferson for the post of collector for New Orleans. Claiborne described Brown as a benevolent young man of promising talents. Claiborne to Jefferson, August 29, 1804, ibid., 279–280; *Register of Civil Appointments in the Territory of Orleans*, ibid., 603; Claiborne to Jefferson, June 1, 1807, ibid., 743. By May 1807 Claiborne had revised his opinion of Brown and described him as "an honest man and an attentive officer," but that he was "greatly influenced in his opinions by men who hate both the Government and the Administration." Claiborne to Jefferson, May 19, 1807, ibid., 735.

45. Clark to Coxe, June 12, 1807, *Transcript of Record, The City of New Orleans Appellant, vs. Myra Clark Gaines, Appeal from the Circuit Court of Louisiana Filed October 19, 1883*; Claiborne to Jefferson, June 17, 1807, Carter, *Territorial Papers*, 9:743; Claiborne to Jefferson, June 28, 1807, ibid., 745–746. In his letter to Coxe describing the duel, Clark added a P.S. to mention that the "secrets of the duel leaked out in Orleans from the Governor's friends" after Claiborne had left New Orleans and that as a consequence Clark was pursued for "90 miles without effect" by a sheriff's deputy. When Clark was "within 6 miles of the place" assigned for the duel, the deputy was informed that Clark had already crossed the Iberville River and gave up his pursuit.

46. Claiborne to Jefferson, June 17, 1807, Carter, *Territorial Papers*, 9:744.

47. Claiborne to Jefferson, May 20, 1807, ibid., 736–737. Claiborne was of the opinion, however, that the superior court had erred in its decision and that the "U. States" were "the legal claimants to the land in question." Ibid.

48. Dargo, *Jefferson's Louisiana*, 74.

49. Ibid., 74–76; Hatcher, *Edward Livingston*, 145.

50. Hatcher, *Edward Livingston*, 147.

51. Claiborne may have suggested this. He had indicated that he believed that the Batture was U.S. property in his letter of May 20, 1807.

52. Claiborne to Mead, November 18, 1806, Rowland, *Letter Books of W. C. C. Claiborne*, 4:35–36.

53. Dargo, *Jefferson's Louisiana*, 77.

54. Claiborne to Madison, October 5, 1807, Carter, *Territorial Papers*, 9:765–766. Claiborne sent a copy of the decision of the court and a translation of an address to him on the subject.

55. Dargo, *Jefferson's Louisiana*, 76–77.

56. Edward Livingston to Robert Livingston, January 28, 1808, Robert Livingston Papers, New York Historical Society.

57. Dargo, *Jefferson's Louisiana*, 79–83.

58. Ibid., 80.

59. Ibid., 81.

60. Ibid., 81–82.

61. Ibid., 82.

62. Ibid., 85.

63. Livingston to Jefferson, May 5, 1808, *Jefferson Papers*; Jefferson to Livingston, May 6, 1808, ibid.; Jefferson to Gallatin, May 6, 1808, ibid.

64. Dargo, *Jefferson's Louisiana*, 89–90.

65. Ibid., 96–98. In 1797, Eppes had married Thomas Jefferson's daughter Maria.

66. Ibid., 98–99.

67. Ibid., 65.

Chapter 7

1. Abernethy, *Burr Conspiracy*, 234, 253–256.

2. Ibid., 255–256.

3. Adams, *John Randolph*, 220–221; Abernethy, *Burr Conspiracy*, 239.

4. Abernethy, *Burr Conspiracy*, 264; Wilkinson, *Memoirs*, 2:7–9.

5. Abernethy, *Burr Conspiracy*, 265–266.

6. Ibid., 266.

7. Ibid.

8. Ibid., 267, 274.

9. Ibid., 269–270.

10. *Louisiana Gazette*, March 8, 1808.

11. Ibid., March 11, March 22, and April 8, 1808.

12. *Louisiana Courier*, July 9, 1810.

13. See Edward Livingston Papers, Box 7, Folder 30, and Box 82, Folder 5.

14. *Louisiana Courier*, April 25 and May 16, 1808.

15. Claiborne to Madison, July 17, 1804, Carter, *Territorial Papers*, 9:753; Claiborne to Madison, October 5, 1807, ibid., 766.

16. Claiborne to Colonel Thomas Cushing, December 29, 1808, Rowland, *Letter Books of W. C. C. Claiborne*, 4:179–180; James Mather to Claiborne, January 8, 1809, Carter, *Territorial Papers*, 9:817–818; Cushing to Claiborne, January 10, 1809, ibid., 819–820; Cushing to Dearborn, January 11, 1809, ibid., 819 n.1. It is questionable whether Claiborne seriously believed in the plot

that Mather described to him. He did not mention it in letters that he wrote to Madison in January 1809.

17. Claiborne to Madison, September 7, 1808, Rowland, *Letter Books of W. C. C. Claiborne*, 4:212.

18. Claiborne to Madison, February 13, 1809, ibid., 316–317.

19. Smith to Claiborne, March 20, 1809, Carter, *Territorial Papers*, 9:830.

20. Dargo, *Jefferson's Louisiana*, 6.

21. Claiborne to Smith, May 15, 1809, Rowland, *Letter Books of W. C. C. Claiborne*, 4:354; Claiborne to Poydras, May 22, 1809, ibid., 339–360.

22. Dargo, *Jefferson's Louisiana*, 156–164; Claiborne to Judge J. White, October 11, 1808, Rowland, *Letter Books of W. C. C. Claiborne*, 4:225–227.

23. Claiborne to Smith, May 18, 1809, Rowland, *Letter Books of W. C. C. Claiborne*, 4:360–361.

24. Robertson to Smith, May 24, 1809, Carter, *Territorial Papers*, 9:841.

25. Paul F. Lachance, "The 1809 Immigration of St. Domingue Refugees to New Orleans: Reception, Integration and Impact," *Louisiana History* 29(2) (1988): 109–113.

26. Claiborne to John Graham, July 19, 1809, Rowland, *Letter Books of W. C. C. Claiborne*, 4:390–391.

27. Ibid.; Lachance, "St. Domingue Refugees," 119–120. Daniel Clark also recognized that Livingston's efforts to aid the St. Domingue refugees was an attempt to bolster his rapidly sinking popularity in Orleans and that it would fail because the refugees saw Claiborne as their savior. "I am afraid you were making a side stroke at popularity when you applied to the Senate in favor of the Cuban refugees, and you will be disappointed in your expectation as they believe they are indebted to Solomon who took on himself to suffer them to land and delivered up their slaves to them, on giving bond they should be forthcoming." Clark to Livingston, July 22, 1809, Edward Livingston Papers.

28. Jefferson to Claiborne, September 10, 1809, *Jefferson Papers*. Jefferson was no longer president when he wrote this, but Claiborne kept him informed of important developments in Orleans Territory until statehood in 1812, and Jefferson continued to advise Claiborne.

29. Lachance, "St. Domingue Refugees," 137.

30. Memorial to Congress by the Legislature, March 10, 1810, Carter, *Territorial Papers*, 9:873–876.

31. Ibid.

32. Claiborne to Poydras, July 18, 1811, Rowland, *Letter Books of W. C. C. Claiborne*, 5:307.

33. Claiborne was fortunate to be in a position to run for governor. Jefferson, acting in capacity as a mediator for Madison, had offered Monroe the post of governor of Orleans in November 1809, but Monroe, as he had done in 1804, 1806, and 1807, refused Jefferson's offer. Prichard, "Selecting a Governor," 343–344.

34. Claiborne to Judge Henry Johnson, June 15, 1811, Rowland, *Letter Books of W. C. C. Claiborne*, 5:277; Claiborne to Paul Hamilton, December 5, 1811, ibid., 397.

35. Claiborne to John Dawson, August 10, 1812, ibid., 6:156. Jacques Villeré's father, Joseph Antoine Villeré, was executed for his involvement in the 1768 revolt against the Spanish in Louisiana. Before he had served as a justice of the peace and a militia officer under the American government, Jacques Villeré was named to Laussat's staff to assist with the transition from French to American government.

36. Jefferson to Claiborne, February 3, 1807, *Jefferson Papers.*

37. Peter J. Kastor, "'Motives of Peculiar Urgency': Local Diplomacy in Louisiana, 1803–1821," *William and Mary Quarterly* 58 (October 2001): 843.

38. Ibid.

39. Ibid., 843–844.

40. Ibid., 844–845.

41. Lachance, "St. Domingue Refugees," 137.

Conclusion

1. Smith, *Republic of Letters*, 2:1287–1288.

2. "An Act Enabling the President to Take Possession of Louisiana," Carter, *Territorial Papers*, 9:89.

3. Boré to Jefferson, February 10, 1804, *Jefferson Papers*; Jefferson to Gallatin, November 9, 1803, ibid.

4. "An Act for the Organization of Orleans Territory," Carter, *Territorial Papers*, 9:204.

5. Claiborne to Madison, March 1, 1804, Rowland, *Letterbooks of W. C. C. Claiborne*, 2:14; "Dr. Watkins Report," February 2, 1804, ibid., 10.

6. Claiborne to Madison, March 10, 1804, ibid., 25; Claiborne to Madison, March 16, 1804, ibid., 42–48.

7. *Moniteur de la Louisiane*, August 9, 1804.

8. *Annals of the Congress*, 8th Congress, 2nd Session, 1014–1017.

9. "An Act for the Government of Orleans Territory," Carter, *Territorial Papers*, 9:405–407.

10. James Brown to Albert Gallatin, December 11, 1805, ibid., 548–549; Brown to Madison, December 23, 1807, ibid., 770.

11. John Watkins to John Graham, September 6, 1805, ibid., 503–504.

12. John W. Gurley to Claiborne, July 25, 1805, ibid., 477.

13. The American government investigated the title of a vast tract of land held by Louis Bouligny known as the Maison Rouge tract (see chapter 5). This investigation, begun under the Act for the Adjustment of Land Claims passed in 1805, continued after Clark's death in 1813. This did not prevent Louis Bouligny from selling his last remaining portion of the land to Clark in 1812 (Clark made two earlier purchases from Bouligny in July 1803 and June 1804), nor did it hinder Clark from selling some of this land in February 1811 and May 1812. Gallatin to Allan R. Magruder, James Brown, and Felix Grundy, July 5, 1805, ibid., 468–469; Mitchell and Calhoun, "Marquis de Mason Rouge," 340–342.

14. Claiborne to Jefferson, November 25, 1806, Carter, *Territorial Papers*, 9:525.

15. "Excerpt from the session of the Legislative Council of May 26, 1806," ibid., 650–657.

16. Ibid., 653; Claiborne to Judge J. White, October 11, 1808, Rowland, *Letter Books of W. C. C. Claiborne*, 4:225–227.

Bibliography

Primary Sources

Manuscript Collections

The Adams Papers Owned by the Adams Manuscript Trust and Deposited in the Massachusetts Historical Society. Massachusetts Historical Society. Boston: 1954.

Addresses of the Mayors of New Orleans. City Archives, New Orleans Public Library.

Clifford-Pemberton Papers. Historical Society of Pennsylvania, Philadelphia.

Coxe Family Papers. Historical Society of Pennsylvania, Philadelphia.

Despatches from the United States Consuls in New Orleans, 1798–1807. Washington, D.C.: National Archives and Records Service, 1958.

Diplomatic and Consular Instructions of the Department of State, 1791–1801. Washington, D.C.: National Archives, 1945.

Gilpin Family Papers. Historical Society of Pennsylvania, Philadelphia.

John W. Gurley Papers. Tulane University, New Orleans.

Thomas Jefferson Papers. Washington, D.C.: Library of Congress, 1974.

Jenkins, William, comp. *Early State Records of the United States.* Washington, D.C.: Library of Congress, 1950.

Pierre Clément Laussat Papers. Historic New Orleans Collection.

Letters of Application and Recommendation during the Administration of Thomas Jefferson, 1801–1809. Washington, D.C.: National Archives, 1962.

Edward Livingston Papers. Princeton University, Princeton, N.J.

Robert Livingston Papers. New York Historical Society, New York.

Louisiana, Court of Probates, 1805–1846. City Archives, New Orleans Public Library.

Madison Papers. Washington, D.C.: Library of Congress, 1964.

Minutes of the Ninth Convention for Promoting Abolition of Slavery and Improving the Condition of the African Race. Philadelphia: Solomon Conrad, 1804.

New Orleans Conseil de Ville, Records, 1804–1836. City Archives, New Orleans Public Library.

New Orleans Municipal Papers, 1803–1813. Tulane University, New Orleans.

State Department Territorial Papers, Orleans Series. Washington, D.C.: National Archives, 1958.

Oliver Wolcott Jr. Papers. Connecticut Historical Society, Hartford.

Published

An Act Erecting Louisiana into Two Territories and Providing for the Temporary Government Thereof. Washington: 1804.

Actes du Conseil Legislatif du Territoire d' Orleans, 1804–1805. New Orleans: De L'imprimerie du
Moniteur, chez J.B.L.S. Fontaine, 1805.

*An Act for Dividing the Territory of Orleans into Counties, and Establishing Courts of Inferior
Jurisdiction therein*. New Orleans: Printed by John Mowry, 1805.

Acts Passed at the First Session of the First Legislature of the Territory of Orleans. New Orleans:
Bradford and Anderson, 1870.

Acts Passed at the First Session of the Legislative Council of the Territory of Orleans. New Orleans: James H. Bradford, 1805.

*Acts Passed at the Sessions of the First–Third Legislature of the Territory of Orleans Held in the
City of New Orleans, 1806–1811*. New Orleans: Bradford and Anderson, 1812.

Adams, Charles, ed. *Memoirs of John Quincy Adams*. Philadelphia: J. B. Lippincott, 1874.

Ames, Seth, ed. *Works of Fisher Ames*. 2 vols. Boston: Little Brown, 1854.

Annals of the Congress of the United States. Washington, D.C.: Gales and Seaton, 1852.

Arrete pour L'Etablissement de l' Autorite Municipale a la Nouvelle Orleans. New Orleans: 1803.

A Bill Further Providing for the Government of the Territory of Louisiana. Washington: 1806,
1810.

Blennerhasset, Harmon. *The Blennerhasset Papers*. Cincinnati: Moore, Wilstach, Keys, 1861.

Brown, Everett S., ed. *William Plumer's Memorandum of the Proceedings in the United States
Senate, 1803–1807*. New York: Macmillan, 1923.

Carter, Clarence, ed. *The Territorial Papers of the United States*. Vol. 5, *The Territory of Mississippi, 1798–1817*. Washington, D.C.: U.S. Government Printing Office, 1937.

———, ed. *The Territorial Papers of the United States*. Vol. 9, *The Territory of Orleans, 1803–1812*.
Washington, D.C.: U.S. Government Printing Office, 1940.

Clark, Daniel. *Proofs of the Corruption of General James Wilkinson*. 1809. Reprint, Freeport,
N.Y.: Books for Libraries Free Press, 1970.

*Collection, . . . the Treaty of Cession between the United States and the French Republic: as also
the laws and ordinances of the Congress for the government of the Territory of Orleans, and
two ordinances of the governor and intendant of Louisiana: by authority*. New Orleans:
Thierry and Dacquency, 1810.

"Despatches from the United States Consulate in New Orleans, 1801–1803, I." *American Historical Review* 32(4) (1927): 801–824.

"Despatches from the United States Consulate in New Orleans, 1801–1803, II." *American Historical Review* 33(8) (1928): 331–359.

Documents Accompanying a Message from the President of the United States, December 2, 1806.
New Orleans: 1806.

*A Faithful Picture of the Political Situation of New Orleans, at the close of the last and beginning
of the present year 1807*. Boston: 1808.

Federal Census of 1810, Territory of Orleans. Baton Rouge: Louisiana Genealogical Society, 1961.

Foner, Philip, ed. *The Complete Writings of Thomas Paine*. New York: Citadel Press, 1945.

Ford, Paul, ed. *The Writings of Thomas Jefferson*. New York: G. P. Putnam's Sons, 1897.

Ford, Worthington, ed. *Journals of the Continental Congress, 1784–1789.* Vol. 1, *1774.* Washington, D.C.: Government Printing Office, 1904.

———, ed. *The Writings of John Quincy Adams.* Vol. 2, *1801–1810.* New York: Greenwood Press, 1968.

Gibbs, George, ed. *Memoirs of the Administrations of Washington and John Adams, Edited from the Papers of Oliver Wolcott, Secretary of the Treasury.* New York: William Van Norden, 1846.

Hacket, Mary, et al., eds. *The Papers of James Madison, Secretary of State Series.* Vol. 3, *1 March–6 October 1802.* Charlottesville: University Press of Virginia, 1995.

———. *The Papers of James Madison, Secretary of State Series.* Vol. 4, *8 October–15 May 1803.* Charlottesville: University Press of Virginia, 1998.

Journal de la Convention d' Orleans de 1811–12. Jackson, Miss.: Jerome Bayone, 1844.

Journal of the House of Representatives of the State of Louisiana, First Session, First Legislature. New Orleans: 1812.

Kline, Mary-Jo. *The Papers of Aaron Burr.* Glen Rock, N.J.: Microfilming Corp. of America, 1977.

La Code Noir ou Edit du Roi. New Orleans: Moniteur, 1803

Laws of the Territory of Louisiana, 1810. Washington, D.C.: Statute Law Book, 1905.

Memorial of the House of Representatives of the Territory of Orleans praying that an Alteration be made in the law of land respecting Titles to Sugar. Washington City: 1806.

Memorial Presented by the Inhabitants of Louisiana to the Congress, Washington: Smith, 1804.

Memorial to the House of Representatives and Legislative Council of the Territory of Orleans on behalf of the inhabitants thereof. Washington City: R. C. Weightman, 1810.

Reflections on the Cause of the Louisianans. Washington: 1804.

Report, in part, of the Committee to whom were referred the petition of the Legislative Council of the Territory of Orleans. Washington: 1806.

Report of the Committee appointed on the Twelfth of November last, on so much of the message of the president of the United States: as relates to the amelioration of the form of government of the territory of Louisiana: to whom was referred the third ultimo, a memorial in the French language, with a translation thereof, from sundry planters, merchants and other inhabitants of the said territory of Louisiana. Washington: 1805.

Rives, John, ed. *Abridgment of the Debates of Congress, from 1789 to 1856.* Vol. 3. New York: D. Appleton, 1857.

———. *Abridgment of the Debates of Congress, from 1789 to 1856.* Vol. 4. New York: D. Appleton, 1858.

Rowland, Dunbar, ed. *The Official Letter Books of W. C. C. Claiborne, 1801–1816.* New York: AMS Press, 1972.

Syrett, Harold, ed. *The Papers of Alexander Hamilton.* New York: Columbia University Press, 1961–1987.

Transcript of Record, The City of New Orleans Appellant, vs. Myra Clark Gaines, Appeal from the Circuit Court of Louisiana Filed October 19, 1883. New Orleans: Tulane University Special Collections.

*View of the Political and Civil Situation of Louisiana; from the Thirtieth of November 1803 to the
First of October, 1804 by a Native, by a Native.* Philadelphia: 1804.

Wilkinson, James. *Memoirs of General Wilkinson.* Washington: 1810.

Newspapers

Louisiana Courier

Louisiana Gazette

Telegraph and Commercial Advertiser

Moniteur de la Louisiane

Orleans Gazette

Union

Secondary Sources

Books and Dissertations

Abernethy, Thomas. *The Burr Conspiracy.* New York: Oxford University Press, 1954.

Adams, Henry. *A History of the United States of America during the Administrations of Thomas
Jefferson.* New York: Library of America, 1986.

———. *John Randolph.* Boston: Houghton, Mifflin, 1894.

Ammon, Henry. *James Monroe: The Quest for National Unity.* New York: McGraw Hill, 1971.

Arthur, Stanley. *Old Families of Louisiana.* New Orleans: Harmanson, 1931.

Austin, Aleine. *Matthew Lyon, "New Man" of the Democratic Revolution, 1749–1822.* University
Park: Pennsylvania State University Press, 1981.

Bemis, Samuel. *Jay's Treaty: A Study in Commerce and Diplomacy.* New Haven, Conn.: Yale
University Press, 1962.

———. *Pinckney's Treaty: America's Advantage from Europe's Distress, 1783–1800.* New Haven,
Conn: Yale University Press, 1960.

Ben-Atar, Doron, and Barbara Oberg. *Federalists Reconsidered.* Charlottesville: University of
Virginia Press, 1998.

Bernhard, Winfred. *Fisher Ames, Federalist and Statesman, 1758–1808.* Chapel Hill: University of
North Carolina Press, 1965.

Brasseux, Carl. *Acadian to Cajun: The Transformation of a People, 1803–1877.* Jackson: University Press of Mississippi, 1992.

———. *A Dictionary of Louisiana Biography, Ten-Year Supplement, 1988–1998.* New Orleans:
Louisiana Historical Society, 1999.

———. *The Founding of New Acadia, The Beginnings of Acadian Life in Louisiana, 1765–1803.*
Baton Rouge: Louisiana State University Press, 1987.

———. *The Road to Louisiana: The St. Domingue Refugees, 1792–1809.* Lafayette: Center for Louisiana Studies, University of Southwestern Louisiana, 1992.

Brown, Everett S. *The Constitutional History of the Louisiana Purchase.* Berkeley: University of
California *Press*, 1920.

Broussard, James. *The Southern Federalists, 1800–1816.* Baton Rouge: Louisiana State University Press, 1978.

Cable, George. *The Creoles of Louisiana.* New York: Charles Scribner's Sons, 1884.

Carrigan, Jo-Ann. "The Safron Scourge: A History of Yellow Fever in Louisiana, 1796–1905." Ph.D. diss., Louisiana State University, 1961.

Chaffin, William. *Brigadier General Benjamin Tupper of the Revolutionary Army and of the Ohio Company.* Marietta, Ohio: Leader Print, 1880.

Clark, John G. *New Orleans 1718–1812: An Economic History.* Baton Rouge: Louisiana State University Press, 1970.

Coffey, Thomas. "The Territory of Orleans, 1804–1812." Ph.D. diss., Saint Louis University, 1958.

Conrad, Glenn, ed. *A Dictionary of Louisiana Biography.* New Orleans: Louisiana Historical Association, 1988.

——. *Land Records of Attakapas.* Lafayette: Center for Louisiana Studies, 1993.

——. *White Gold: A Brief History of the Louisiana Sugar Industry, 1795–1995.* Lafayette: Center for Louisiana Studies, 1990.

Cooke, Jacob E. *Tench Coxe and the Early Republic.* Chapel Hill: University of North Carolina Press, 1978.

Cox, Isaac. *The West Florida Controversy, 1798–1813.* Baltimore: Johns Hopkins University Press, 1918.

Dangerfield, George. *Chancellor Robert R. Livingston of New York.* New York: Harcourt and Brace, 1960.

Dargo, George. *Jefferson's Louisiana: Politics and the Clash of Legal Traditions.* Cambridge, Mass.: Harvard University Press, 1975.

Dawson, Joseph. *The Louisiana Governors.* Baton Rouge: Louisiana State University Press, 1990.

DeConde, Alexander. *This Affair of Louisiana.* New York: Charles Scribner's Sons, 1976.

De Villiers, Gladys. *The Opelousas Post: A Compendium of Church Records Relating to the First Families of Southwest Louisiana, 1776–1806.* Cottonport, La.: Polyanthos, 1972.

Dubester, Henry. *An Annotated Bibliography of Censuses of Population taken after the year 1790 by States and Territories of the United States.* Washington, D.C.: Library of Congress, 1948.

Du Pratz, Le Page. *The History of Louisiana.* Baton Rouge: Louisiana State University Press, 1975.

Eblen, Jack. *The First and Second United States Empires, Governors and Territorial Government, 1784–1912.* Pittsburgh: Pittsburgh University Press, 1968.

Elkins, Stanley, and Eric McKitrick. *The Age of Federalism.* London: Oxford University Press, 1993.

Ellsworth, Lucius. *The Americanization of the Gulf Coast, 1803–1850.* Pensacola, Fla.: Pensacola Preservation Board, 1971.

Este, William. *"Honest" Judge William Miller, commissioner and agent, on the part of the Republics of France and the United States, to receive possession of the post and depending territory of Rapides Louisiana, in 1804, commissioned a judge under the new regime.* New York: Este, 1892.

Fischer, David. *The Revolution of American Conservatism: The Federalist Party in the Era of Jeffersonian Democracy.* New York: Harper and Row, 1965.

Formisano, Ronald. *The Transformation of Political Culture: Massachusetts Parties, 1790's–1840's.* New York: Oxford University Press, 1983.

Forsyth, Alice. *Louisiana Marriages.* New Orleans: Polyanthos, 1977.

Fortier, Alcee. *A History of Louisiana: The American Domination, 1803–1861.* New York: Manzi, Joyant, 1903.

Fuller, Hubert. *The Purchase of Florida.* Cleveland: Burrows Brothers, 1906.

Gayarre, Charles. *History of Louisiana: The American Domination.* New York: William J. Widdleton, 1866.

Goodman, Paul. *The Democratic Republicans of Massachusetts: Politics in a Young Republic.* Cambridge, Mass.: Harvard University Press, 1964.

Hall, Gwendolyn. *Afro-Louisiana History and Genealogy, 1699–1860.* Baton Rouge: Louisiana State University Press, 2000.

Harmon, Nolan, Jr. *The Strange Case of Myra Clark Gaines.* Baton Rouge: Louisiana State University Press, 1946.

Harrison, Lowell. *John Breckinridge, Jeffersonian Republican.* Louisville: Filson Club, 1969.

Hatcher, William B. *Edward Livingston: Jeffersonian Republican and Jacksonian Democrat.* Baton Rouge: Louisiana State University Press, 1940.

Hatfield, Joseph. *William Claiborne: Jeffersonian Centurion in the American Southwest.* Lafayette: University of Southwestern Louisiana, 1976.

Hendrix, James. "The Efforts to Re-open the African Slave Trade in Louisiana." M.A. thesis, Louisiana State University, 1968.

Howard, Clinton N. *The British Development of West Florida.* Berkeley: University of California Press, 1947.

Hunt, Charles Haven. *Life of Edward Livingston.* New York: D. Appleton, 1864.

Jeansonne, Glen, ed. *A Guide to the History of Louisiana.* Westport, Conn.: Greenwood Press, 1982.

Johnson, Cecil. *British West Florida, 1763–1783.* New Haven, Conn.: Yale University Press, 1943.

Kerber, Linda. *Federalists in Dissent: Imagery and Ideology in Jeffersonian America.* Ithaca, N.Y.: Cornell University Press, 1970.

Kukla, John. *A Guide to the Papers of Pierre Clément Laussat.* New Orleans: Historic New Orleans Collection, 1993.

Kurtz, Stephen. *The Federalists: Creators and Critics of the Union, 1780–1801.* N.p.: Problems in American History Series, n.d.

Laussat, Pierre Clément. *Memoirs of My Life.* Ed. Robert Bush; trans. Agnes-Josephine Pastawa. Baton Rouge: Louisiana State University Press, 1978.

Lawson, Phiip. *The Imperial Challenge: Quebec and Britain in the Age of the American Revolution.* Montreal: McGill-Queen's University Press, 1989.

Le Breton, Marie. "A History of the Territory of Orleans, 1803–1812." Ph.D. diss., Louisiana State University, 1969.

Lomask, Milton. *Aaron Burr: The Conspiracy and Years of Exile, 1805–1836*. New York: Farrar, Strauss, Giroux, 1982.

Malone, Dumas, ed. *Dictionary of American Biography*. Vol. 6. New York: Scribner, 1961.

———. *Jefferson the President, First Term, 1801–1805*. Boston: Little, Brown, 1970.

———. *Jefferson the President, Second Term, 1805–1809*. Boston: Little, Brown, 1974.

Martin, Francois-Xavier. *The History of Louisiana from the Earliest Period*. New Orleans: James A. Gresham, 1882.

McCaleb, Walter. *New Light on Aaron Burr*. Austin: University of Texas Press, 1963.

McMichael, Andrew. *Atlantic Loyalties: Americans in Spanish West Florida, 1785–1810*. Athens: University of Georgia Press, 2008.

Melville, Annabelle. *Louis William Dubourg: Bishop of Louisiana*. Chicago: Loyola University Press, 1986.

Miller, John. *The Wolf by the Ears: Thomas Jefferson and Slavery*. New York: Free Press, 1977.

Moore, Glover. *The Missouri Controversy, 1819–1821*. Louisville: University of Kentucky Press, 1953.

Moore, John Preston. *Revolt in Louisiana: The Spanish Occupation, 1766–1770*. Baton Rouge: Louisiana State University Press, 1976.

Neatby, Hilda. *Quebec: The Revolutionary Age, 1760–1791*. Toronto: McClelland and Stewart, 1966.

Newton, Lewis W. *The Americanization of French Louisiana: A Study of the Process of Adjustment between the French and the Anglo-American Populations of Louisiana, 1803–1860*. New York: Arno Press, 1980.

Onuf, Peter. *Jefferson's Empire: The Language of American Nationhood*. Charlottesville: University Press of Virginia, 2000.

Phelps, Albert. *Louisiana: A Record of Expansion*. Boston: Houghton Mifflin, 1905.

Philbrick, Francis. *The Rise of the West, 1754–1830*. New York: Harper and Row, 1965.

Pitot, James. *Observations on the Colony of Louisiana, from 1796–1802*. Trans. Henry C. Pitot. Baton Rouge: Louisiana State University Press, 1979.

Purcell, Richard. *Connecticut in Transition, 1775–1818*. Washington, D.C.: American Historical Association, 1918.

Rea, Robert R. *Major Robert Farmar of Mobile*. Tuscaloosa: University of Alabama Press, 1990.

Renaut, F. P. *La Question de la Louisiane, 1796–1806*. Paris: Societe de l' Histoire des Colonies Francaises, 1918.

Rightor, Stanley. *Standard History of New Orleans, Louisiana*. Chicago: Lewis Publishing, 1916.

Robertson, James. *Louisiana Under the Rule of Spain, France, and the United States*. Vol. 2. Cleveland: Arthur H. Clark, 1911.

Robinson, William. *Jeffersonian Democracy in New England*. New York: Greenwood Press, 1968.

Roeder, Robert. "New Orleans Merchants, 1790–1837." Ph.D. diss., Harvard University, 1959.

Russell, Sarah. "Cultural Conflicts and Common Interests: The Making of the Sugar Planter Class in Louisiana, 1795–1853." Ph.D. diss., University of Maryland, 2000.

Sharp, Roger. *American Politics in the Early Republic: The New Nation in Crisis.* New Haven, Conn.: Yale University Press, 1993.

Smith, James Morton, ed. *The Republic of Letters: The Correspondence between Thomas Jefferson and James Madison, 1776–1826.* Vol. 2, *1790–1804*. New York: W. W. Norton, 1995.

Swanson, Richard. "The Government of Orleans Territory: The Years of Transition to American Rule, 1803–1806." M.A. thesis, University of Wisconsin, 1977.

Toups, Gerard. *The Provincial, Territorial, and State Administrations of William C. C. Claiborne, Governor of Louisiana, 1803–1816.* Ann Arbor, Mich.: University Microfilms, 1979.

Turner, Lynn W. *William Plumer of New Hampshire, 1759–1850.* Chapel Hill: University of North Carolina Press, 1962.

Usner, Daniel. *Indians, Settlers and Slaves in a Frontier Exchange Economy.* Chapel Hill: University of North Carolina Press, 1992.

Young, James. *The Washington Community, 1800–1828.* New York: Columbia University Press, 1966.

Walling, Kurt-Friedrich. *Republican Empire, Alexander Hamilton and Free Government.* Lawrence: University of Kansas Press, 1999.

Whitaker, Arthur. *The Mississippi Question, 1795–1803.* New York: D. Appleton-Century, 1934.

Wilkinson, James. *Memoirs of My Own Times.* Philadelphia: printed by Abraham Small, 1816.

Wilson, E. *Louisiana in French Diplomacy, 1759–1804.* Norman: University of Oklahoma Press, 1934.

Zink, Frances. *Julien Poydras.* Lafayette: University of Southwestern Louisiana, 1968.

Articles

Baur, John E. "International Repercussions of the Haitian Revolution." *Americas* 26(4) (1970): 394–418.

Beauford, Gertrude. "De Luziere, De Lauses, St. Vrain and Derbigny." *DAR Magazine* 114(5) (1980): 688–691.

Beerman, Eric. "Victory on the Mississippi." Ed. and trans. Gilbert C. Din. In *The Louisiana Purchase Bicentennial in Louisiana History.* Vol. 2, *The Spanish Presence in Louisiana, 1763–1803*, ed. Gilbert C. Din, 192–202. Lafayette: Center for Louisiana Studies, University of Southwestern Louisiana, 1996.

Bowman, Albert H. "Pichon, the United States and Louisiana." *Diplomatic History* 1(3) (Summer 1977): 257–270.

Brown, Everett. "The Orleans Territory Memorialists to Congress, 1804." *Louisiana Historical Quarterly* (January 1917): 99–102.

———. "The Senate Debate on the Breckinridge Bill for the Government of Louisiana, 1804." *American Historical Review* 22(2) (1917): 340–364.

Carr, David. "The Role of Congress in the Acquisition of the Louisiana Territory." *Louisiana History* 26(4) (1985): 369–383.

Casino, Joseph J. "Anti-Popery in Colonial Pennsylvania" In *Early American Catholicism, 1634–1820*, ed. Timothy Walch. New York: Garland, 1988.

Chaput, Donald. "The Pirote de Bellastre Family." *Louisiana History* 21(1) (1980): 67–76.

Christian, Marcus. "Demand by Men of Color for Rights in Orleans Territory." *Negro History Bulletin* 36(3) (1973): 54–57.

Coffey, Thomas. "Spanish Intrigue in the Territory of Orleans." *Red River Valley Historical Review* 3(4) (1978): 64–75.

Couch, Randal. "William Charles Cole Claiborne: An Historiographical Review." *Louisiana History* 36(4) (1995): 453–465.

Debien, Gabriel, and Rene Legradeur. "St. Domingue's Colonist Refugees in Louisiana, 1792–1804, Part 3: 1798–1803." *Louisiana Review* 10(1) (1981): 11–49.

Estaville, Lawrence. "The Louisiana French Region." *Southern History* 1(1) (1990): 61–65.

Everett, Donald. "Free Persons of Color in Colonial Louisiana." *Louisiana History* 7(1) (1966): 21–50.

Gitlin, Jay. "Crossroads on the Chinaberry Coast: Natchez and the Creole World of the Mississippi Valley." *Journal of Mississippi History* 54(4) (1992): 365–384.

Holmes, Jack. "Martin Duralde: Observations." *Revue de Louisiane* 9(1) (1980): 69–84.

Ingersoll, Thomas. "Free Blacks in a Slave Society." *William and Mary Quarterly* 48(2) (April 1991): 173–200.

Kendall, John. "Early New Orleans Newspapers." *Louisiana Historical Quarterly* 10 (1927): 383–401.

Lachance, Paul. "The 1809 Immigration of St. Domingue Refugees to New Orleans: Reception, Integration and Impact." *Louisiana History* 29(2) (1988): 109–141.

———. "Intermarriage and French Cultural Persistence in Late Spanish and Early American New Orleans." *Social History* 15(29) (1982): 47–81.

———. "The Politics of Fear: French Louisianans and the Slave Trade, 1786–1809." *Plantation Society in the Americas* 1(2) (1979): 162–197.

Legan, Marshall. "Judge Henry Bry: Genevan on the Ouchita." *North Louisiana Historical Journal* 3(3) (1972): 81–86.

Melville, Annabelle. "John Caroll and Louisiana, 1803–1815." *Catholic Historical Review* 64(3) (1978): 398–440.

Padgett, James, ed. "Letters of Edward Livingston to Presidents of the United States." *Louisiana Historical Quarterly* 19 (October 1936): 938–963.

Prichard, Walter. "Selecting a Governor for the Territory of Orleans." *Louisiana Historical Quarterly* 27(4) (April 1948): 933–963.

Rooney, William. "Thomas Jefferson and the Marine Hospital." *Journal of Southern History* 22(2) (May 1956): 167–182.

Scanlon, James. "A Sudden Conceit: Jefferson and the Louisiana Government Bill of 1804." *Louisiana History* 9(2) (1968): 139–162.

Sheperd, William. "Wilkinson and the Beginnings of the Spanish Conspiracy." *American Historical Review* 9 (October 1903–July 1904): 168–182.

Vincent, Bernard. "Thomas Paine and the Louisiana Purchase." *Plantation Society in the Americas* 3(2) (1993): 63–72.

Whitaker, Arthur, ed. "Another Dispatch from the United States Consulate in New Orleans."
  American Historical Review 38(2) (January 1933): 291–295.

———. "The Commerce of Louisiana and the Floridas at the End of the Eighteenth Century."
  Hispanic American Review 8(2) (May 1928): 190–203.

Young, Tom. "The United States Army and the Institution of Slavery in Louisiana, 1803–1812."
  Louisiana Studies 13(3) (1974): 201–227.

Index

Nicholson, Sen. Joseph, 52, 53, 84, 85

Northwest Ordinance, 9, 10, 35–37, 43, 50, 88–90, 95, 149, 153, 156, 163

Northwest Territory, 43

Ogden, Peter, 123, 124

Ohio, 39, 118

O'Reilly, Gen. Alexander, 5, 13

Orleans Territory, 9, 10, 36, 37, 39, 40, 53, 59, 60, 62, 64–67, 73, 82, 84, 86, 90, 93–98, 100–103, 105–10, 116–19, 121, 122, 124, 126–31, 133, 135, 137, 140–45, 147, 149, 150, 152–60, 162, 163, 172n23; Eastern District, 98, 100, 102, 104, 158; Western District, 98, 99, 104. *See also* government: territorial

Ouachita River, 63, 98, 99

Paine, Tom, 41; *To the French Inhabitants of Louisiana*, 85

Peace of Basle, 15

Pennsylvania, 49

Pensacola, 6, 8, 13, 79, 104

Petit, Pierre, 65, 176–77n43

Pichon, Louis-André, 23

Pickering, Timothy, 16–18, 41, 42, 46, 85, 86

Pinckney, Thomas, 14

Pinckney Treaty, 14, 18

Pitot, James, 64, 65, 69, 92, 121

plantation/plantation economy, 3, 63, 166–67n8

Plumer, Sen. William, 39, 44, 85–86

Pollock, George, 78, 84, 179n1

Pollock, Jacinto, 15

Pollock, Oliver, 13, 15

Portell, Capt. Thomas, 136

Potter, Samuel, 42

Power, Thomas, 135

Poydras, Julien, 62, 73, 78, 84, 92, 107, 140, 142, 146, 147, 150, 152, 161, 180n32

Prevost, Judge John, 76, 90–91, 135

Price, Chandler, 32

Protestants, 40

Quebec Act, 40, 41, 72

Randolph, John, 85, 86, 88, 89, 94, 95, 108, 109, 117, 136, 137, 150, 156

Reflections on the Cause of Louisianans respectfully submitted by their agents, 86

Remonstrance of the People of Louisiana, 65, 68–74, 76, 77, 106, 135, 143, 148, 150, 155, 156, 159, 162

Report, 94, 95

Republicans, 10, 39, 42, 44, 48, 50, 53, 73, 150, 156, 162, 163

Rhea, Rep. John, 52

right of deposit, 15, 18, 23

Robertson, Thomas, 143–44

Rodney, Caesar, 129

Roman (Romain), John, 75, 179n1

Roman Catholics, 40, 41

Ross, George, 125, 127

Roustan, Antoine, 21, 22

Sauvé, Pierre, 9, 56, 68, 77, 101, 109, 111, 155, 156, 159, 160

Senate, the, 9, 16, 32, 36–39, 41–45, 47–49, 51–53, 56, 59, 87–90, 95, 106, 107, 116, 117, 133, 141, 146–48, 150, 152, 154, 156

Seven Years' War, 12

Sheffey, Rep. Daniel, 133

shipping, 18, 20, 21, 23, 39, 49, 137

Skipwith, Fulwar, 32

slaves/slavery, 3, 4, 6, 9, 12, 43–46, 50–52, 55, 56, 58–60, 62, 67, 71, 85, 89, 105, 106, 141, 142, 144, 145, 151, 152, 154, 157, 162, 185n31

Sloan, Rep. James, 51

Smith, Sen. Israel, 42, 44, 45

Smith, Sen. John, 42, 45

Smith, Robert, 140, 143

Smith, Sen. Samuel, 44

smuggling, 4, 21, 106, 141, 142, 157

Someruelos, Marquis de, 17, 18

South Carolina, 8, 44, 49, 56, 106, 157

Spain, 4–8, 12–20, 24–26, 29, 30, 32, 34, 54, 86,
    99, 108, 109, 136, 137, 146, 167n27, 178n65,
    185n40, 187n16

Spanish, the, 3–8, 13–24, 26–28, 31, 34, 40, 52,
    54, 59, 65, 67, 70, 77, 80, 81, 83, 98–100,
    102–4, 108, 117, 119, 127, 129, 130, 132, 135,
    137, 143, 151, 153, 158, 160, 167n27, 184n23

Spanish Crown, 4, 5, 98

Spence, Lt. Robert T., 137

St. Domingue, 19–21, 44, 50, 55, 59, 69, 106,
    107, 112, 142–45, 151, 157, 162

Stirling, Capt. James, 151

sugar, 3, 13, 14, 24, 28, 55, 57, 62, 104, 112, 166–
    67n8

Sumter, Thomas, Jr., 32

Swartout, Samuel, 118, 121, 124

Talleyrand, Charles-Maurice de, 20

Tennessee, 39, 49, 91, 92, 118, 122

Texas, 13, 100, 108, 109, 120

Thatcher, Rep. George, 105

Thierry, Jean Baptiste, 139

Tiffin, Edward, 119

timber/timber products, 5, 104

tobacco, 5, 12, 14

Tracy, Sen. Uriah, 88

Treaty of Fontainebleau, 5

Treaty of Paris, 6, 8, 89

Trist, Hore Browse, 73

Tupper, Benjamin, 56, 62, 174nn5–6

Tyler, Gov. John, 133

Ulloa, Antonio de, 4, 13

United States Congress, 3, 6, 8, 10–12, 14, 24,
    27, 32, 35–43, 48, 54–59, 61–70, 72, 77–79,

82, 85–90, 93–95, 99, 103, 104, 107, 111, 112,
    114, 115, 117, 118, 120, 122, 124–27, 133, 136,
    140–47, 148, 150, 152–62

Ventura Morales, Juan, 16, 70, 99

Victor, Claude Emmanuel, 20–22

*View of the Political and Civil Situation of
    Louisiana; from the Thirtieth of November
    1803 to the First of October, 1804 by a Na-
    tive*, 80

Villars, Joseph, 101, 160, 184n17

Washington, D.C., 9, 19, 30, 31–53, 56–58, 65,
    69, 74–96, 102, 104, 109, 111, 114–16, 118–
    22, 126, 128–30, 132, 133, 138, 140, 142, 144,
    145, 148, 150, 152, 154, 156, 158–63

Washington, George, 15

Watkins, Dr. John, 54, 55, 57, 58, 62, 73, 75, 82,
    83, 108, 111, 121, 122, 123, 125, 127, 140, 147,
    154, 157, 175n10, 184n15, 187n23

Wilkinson, Gov. James, 4, 14, 16, 22, 27, 29, 30,
    34, 69, 76, 90, 99, 114–25, 127, 130, 132,
    135–40, 149, 161, 188n26, 188n29, 188n35

Wolcott, Oliver, Jr., 39

Workman, James, 123

Worthington, Sen. Thomas, 41, 42

Wykoff, William, 75, 78

CPSIA information can be obtained at www.ICGtesting.com
Printed in the USA
BVOW010539190213

313597BV00002B/4/P